The Cuisine of Armenia

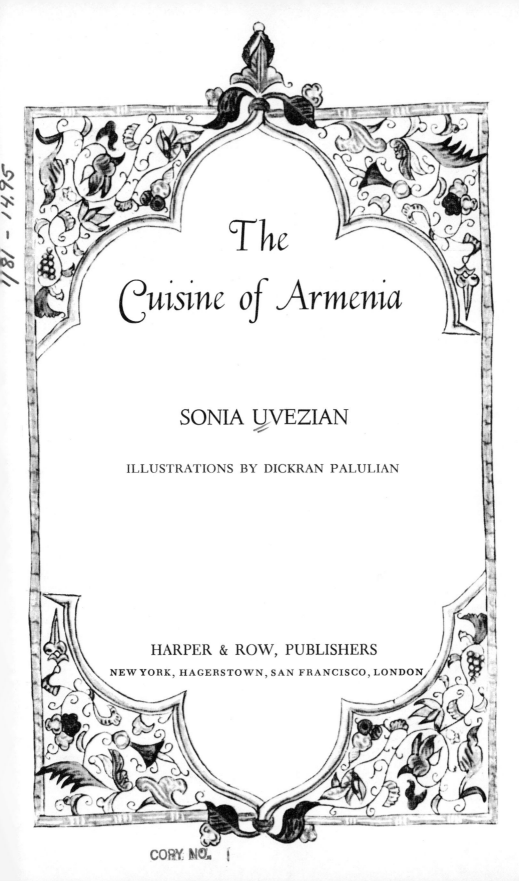

The Cuisine of Armenia

SONIA UVEZIAN

ILLUSTRATIONS BY DICKRAN PALULIAN

HARPER & ROW, PUBLISHERS

NEW YORK, HAGERSTOWN, SAN FRANCISCO, LONDON

641.5
U

Designed by C. Linda Dingler

Library of Congress Cataloging in Publication Data

Uvezian, Sonia.
  The cuisine of Armenia.
  1. Cookery, Armenian. I. Title
TX723.4.U93 1974   641.5'9566'2   73-4132
ISBN 0-06-014472-6

77 78 79 80 10 9 8 7 6 5 4 3 2

To immortal Armenia

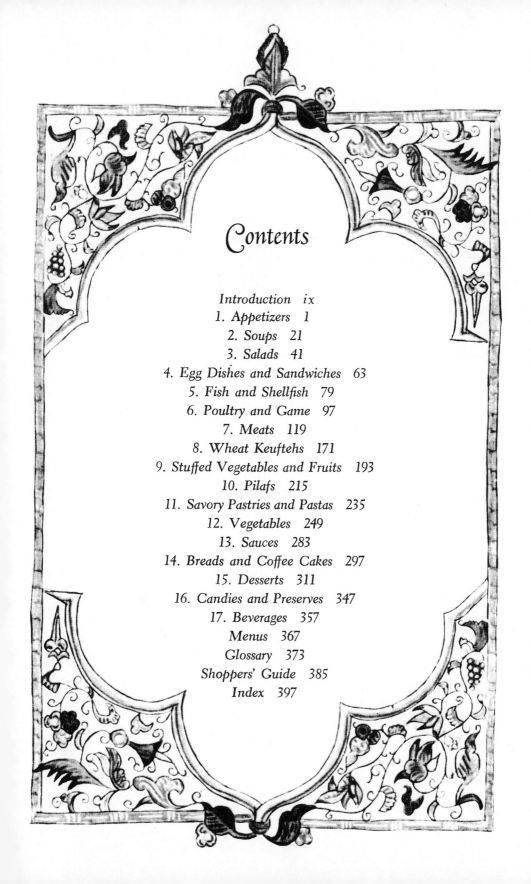

Contents

Introduction

Food and its preparation are one of the cornerstones of Armenian culture. Among my most vivid childhood memories are those of the sights and aromas in our kitchen, where I spent many hours watching delicacies being concocted daily by the grown-ups. There was a good deal of folklore in the old Armenian recipes that were handed down from mother to daughter, the amount of the ingredients often being determined "by the measure of the eye." This is true of all Middle Eastern cookery, and in fact Armenian cuisine includes the majority of the best Middle Eastern dishes.

Armenia, land of the Tigris and Euphrates rivers, has existed under different names since very ancient times and is referred to in the Bible as the land of Mount Ararat, where Noah's Ark is believed to have landed after the Deluge. The powerful Hittite Empire of the second millennium B.C. and the kingdom of Urartu, around 900 to 700 B.C., preceded the Armenian nation. The name "Urartu" survives in the word "Ararat," and archaeologists have discovered that there was once an Urartuan citadel called Erebuni within what is now Yerevan, the capital of Soviet Armenia.

Because of its strategic location in the line of trade routes between the Black and Caspian seas, Armenia was for many centuries a battleground of both eastern and western armies, which conquered its territory time and again. Early in the fourth century Armenia became the first nation to be converted to Christianity, an event that further increased the storminess of its history. Yet throughout the centuries, Armenians have maintained their individuality down to the present time; now their country is divided among Turkey, Iran, and the Soviet Union, and many Armenians are dispersed the world over. Some four

ix

hundred thousand live in the Middle East, including an important community in Lebanon in which I spent the early part of my life, and many thousands have found their way to America.

Basically a high plateau furrowed by the Caucasus and other mountain ranges, Armenia contains many rivers, streams, and lakes. Its soil is fertile and its climate, though extreme, is conducive to exuberant productivity. There are areas of majestic scenery, and the many kinds of flowers are renowned for their beauty. Both song and game birds abound, and grains and vegetables are cultivated, as are a large variety of fruits of exceptional quality, including apricots and cherries, both of which originated in Armenia. Cattle and sheep are raised in quantity; in ancient times Armenian horses were as highly prized as Arabian horses are today.

Although Soviet Armenia, the only part of Armenia which is recognized today as a geographic entity, is one of the most modern and progressive parts of Russia, two of its important industries have existed since antiquity: winemaking and the manufacture of rose petal preserves.

Armenian cuisine is a very old one, with a history going back thousands of years. Excavations reveal that ancient Urartuans and Armenians had a well-developed agricultural system. Domestic fowl and animals, especially cattle and sheep, were raised and used for food. Many kinds of fish, wild animals, and birds were also eaten. Grains such as wheat, rye, barley, and millet were cultivated. Not only were various types of bread made from the grains, but the production of beer was also important. Lentils and different kinds of beans were grown, as well as many other vegetables, and the use of vegetable oil was known. Besides grapes for eating and winemaking, many other fruits were cultivated. Some fruits were dried. Dairy products such as butter, cheese, milk, and yogurt were an important part of the diet, and the ancient peoples made extensive use of herbs and spices. Through the centuries, Armenian historians have described many dishes that are still eaten today.

The combination of many influences plus pride in national heritage has given Armenians a richly varied cuisine that, in addition to preserving its many original dishes, has skillfully assimilated foods of the other cultures that left their imprint on the land. Conversely, as Armenians settled throughout the Middle East, many of their recipes became part of the cuisines of other countries in the area. The recipes in this book are not confined to a few regions of Armenia; rather, an attempt has been made to include a representative collection of the best dishes from the entire country, as well as other areas of the Middle East in which Armenians have lived for centuries.

The long Turkish occupation of Armenia accounts for many Turkish names for Armenian dishes, a fact which explains the presence of numerous Turkish titles in this book. Also, in cases where a particular dish is known by both Armenian and Turkish (and occasionally by Arabic) names, I have placed the Armenian title first.

Armenian cuisine is exotic in flavor without being extreme, a characteristic that enables one to incorporate it very successfully into an international menu if one wishes. Although spices play an important role, they are used more sparingly than in some of the other Middle Eastern cuisines. Herbs and spices commonly used include allspice, caraway, cardamom, cayenne, cinnamon, cloves, coriander, cumin, garlic, *mahlab* (an aromatic spice derived from black cherry kernels), paprika, black and white pepper, saffron, sesame, *sumakh* (sumac or barberry), bay leaf, basil, dill, mint, oregano, parsley, savory, tarragon, and thyme. In the recipes fresh herbs should be used unless dried herbs are specified as a substitute. Armenians cook with olive and vegetable oils. Regular butter, as well as clarified butter, are also used extensively. Often *kyurdyuk*, lamb fat procured from fat-tailed sheep native to the Middle East, the Caucasus, and Central Asia, is melted and used for cooking instead of butter; however, butter or margarine is an acceptable substitute.

From ancient times cheese has been a basic Armenian food served at every meal, and today, as in ancient Urartu, dairy products are an important industry in Soviet Armenia. Armenian cheese is famous throughout the Soviet Union, and many kinds are produced from cows, sheep, and water buffalo, including *kanach banir*, or *muklats banir*, a green cheese similar to Roquefort, and *brindze*, a white cheese made from sheep's milk, which is similar to feta.

Rice and bulghur (cracked wheat) are the most widely used cereals. Potatoes are also used, often in combination with meat, other vegetables, and fruits. Eggplant, a favorite vegetable, is prepared in a great variety of ways. Stock items include chick-peas, lentils, barley, various beans, macaroni, *tahini* (sesame seed paste), *titvash*, or *tourshou* (homemade pickles), yogurt, cheese, home-cured olives, *basterma* (spicy dried beef), *yershig*, or *soudjuk* (Armenian sausage), Armenian coffee, tea, and Armenian bread. Almonds, walnuts, and pistachios are plentiful in Armenia and along with pine nuts and currants turn up as frequent ingredients in appetizers, pilafs, stuffings, fruit compotes, cakes, and pastries.

Lamb is the preferred meat, although beef, veal, and pork are also used. Cooking on a spit over charcoal or wood embers is a favorite way of preparing meat, poultry, game birds, and fish and has been so for thousands of years. Salads are popular and are eaten daily, sometimes as a main course during the warm summer months. Fresh fruit is the usual dessert, as well as the most popular snack next to cheese, olives, and bread. Cakes, pastries, and certain puddings are eaten as a rule at teatime and on holidays. Rosewater, orange flower water, and honey are used to flavor many desserts and pastries. There are also many delectable meatless dishes intended for the Lenten season which can be enjoyed at any time of the year.

Of special appeal to the modern cook are the many recipes that can be prepared in advance; also, the nutritional content of Armenian cuisine is of a high order, so that one is assured of healthful, well-balanced meals. Most of the ingredients in the recipes that follow are available at supermarkets throughout the country. The few remaining Armenian ingredients may be purchased from the stores listed in the Shoppers' Guide (pages 385–95).

Although Armenians eat three meals a day, for many, many centuries breakfast has been simple, most likely consisting for the Armenian peasant of no more than bread and cheese. Lunch has also characteristically been moderate: usually bread, cheese, yogurt, or soup. The main meal occurs at dinner, and from the accounts of Armenian historians through the ages, it was often an imposing affair.

A typical modern-day Armenian dinner usually begins with a first course that may range anywhere from a quickly assembled selection of hors d'oeuvres from the pantry—roasted and salted almonds or pistachios, home-cured olives, *titvash*, goat's cheese or string cheese in brine, slices of *yershig*, or *soudjuk*, and *basterma* and Armenian bread—to a vast array of *meza* (appetizers) including *boeregs* (hot, flaky turnovers stuffed with meat, cheese, or vegetables), cold *dolmas* (vegetables stuffed with rice and olive oil), *midia dolma* (stuffed mussels), cold vegetable salads, eggplant and chick-pea dips, and many others. *Oghi*, or *raki*, an alcoholic drink similar to anisette, often accompanies the *meza* as an aperitif.

xii

The second course would be a meat, chicken, or vegetable soup, usually prepared with a tomato, egg and lemon, or yogurt sauce flavored with onion or garlic and herbs. In summer *jajik*, a refreshing iced cucumber and yogurt soup, is frequently served.

This is followed by a main course of meat, chicken, or fish. Lamb dishes are the most popular and numerous. There are many varieties of kebabs (meat dishes), stews, casseroles, *keuftehs* (meat or vegetable mixtures usually shaped into patties or balls), and meat *dolmas* (vegetables or fruits stuffed with meat and rice or cracked wheat). The meat course is served with a rice or cracked wheat pilaf and hot or cold vegetables such as artichokes, eggplant, zucchini, or beans.

Dessert usually consists of fresh fruit and cheese or a fruit compote followed by Armenian coffee or tea. On special occasions there would be a helping of the richer pastries like *baklava*, *kurabia*, or *kadayif*. Throughout the meal red and white wines are served. Wonderful Armenian brandies or a homemade cherry cordial end the meal.

This book is a response to the large number of requests for Armenian recipes I have received. They have come not only from my dinner guests, who would enthusiastically comment on how unusual and delicious the food they were served was, but also from people I met who were already acquainted with Armenian cuisine and who lamented their inability to locate recipes for the delectable dishes they so fondly remembered. Over the years I came to realize more and more the need for a book that would provide clear and simple directions for making Armenian dishes, retaining their authenticity while using ingredients and materials readily available.

In addition to the many authentic Armenian recipes listed here, I have included some of my own improvisation, indicated by ornaments, that have been inspired by the Armenian style of cooking. Armenians have traditionally used earthenware utensils for most of their cooking needs; for our modern times enameled cast iron utensils are recommended.

The use of spices, seasonings, and herbs is in the final analysis a matter of individual taste, and no experienced Armenian cook would think of treating the matter rigidly. The reason for stating specific amounts is merely to give the beginner something to go by until he has become familiar enough with the cuisine to have developed his own "measure of the eye."

1. Appetizers

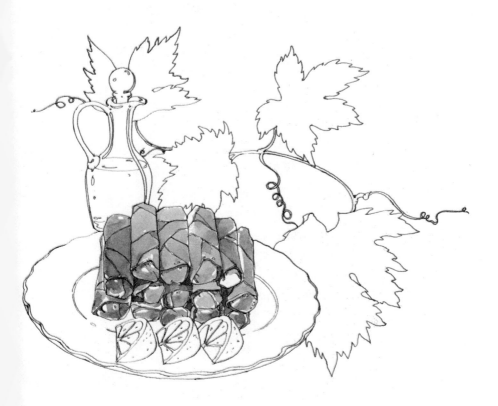

Grapevine Leaves Stuffed with Rice and Olive Oil (page 9)

Appetizers, or *meza*, as they are called, constitute a delightful aspect of Armenian cuisine, covering a wide range of foods both hot and cold. They may be served at the start of a meal or with drinks at parties, when a full table of *meza* would by American standards be considered a buffet dinner. For the first course of a dinner it is best either to serve generous portions of one or two appetizers at the table or to pass around a few *meza* with cocktails before the meal.

A satisfying appetizer involving little effort could consist of feta cheese and crusty bread, alone or in combination with *basterma* (spicy dried beef) and Middle Eastern olives (also known as "Greek olives"), all of which may be purchased already prepared and thus provide a quick yet authentic *meza*.

Eggplant Caviar or Carp Roe Dip served with Armenian Thin Bread (page 301) or crackers makes a delicious dip with cocktails. Stuffed Mussels is an unusual and outstanding first course. For a hot fish appetizer try Fried Mussels with Garlic and Nut Sauce.

If one wishes to avoid last-minute preparation, *boeregs*, which use paper-thin pastry and various stuffings, can be prepared the day before, refrigerated overnight, and baked in the oven just before serving. The cold vegetables and rice-stuffed *dolmas* are also excellent appetizers to prepare in advance and keep in the refrigerator until serving time. Among these Artichokes with Olive Oil (page 254) and Grapevine Leaves Stuffed with Rice and Olive Oil (page 9) are particular favorites. Meat and Egg Rolls is another excellent appetizer that may be prepared in advance and refrigerated.

For other dishes that can also be served as appetizers, consult the various chapters, following your inclinations and using your judgment.

3

FRIED ALMONDS

Dabgvadz Noush

These savory nuts are often included in the numerous dishes which comprise the *meza*, primarily to provide an interesting embellishment and a moment's excitement to the palate.

Unshelled almonds or whole blanched almonds
Olive oil
Salt

If using unshelled almonds, remove the shells and place the almonds in boiling water for about half a minute. Drain the almonds and rinse under running cold water. Peel at once by squeezing the nuts between the fingers until the skins slip off. Drain on absorbent paper.

Cover the bottom of a skillet with olive oil and heat over moderate flame. Add the almonds and sauté, stirring frequently, until golden brown on both sides. Drain on absorbent paper, sprinkle with salt, and serve.

These keep well for several weeks in tightly covered jars stored in a cool, dry place.

NOTE: The almonds may also be sautéed in butter instead of olive oil with excellent results.

TOASTED PUMPKIN SEEDS

Khorovadz Titoumi Good

Like the Fried Almonds, above, these delicious, slightly salty seeds appear on the *meza* as an extra flourish to tantalize the appetite. Once you have tasted them you will never again throw away the seeds from a pumpkin.

1 cup pumpkin seeds
1½ cups cold water
¼ cup salt

Place the pumpkin seeds in a colander and rinse thoroughly under running cold water. Drain and place in a heavy saucepan. Add the cold water and salt and bring to a boil over high heat, stirring constantly, until salt is dissolved. Lower the heat and simmer 30 minutes.

Drain the seeds well and spread on an ungreased baking sheet. Toast in a preheated 300° oven, stirring occasionally, 20 to 30 minutes or until both the outsides and insides of the seeds are toasted and crisp. To determine whether insides are done, gently crack a seed open between your teeth and eat it, discarding the shell. Test seeds frequently as the end of the baking period approaches to avoid overtoasting. Serve alone or mixed with roasted and salted chick-peas and nuts.

Makes 1 cup

NOTE: Melon or sunflower seeds may be toasted in the same manner as the pumpkin seeds.

EGGPLANT CAVIAR

This popular dish, also known as "poor man's caviar," is made in many different ways throughout the Middle East and the Caucasus.

1 large eggplant (about 2 pounds)
7 tablespoons olive oil
1 large onion, finely chopped
½ cup finely chopped green pepper
1 large clove garlic, finely chopped
3 medium ripe tomatoes, peeled, seeded, and finely chopped
Salt and freshly ground black pepper to taste
2 tablespoons freshly squeezed and strained lemon juice

Cut the stem and hull from the eggplant and discard. Bake eggplant in a preheated 425° oven about 1 hour, turning several times, until the flesh is very soft and the skin is charred.

Meanwhile, in a small skillet heat 4 tablespoons of the olive oil over moderate heat. Add the onion and fry, stirring frequently, until soft but not browned. Add the green pepper and garlic and continue to cook, stirring often, 5 minutes. When the eggplant is cool enough to handle, peel off the skin and slit it open. Scoop out the seeds and discard.

Place the eggplant pulp in a bowl and mash it. Stir in the contents of skillet, tomatoes, and salt and pepper and mix well. Place the remaining 3 tablespoons olive oil in the skillet and heat over moderate heat. Add the eggplant mixture and bring to a boil, stirring continuously, then reduce the heat, cover, and simmer 1 hour. Uncover and cook 30 minutes, stirring occasionally, until all moisture in the pan has evaporated and the mixture has thickened. Stir in the lemon juice and taste for seasoning. Pour into a serving bowl, cover with clear plastic wrap, and chill. Serve with *lavash* (Armenian Thin Bread, page 301) or sesame seed crackers.

Serves 6 to 8

CARP ROE DIP

Tarama

    3 slices white bread, trimmed of crusts
 ¼ cup *tarama* (salted carp roe)
    2 tablespoons freshly squeezed and strained lemon juice
    3 tablespoons grated onion
 ½ cup olive oil (approximately)

Hand method: Soak the bread in water, squeeze it dry, and place in a shallow bowl. Gradually add the *tarama* a little at a time, mashing and mixing it with a spoon. Beat in the lemon juice, onion, and enough of the olive oil a tablespoon at a time to make a smooth and creamy mixture (you may not need all the oil). Taste for seasoning, cover, and refrigerate.

Blender method: Soak the bread in water and squeeze dry. Place it and the *tarama* in the container of an electric blender and blend until smooth. Keeping the motor running, remove the cover and add the lemon juice, onion, and enough of the olive oil in a slow, steady stream to make a thick, smooth mixture (you may not need all the oil). Taste for seasoning, cover, and refrigerate.

Serve *tarama* as a dip with crusty bread or crackers, accompanied if you wish by a side dish of tomatoes and black olives (preferably the Greek variety). Slices of hard-cooked egg and tomato on lettuce, dressed with *tarama* and garnished with black olives, make a good hors d'oeuvre. Or peel small cucumbers and slice them lengthwise in half, scoop out the seeds, and stuff with *tarama*; serve chilled, decorated with sliced olives. *Tarama* is also often served as part of a platter of assorted appetizers such as stuffed grapevine leaves, feta cheese, *basterma,* and olives.

Serves 6 to 8

NOTE: Red caviar may be substituted for the salted carp roe.

ROASTED PEPPERS

Khorovadz Bighbegh

Although this dish may be prepared indoors, it has a superior flavor when the peppers are roasted over an open flame.

    4 large green peppers
    ¼ cup finely chopped onion
    Salt and freshly ground black pepper to taste
    3 tablespoons olive oil
    1 tablespoon red wine vinegar

Impale the peppers on long-handled forks or skewers and turn them over a charcoal or wood fire until the skins are blackened and the peppers are cooked through. The peppers may also be broiled or baked in a preheated 450° oven about 25 to 30 minutes.

Peel off the skins while the peppers are still hot. Cut out the stems and white membrane and discard the seeds. Cut the peppers lengthwise into quarters and place in a serving bowl. Sprinkle with the onion, and salt and pepper. Mix the olive oil and vinegar and add to the peppers. Toss gently but thoroughly. Taste for seasoning. Serve cold as an appetizer or as an accompaniment to grilled fish or meats.

Serves 4

MIXED PICKLES

Titvash or Tourshou

Pickled vegetables accompany almost every Armenian meal. In the Middle East during the summer when vegetables are plentiful, many families pack huge amounts of *titvash* into large jars to provide the coming year's supply. Among the vegetables pickled are cucumbers, carrots, cauliflower, celery, onions, green beans, tomatoes, eggplants, cabbage, and green, red, and yellow peppers.

VEGETABLES

    1 small head cauliflower, separated into flowerets
    4 carrots, quartered lengthwise and cut into 3- to 4-inch pieces
    4 tiny cucumbers or green tomatoes
    ¼ pound green beans, trimmed
    2 sweet yellow or green peppers, quartered, seeded, and deribbed
    2 1-inch pieces hot red pepper (optional)
    2 large cloves garlic, peeled and halved
    4 fresh dill sprigs
    Grapevine leaves (optional)

> 4 cups water
> 1 cup cider vinegar
> ¼ cup salt (not iodized)

Wash the vegetables and pack into 2 sterilized quart jars, adding 1 clove garlic, 2 dill sprigs, and a few grapevine leaves to each jar.

In a saucepan combine the water with the vinegar and salt. Bring to a boil and pour over the vegetables in the jars to cover. Seal and store in a cool place 4 weeks.

Makes 2 quarts

NOTE: Sweet red peppers or pimientos are especially good pickled. To prepare, wash the peppers and cut lengthwise in half, leaving the seed pods on. Pack into sterilized jars, adding 1 clove garlic and 2 dill sprigs to each jar. Cover with hot brine, seal, and store as above.

GRAPEVINE LEAVES STUFFED WITH RICE AND OLIVE OIL

*Tzitayoughov Derevapatat, Derevi Dolma (Sarma)
or Yalanchi Dolma*

This is a splendid appetizer, cherished throughout the Caucasus and the Middle East.

> 2 cups grated onion
> ½ cup uncooked long-grain white rice
> 2 tablespoons pine nuts
> 2 tablespoons dried currants
> 2 tablespoons chopped parsley
> 2 tablespoons finely chopped fresh dill (1 tablespoon dried dill weed may be substituted)

1 tablespoon finely chopped fresh mint leaves (optional)
6 tablespoons olive oil
2½ tablespoons freshly squeezed and strained lemon juice
Salt and freshly ground black pepper to taste
60 fresh, tender grapevine leaves or 60 preserved grapevine leaves (a one-pound jar)
1 cup water
1 lemon, cut into wedges

Place the onion, rice, pine nuts, currants, parsley, dill, mint, olive oil, 1 tablespoon of the lemon juice, and the salt and pepper in a bowl and mix well. Taste for seasoning and set aside.

If using fresh grapevine leaves, soak them in boiling salted water 2 minutes to soften, then rinse under cold water. Rinse preserved grapevine leaves in hot water to remove brine. Spread the washed leaves on absorbent paper to drain.

Cover the bottom of a heavy casserole with 10 of the leaves to prevent the stuffed leaves from burning during cooking. Stuff each of the remaining 50 leaves as follows: Remove the stem, if any, and spread the leaf on a plate, stem end toward you, dull side up. Place about 1 teaspoon (or more for larger leaves) of the rice mixture near the stem end. Fold the stem end over the stuffing, then fold over the sides to enclose the stuffing securely. Beginning at the stem end, roll the grape leaf firmly away from you toward the tip, forming a cylinder.

Layer the stuffed leaves seam sides down and close together in neat rows in the casserole. Sprinkle the remaining 1½ tablespoons lemon juice over them and add the water. Gently place an inverted plate over the top to keep the stuffed leaves in place while cooking. Bring to a boil over moderate heat, reduce heat to low, cover, and simmer about 50 to 60 minutes or until the stuffing is very tender. If necessary, more water may be added. Remove from the heat and cool to room temperature. Remove plate and arrange the *sarmas* on a serving platter. Cover and chill. Serve cold, garnished with the lemon wedges.

Makes 50 (Serves 10 to 12)

10

The following are two popular stuffings for grapevine or cabbage leaves used by Armenians living in the Caucasus. In addition to the herbs listed below they add chopped fresh coriander (also known as *cilantro* or Chinese parsley). In the Pea and Rice Stuffing the minced apricot or plum fruit roll is a substitute for native sour plums, which are unavailable outside the Caucasus.

Lentil and Bulghur Stuffing

Mix together ¼ cup boiled and drained washed lentils; ¼ cup coarse bulghur, soaked in warm water for 30 minutes and drained; 1 medium onion, minced and fried in vegetable oil; 2 tablespoons dried currants; 2 tablespoons minced dried apricots; ¼ cup each finely chopped fresh mint and savory; and salt and pepper to taste.

Pea and Rice Stuffing

Mix together ½ cup fresh or thoroughly defrosted frozen peas; 2 tablespoons uncooked long-grain white rice, soaked in hot water for 30 minutes and drained; 1 small onion, minced and fried in vegetable oil; 2 tablespoons dried currants; 2 tablespoons minced apricot or plum fruit roll; ¼ cup each finely chopped fresh mint and savory; and salt and pepper to taste.

Using either stuffing, follow the directions on page 10 for filling the leaves. Layer the stuffed leaves in a casserole, put 4 or 5 dried apricots, chopped, around them, and pour in 1 cup water and a tablespoon of vegetable oil. Place an inverted plate over top and cook as directed. Serve cold, sprinkled with finely chopped fresh parsley, savory, or mint.

FRIED MUSSELS

Dabgvadz Midia

24 large mussels in their shells
⅓ cup seasoned flour
 2 eggs, beaten
Olive oil for frying
Garlic and Nut Sauce (page 290)
Lettuce leaves (optional)

Scrub the mussels well and pry open with the point of a knife. Trim off the beards, scoop out the flesh, and discard the shells. Wash and dry the mussels thoroughly. Dip first in the seasoned flour, then in the beaten egg. Deep-fry in hot olive oil until golden brown on both sides, about 1 minute. Serve hot, on wooden picks, with a bowl of the sauce for dipping as an accompaniment to cocktails. The mussels can also be served hot on lettuce leaves, with the sauce, as a first course.

Serves 8

STUFFED MUSSELS

Midia Dolma

This is an elegant and distinguished hors d'oeuvre which will stimulate not only the palate but the conversation as well.

36 large mussels in their shells
½ cup olive oil
 3 cups finely chopped onion
½ cup uncooked long-grain white rice, washed and drained
¼ cup dried currants

12

¼ cup pine nuts
½ teaspoon allspice
¼ teaspoon cinnamon
Salt and freshly ground black pepper to taste
  2 cups water
  1 tablespoon freshly squeezed and strained lemon juice
  2 lemons, cut into wedges

Scrub the mussel shells with a stiff brush or stainless steel scouring pad under running cold water. Using a sharp knife, pry the shells open until loose but not separated. Remove the beards and any bits of black waste matter. Leaving the mussels in their shells, rinse carefully under running cold water to remove sand and clean the insides of the shells. Soak the mussels in cold water for 1 hour.

Meanwhile, in a heavy skillet heat the olive oil over moderate heat. Add the onion and sauté until golden brown, stirring frequently. Remove from the heat and stir in the rice, currants, nuts, allspice, cinnamon, and salt and pepper. Mix well, taste for seasoning, and set aside to cool.

Lift the mussels out of the water into a sieve and rinse again under running cold water. Drain well. Place 1 tablespoon of the rice mixture in each shell, then close it tightly by tying firmly with a piece of string.

Arrange the stuffed mussels side by side in layers in a heavy casserole. Pour in the water and lemon juice. Place an inverted plate over the top to keep the mussels from moving during cooking. Bring to a boil over moderate heat, then reduce the heat to low. Cover and simmer about 1 hour or until rice stuffing is tender. Uncover and let the mussels cool to room temperature in the casserole. Using a perforated spoon, remove the mussels from the casserole, discarding the liquid in which they were cooked. Cut off the strings and arrange the mussels on a serving platter. Cover and chill. Serve cold, garnished with the lemon wedges.

Serves 9

CUMIN FINGERS

Chamanov (Kimionov) Keufteh

1 pound ground lamb
1 large onion, grated
1 egg
½ cup fresh bread crumbs
½ cup finely chopped parsley
1 teaspoon ground cumin
Salt to taste
Vegetable oil for frying

Put all ingredients except the oil in a bowl and knead thoroughly until the mixture is smooth. Form into "fingers" 2 inches long and ½ inch wide and deep-fry in hot oil until golden brown, about 2 minutes. Serve hot.

Serves 12 to 16

NOTE: You may substitute 1 tablespoon curry powder for the cumin with excellent results.

MEAT AND EGG ROLLS

Here is a flavorful, decorative, and substantial appetizer which is also a perfect picnic or buffet dish.

1¼ pounds lean lamb, ground 3 times or pounded with a wooden mallet until pasty
1 large clove garlic, crushed

⅛ teaspoon cinnamon
⅛ teaspoon nutmeg
½ teaspoon curry powder
Salt, freshly ground black pepper, and cayenne to taste
  4 hard-cooked eggs
¼ cup tomato paste
¼ cup water
  2 tablespoons melted butter
Beef broth
Parsley sprigs

Combine the lamb, garlic, cinnamon, nutmeg, curry powder, and salt, black pepper, and cayenne in a deep bowl and knead until thoroughly blended. Divide into 4 equal parts. Form one part into a 3½-by-5½-inch rectangle, shorter side toward you, and place 1 hard-cooked egg crosswise in the center. Fold the lower edge of meat over the egg and roll up like a jelly roll. Pinch the ends of the roll together to seal and enclose the egg securely. Repeat the shaping and rolling procedure with the remaining 3 parts. With hands moistened with water, smooth the surface of the meat rolls and place in a buttered shallow baking dish just large enough to hold them comfortably in one layer.

Combine the tomato paste and water. Brush the rolls with the melted butter and spoon the tomato paste mixture over them. Bake in a preheated 350° oven about 45 minutes or until browned, turning and basting the rolls every 10 minutes with the beef broth and pan juices. When the rolls are done, transfer them to a plate, cool to room temperature, cover, and refrigerate until thoroughly chilled. Slice and arrange on a flat serving platter. Garnish with the parsley sprigs.

Serves 8

NOTE: The meat rolls may also be served hot as a main course (serves 4) accompanied by their own sauce, Plain Rice Pilaf (page 219) or fried potatoes, and a green salad.

Variation: Instead of stuffing rolls with whole hard-cooked eggs, stuff each with a mixture of 1 tablespoon each chopped hard-cooked egg whites and chopped pistachio nuts, salted to taste.

FRIED LIVER

Dabgvadz Giger

1 pound calf's liver
¼ cup olive oil
⅓ cup flour
6 scallions, trimmed and sliced, including 2 inches of the
green tops
¼ cup chopped parsley
1 tomato, seeded and chopped
Salt and freshly ground black pepper to taste

Wash and dry the liver and cut into bite-size pieces. Heat the olive oil in a heavy 10-inch skillet. Dip liver in the flour and fry quickly in the hot olive oil, turning to brown on all sides, about 1 or 2 minutes. Do not overcook. Transfer to a platter and keep warm. To the oil remaining in the skillet add the scallions and sauté, stirring constantly, until soft. Add the parsley and tomato to the scallions, mix, and pour over the liver. Season with the salt and pepper and serve hot.

Serves 8

Variation: Omit the tomato. Serve the fried liver with 3 tablespoons freshly squeezed and strained lemon juice over it.

PHYLLO PASTRY BOEREGS

Fit for a royal palate, the savory or sweet pastries known as *boeregs* are delicious as well as versatile. They can be prepared with paper-thin phyllo pastry or a homemade dough, using a meat, cheese, or vegetable filling for an appetizer and fruit, nuts, or cream for the dessert version.

These delectable pastries are equally good served with afternoon tea, and some of the recipes make excellent luncheon or supper dishes when served in larger portions and accompanied by a green salad. For *boereg* recipes using homemade dough, consult Chapter 11.

NOTE: Before making *boeregs*, please read the entry on phyllo in the Glossary.

BOEREG ROLLS

Phyllo pastry sheets as needed, allowing 8 sheets per cup of filling
Melted butter
Cheese Filling, Meat Filling, or Spinach-Cheese Filling (pages 18–19)

Cut the phyllo sheets into quarters. Pile the sheets on top of one another and cover with a barely dampened kitchen towel to prevent drying. Taking one sheet at a time, brush with the melted butter and place about ½ tablespoon filling on it, centered 1 inch from the lower edge. Fold the lower edge of the sheet over the filling and roll several times. Bring both sides over the filling, brushing each with butter, then roll up the length of the strip like a jelly roll. Secure the seam by brushing with melted butter. Place seam side down on a lightly buttered baking sheet. Repeat this procedure with the remaining phyllo sheets and filling. Brush the tops of the rolls with melted butter. Bake in a preheated 350° oven about 15 to 20 minutes or until golden brown. Serve hot, allowing 4 *boeregs* per person.

NOTE: For larger rolls cut the phyllo sheets in half crosswise instead of cutting them into quarters. Fill, using 2 tablespoons filling per *boereg*. Roll and bake as above. Allow 2 *boeregs* per person.

BOEREG TRIANGLES

**Phyllo pastry sheets as needed, allowing 8 sheets per cup of filling
Melted butter
Cheese Filling, Meat Filling, or Spinach-Cheese Filling
(below and opposite page)**

Cut the phyllo sheets into quarters lengthwise. Stack and cover with a barely dampened kitchen towel to prevent drying. Brush 2 strips with the melted butter and carefully place one over the other, buttered sides up. Place about 1 tablespoon filling on a bottom corner and fold over to form a triangle. Continue folding in triangles the length of the strip. Secure the seam by brushing with melted butter. Place seam side down on a lightly buttered baking sheet. Repeat this procedure with the remaining phyllo strips and filling. Brush the tops of the triangles with melted butter. Bake in a preheated 350° oven about 15 to 20 minutes or until golden brown. Serve hot, allowing 4 *boeregs* per person.

NOTE: For smaller cocktail-size *boeregs*, cut the phyllo sheets into narrower strips and reduce the amount of filling per strip accordingly.

FILLINGS FOR BOEREGS

CHEESE FILLING

> 2 eggs
> 8 ounces small-curd cottage cheese, drained, or Muenster cheese, grated
> 4 ounces freshly grated feta cheese
> Salt to taste
> ¼ cup finely chopped parsley (optional)

18

Place the eggs in a mixing bowl and beat slightly. Add the cheeses and salt (if needed; feta is salty) and blend well. Mix in the parsley.

Makes about 1 cup

MEAT FILLING

- 2 tablespoons butter
- 1 medium onion, finely chopped
- ½ pound lean ground lamb
- 1 small tomato, peeled, seeded, and finely chopped
- Salt and freshly ground black pepper to taste
- 2 tablespoons finely chopped parsley
- 2 tablespoons pine nuts
- 2 teaspoons finely chopped fresh basil or ½ teaspoon dried basil or oregano

Melt the butter in a skillet over moderate heat. Add the onion and sauté, stirring frequently, until soft but not browned. Add the meat, and breaking it up with the back of a spoon or fork, continue to sauté until no longer pink. Add the tomato and salt and pepper and cook, stirring occasionally, until meat turns brown, about 10 minutes. Mix in the parsley, pine nuts, and basil. Taste for seasoning and cool.

Makes about 2 cups

 Variation: Omit the parsley and basil. Sauté 1 large clove garlic, minced, along with the meat. Add ½ teaspoon curry powder (or to taste) with the tomato.

SPINACH-CHEESE FILLING

- 3 tablespoons olive oil
- 1 small onion, finely chopped
- ½ pound spinach, washed, thoroughly drained, and finely chopped
- 1 tablespoon milk
- ¾ cup freshly grated feta cheese
- ¼ cup freshly grated Parmesan or Romano cheese
- Salt and freshly ground black pepper to taste
- 1 small egg, lightly beaten

Heat the olive oil in a skillet over moderate heat. Add the onion and sauté, stirring frequently, until soft but not browned. Add the spinach, and stirring frequently, simmer 10 minutes or until most of the liquid in the skillet has evaporated. Remove the skillet from the heat and mix in the milk. Cool to room temperature, then stir in the cheeses, salt and pepper, and egg. Taste for seasoning.

Makes about 1 cup

2. Soups

Chilled Yogurt and Cucumber Soup (page 27)

Armenian cuisine has a large repertoire of soups, ranging from simple vegetable, meat, or fish broths to the rich meat and vegetable combinations of the Caucasus known as *bozbash*, which may also incorporate fruit. A remarkable variety of ingredients is used in preparing soups, including such unusual foods as plum paste, pomegranate seeds, pumpkin, tripe, trout, venison, and walnuts.

Soups play an important role in the Armenian diet, particularly in the cold winter months, when a hot broth or light soup is certain to be included in the meal. The more substantial soups, such as the last eight in this chapter, are often served as the main course of a lunch or supper.

One of the oldest and most delicious of all soups is Targhana Soup, which has a unique flavor and is very satisfying on a wintry night. Another equally popular and unusual soup is *jajik*, Chilled Yogurt and Cucumber Soup, which may either precede a summer meal or accompany the main course. Both of these soups employ yogurt in their preparation, as do a number of other Armenian soups, such as the *spas* of the Caucasus, which may be made with barley, rice, wheat, lentils, or asparagus. Tomatoes and sometimes saffron are also used to flavor and color soups. Sugar-sweetened cold soups, made with apricots, cornelian cherries (*kizil*), currants, mulberries, and sweetbriar, are also popular and can be served as either a first course or dessert.

Cubed Armenian Thin Bread (page 301), toasted or fried with a little butter; onions or garlic, sautéed in butter; and chopped fresh basil, coriander, mint, parsley, and tarragon are common garnishes for soups. Also, egg and lemon sauce is added to many soups at the finish, giving them a tart flavor and thickening the consistency.

23

TARGHANA SOUP

Targhana Abour

This wholesome, hearty soup is a winter favorite of Armenian villagers.

    8 cups beef broth or water
    1 cup *targhana* (below)
    ¼ cup butter
    1½ cups finely chopped onion
    1 tablespoon crushed dried mint
Salt to taste
    2 cups unflavored yogurt

In a saucepan over high heat bring the beef broth to a boil. Add the *targhana* and reduce the heat to medium. Cook about 40 minutes or until the *targhana* is tender.

Meanwhile, melt the butter in a small skillet. Add the onion and sauté until golden brown, stirring frequently. Mix in the mint and salt. Remove from the heat and keep warm. When the *targhana* is done, stir the contents of the skillet into it, reduce the heat to low, and simmer 5 minutes. Remove from the heat, gradually stir in the yogurt until amalgamated, and serve at once.

Serves 8

TARGHANA

    ⅓ ounce compressed yeast (½ cake)
    1 cup warm water
    2 cups all-purpose flour, sifted

24

½ teaspoon salt
1⅓ cups coarse bulghur
1 cup unflavored yogurt

Dissolve the yeast in ¼ cup of the water, then mix in the remaining ¾ cup water. Add the flour, salt, bulghur, and yogurt and mix until well blended. Cover with a kitchen towel and let stand overnight. The following day form the dough into egg-size pieces, flatten them out to about a ⅛-inch thickness in the palms of your hands, and place on a cloth to dry. (Armenians living in the Middle East usually place the *targhana* outdoors in a windy spot to dry in the sun, but a warm oven may be used for this purpose.) When dried on one side, turn them over. When thoroughly dried, break into small bits and store in airtight jars to be used as needed.

Makes about 3 cups

YOGURT SOUP WITH BARLEY

Tanabour

If you like yogurt, you will love this soup. When prepared with rice it is considered a cure for all ailments.

½ cup pearl barley
4 cups beef broth or water
Salt to taste
¼ cup butter
1 medium onion, finely chopped
2 tablespoons finely chopped fresh mint leaves
2 tablespoons finely chopped parsley
1 to 2 cups unflavored yogurt (depending on thickness desired)
1 egg, beaten

Soak the barley in water overnight to soften. Drain. In a saucepan bring the beef broth to a boil over high heat. Add the barley and salt, lower the heat, and cook until tender.

Meanwhile, in a small skillet melt the butter over moderate heat. Add the onion and sauté until golden brown, stirring frequently. Remove from the heat, stir in the mint and parsley, and add to the soup. Mix well.

Pour the yogurt into a deep bowl and stir with a large spoon until smooth. Beat in the egg. Gradually stir a little hot broth from the saucepan into the yogurt mixture. Slowly pour the mixture into the saucepan. Stir constantly over low heat until well blended and heated through. Do not let the soup boil. Serve hot or cold.

Serves 4

Use 2 tablespoons each butter and minced onion. Reserve the mint and parsley for finishing the soup. Do not sauté the onion. Stir the onion and butter into the yogurt and broth mixture and simmer 1 or 2 minutes. Serve hot, sprinkled with the herbs, or chill thoroughly and sprinkle with the herbs just before serving. Caucasian Armenians make a similar soup called *spas*, using fresh mint or coriander.

Yogurt and Rice Soup

Substitute uncooked long-grain white rice for the barley. Soaking is not necessary. Use 3 to 4 cups yogurt.

Yogurt and Noodle Soup

Titmaj Abour

Substitute 1½ cups ¼-inch-wide egg noodles for the barley and 1 tablespoon crushed dried mint leaves for the fresh mint. Omit the parsley. Also, if you like garlic, substitute 1 large clove garlic, mashed with ¼ teaspoon salt, for the onion. Use 3 to 4 cups yogurt.

CHILLED YOGURT AND CUCUMBER SOUP

Jajik

This is a light and refreshing soup of inspired simplicity, renowned throughout the Middle East.

    2 medium cucumbers (about ½ pound each)
    4 cups unflavored yogurt
    ¾ cup ice water
    Salt to taste
    2 tablespoons finely chopped fresh mint leaves
    2 tablespoons finely chopped scallions, including 2 inches of the
        green tops
    4 ice cubes or ¾ cup crushed ice

Peel the cucumbers and cut lengthwise into eighths. Cut out the seeds if too large and discard. Slice the cucumbers crosswise into ¼-inch pieces.

Pour the yogurt into a deep bowl and stir with a large spoon until smooth. Add the ice water and blend gently but thoroughly. Add the cucumbers and salt and stir well. Taste for seasoning and refrigerate for several hours until thoroughly chilled.

Just before serving, sprinkle the soup with the mint and scallions. Serve in individual soup bowls, adding 1 ice cube to each bowl. (If using crushed ice, add with mint and scallions.)

Serves 4

VARIATION

Matsnabrdosh

The Caucasian variation of *jajik* is prepared by mixing equal amounts of yogurt and ice water and adding diced cucumbers, sliced hard-cooked eggs, chopped scallions, minced fresh herbs (dill, parsley, coriander), and salt to taste. *Matsnabrdosh* is served cold, with an ice cube or two added to each serving.

LENTIL SOUP I

Vosbabour

1 cup dried lentils
6 cups water
¼ cup olive oil
2 medium onions, thinly sliced
Salt and freshly ground black pepper to taste
2 teaspoons freshly squeezed and strained lemon juice
1 tablespoon chopped parsley or fresh tarragon

Wash the lentils in a sieve under running cold water. In a large heavy pot bring the water to a boil over high heat. Add the lentils, reduce the heat to low, and simmer until tender, about 20 to 40 minutes. Heat the olive oil in a skillet over moderate heat. Add the onions and sauté until golden brown, stirring frequently. Add to lentils, season to taste, and cook 10 minutes. Remove from heat, add lemon juice, sprinkle with parsley or tarragon, and serve.

Serves 4

VARIATION

Lentil-Bulghur Soup

¼ cup coarse bulghur may be added with the lentils. Chicken or beef broth may be substituted for the water, and butter for the olive oil.

LENTIL SOUP II

Vosbabour

A wonderfully rich and creamy soup, enlivened by the magic taste and aroma of tarragon.

28

1 cup dried lentils
2 tablespoons butter
1 large onion, cut lengthwise in half and thinly sliced
4 cups beef broth, more if needed
1 bay leaf
1 teaspoon paprika
Salt and cayenne to taste
2 tablespoons finely chopped fresh tarragon leaves

Wash the lentils in a sieve under running cold water. In a heavy saucepan melt the butter over moderate heat. Add the onion and sauté until soft but not browned, stirring frequently. Stir in the lentils and cook 2 to 3 minutes. Add the broth, bay leaf, paprika, and salt and cayenne and simmer until the lentils are very soft, adding more beef broth if necessary. Discard the bay leaf. Purée the soup with a food mill or in a blender. If the soup seems too thick, stir in a little additional hot beef broth. Return to the saucepan and cook over low heat a few minutes until heated through, stirring constantly. Taste for seasoning. Sprinkle with the tarragon before serving.

Serves 4

TOMATO SOUP WITH WHEAT

Tzavarabour

3 tablespoons butter
4 medium ripe tomatoes, peeled, seeded, and finely chopped, or
    1 16-ounce can tomatoes, finely chopped
½ cup coarse bulghur
4 cups boiling water
Salt and freshly ground black pepper to taste
½ pound spinach, washed, drained, stemmed, and coarsely
    chopped
1 medium clove garlic, crushed
2 tablespoons freshly squeezed and strained lemon juice
2 teaspoons crushed dried mint

In a saucepan melt the butter over moderate heat. Add the tomatoes and cook 5 minutes, stirring and mashing. Add the bulghur and cook 5 minutes, stirring occasionally. Add the boiling water, salt and pepper, spinach, and garlic, and bring to a boil, stirring constantly. Cover the pan and simmer 30 minutes or until bulghur is tender but not mushy. Stir in the lemon juice and mint 5 minutes before the soup is done.

Serves 6

Tomato Soup with Rice

Substitute uncooked long-grain white rice for the bulghur if you like, but omit the spinach, garlic, lemon juice, and mint. Serve the soup sprinkled with 2 tablespoons finely chopped parsley.

CHICKEN SOUP WITH EGG AND LEMON SAUCE

Havabour

One of the great classic soups of the Armenian cuisine, distinguished in its simplicity.

6 cups Homemade Chicken Stock (opposite page) or canned or reconstituted instant chicken broth
2 eggs
2 to 3 tablespoons freshly squeezed and strained lemon juice
Salt to taste
2 tablespoons finely chopped parsley

In a saucepan bring the chicken stock to a boil over high heat. Reduce the heat to low and keep soup at a simmer. Meanwhile, in a small bowl beat the eggs until frothy. Gradually beat in the lemon juice. Slowly pour in ½ cup of the simmering stock, beating constantly. Return the egg-lemon mixture to the simmering stock, stirring constantly. Simmer a few minutes longer until the broth thickens slightly. Do not allow the soup to boil, or the eggs will curdle. Taste for seasoning and add salt if necessary (it may not be). Serve immediately, sprinkled with the parsley.

Serves 4 to 6

NOTE: If you use a homemade chicken stock, you may add 1 cup small slivers of chicken to the finished soup.

Chicken Soup with Rice and Egg and Lemon Sauce

Add ½ cup uncooked long-grain white rice or broken vermicelli pieces to the boiling stock. Lower the heat and cook until tender but not mushy. Prepare the egg-lemon mixture and continue as above.

Chikhirtma

This is a similar soup of Caucasian Armenian origin. To prepare, have the chicken stock at a simmer as above. In a small skillet sauté 1 medium-size onion, minced, in 1 tablespoon butter until golden brown. Sprinkle with 1 tablespoon flour and cook, stirring, 1 minute. Stir a little of the stock into the contents of the skillet, then add to remaining stock in saucepan and cook as above. If you wish, you may dissolve a pinch of saffron in ¼ cup hot water and add it to the stock. Then prepare the egg-lemon mixture and continue as above. Serve the soup sprinkled with fresh coriander. *Chikhirtma* can also be made with lamb stock and slivers of lamb.

HOMEMADE CHICKEN STOCK

1 4-pound stewing chicken
Cold water
1 large onion, sliced
Salt and freshly ground black pepper to taste

Place the chicken in a large pot and cover with cold water. Bring to a boil over high heat. Skim off the scum that rises to the top. Add the onion and salt and pepper, cover the pot, and reduce the heat to low. Simmer 1½ to 2 hours or until the bird is tender. Transfer the chicken to a plate and remove the skin. Cut the meat into slivers. Strain the stock. Use the meat and stock as needed.

Makes about 2 quarts

MEATBALL SOUP WITH RICE

Gelorig

Many variations of this widely appreciated soup exist throughout the Middle East and the Caucasus. The ones given below are among the best.

     1 pound lean lamb or beef, ground twice
     2 tablespoons uncooked long-grain white rice
     1 small onion, grated
     2 tablespoons finely chopped parsley
   Salt and freshly ground black pepper to taste
     6 cups lamb or beef broth
     3 medium ripe tomatoes, peeled, seeded, and puréed, or
       3 tablespoons tomato paste
     2 tablespoons butter
     1 medium clove garlic
     ¼ teaspoon salt
     1 tablespoon crushed dried mint

In a mixing bowl combine the meat, rice, onion, parsley, and salt and pepper. Knead with the hands until well blended. Taste for seasoning. Shape the mixture into balls about 1 inch in diameter and set aside.

In a heavy saucepan bring the broth and tomatoes to a boil over moderate heat. Season with additional salt and pepper. Add the meat-

32

balls to the broth and bring to a boil. Reduce the heat, cover, and simmer 30 minutes or until tender.

Meanwhile, in a small skillet melt the butter over moderate heat. Mash the garlic together with salt and add to the skillet. Sauté briefly, stirring constantly, until the garlic is lightly browned. Mix in the mint and pour the contents of the skillet into the soup. Taste for seasoning and serve at once.

Serves 4

Meatball Soup with Rice and Egg and Lemon Sauce

The above soup is sometimes served with an egg and lemon sauce. To prepare, omit the tomatoes, and instead of finishing with the butter, garlic, salt, and mint, add Egg and Lemon Sauce (page 292).

Kololik

This is the Caucasian Armenian version of the soup. Omit the tomatoes, butter, garlic, salt, and mint. Add meatballs, ½ cup uncooked long-grain white rice, 1 small onion, minced and fried, and ¼ cup finely chopped fresh tarragon to the broth and cook until the rice is tender. Serve as is, or add Egg and Lemon Sauce (page 292), or pour a beaten egg in a slow, steady stream into the soup, bring to a boil once, and serve immediately.

MEATBALL SOUP WITH CRACKED WHEAT

Kololik Gekharkuni

Cognac imparts an aristocratic touch to this substantial Caucasian Armenian soup.

    1 pound lean ground beef
    Salt and freshly ground black pepper to taste

SOUPS   33

2 tablespoons Cognac
1 egg, beaten
2 tablespoons finely chopped fresh coriander or parsley
1 tablespoon milk
2 tablespoons flour (approximately)
8 cups beef broth, salted to taste
½ cup medium bulghur
¼ cup butter
1 small onion, finely chopped

Pound the meat until pasty and season with the salt and pepper. Continue beating until light, moistening the meat with cognac, adding it 1 teaspoon at a time. Add the egg, coriander, milk, and flour and beat until thoroughly blended. Taste for seasoning. Form the mixture into balls about 1 inch in diameter. If the mixture does not hold together, a little more flour may be added.

In a heavy saucepan bring the beef broth to a boil over high heat. Add the bulghur and meatballs and lower the heat. Cook until the bulghur is tender and the meatballs rise to the surface.

Meanwhile, in a small skillet melt the butter over moderate heat. Add the onion and sauté until lightly browned, stirring frequently. Pour the contents of skillet into the soup and taste for seasoning.

Serves 4

DUMPLING SOUP

Mantabour or Shish Barak

Manti could be described as the Armenian counterpart of Italian ravioli, Chinese won ton, or Jewish kreplach. It may be made with either a yogurt or a tomato broth.

It is best to use homemade dough for the dumplings, but if you are pressed for time, you may use won ton wrappers, available at most Oriental grocery stores.

Dumplings

DOUGH

> 3¼ cups all-purpose flour
> 1 egg
> 2 tablespoons melted butter
> 1 cup water
> Pinch salt

MEAT FILLING

> 1 pound lean ground lamb
> 2 medium onions, grated
> ⅓ cup finely chopped parsley
> Salt and freshly ground black pepper to taste

In a large mixing bowl combine the flour, egg, melted butter, water, and salt. Knead, sprinkling with additional flour if needed to prevent the dough from sticking, until smooth and elastic. Divide the dough into 2 equal parts, shaping each into a ball. Cover with a kitchen towel and let rest at room temperature 30 minutes.

Combine the lamb, onions, parsley, and salt and pepper in a bowl. Knead with the hands until well blended and smooth. Taste for seasoning and set aside.

On a lightly floured surface roll out one ball of dough about 1/16 inch thick. Cut into 1½-inch squares. Place about ½ teaspoon of the meat filling just above the lower left corner of each square. Moisten the edges of each square with a finger dipped lightly in cold water. Fold the dough over the filling so that each square forms a triangle, pinching the edges together to seal. Dip your fingers in water and bring the two outer corners of each triangle together, pinching firmly. Repeat with the second ball of dough and the remaining filling.

The dumplings may be cooked in either the Yogurt Broth or the Tomato Broth (following page).

Yogurt Broth

    3 quarts lamb or beef broth
Salt and freshly ground black pepper to taste
½ cup butter
    1 large onion, finely chopped
    2 tablespoons crushed dried mint
    6 cups unflavored yogurt

In a large, heavy pot bring the broth to a rolling boil over high heat. Add salt and pepper and drop the dumplings into the broth. Reduce the heat and cook 10 minutes or until tender.

Meanwhile, in a small skillet melt the butter over moderate heat. Add the onion and fry until golden brown, stirring frequently. Mix in the mint. Remove from the heat and keep warm.

Pour the yogurt into a deep bowl. Gradually stir up to 6 cups of the broth from the pot into the yogurt until well amalgamated. Slowly pour the yogurt mixture into the saucepan and stir until well mixed. Do not let the soup boil. Pour the contents of the skillet into the soup, stir, and simmer over low heat 1 or 2 minutes longer. Taste for seasoning. Serve at once.

Serves 6 as a main course

Tomato Broth

    3 quarts lamb, beef, or chicken broth
    4 large ripe tomatoes, peeled, seeded, and pureed, or
        4 tablespoons tomato paste
Salt to taste
    6 tablespoons butter
    2 large cloves garlic
½ teaspoon salt
    2 tablespoons crushed dried mint

In a large heavy pot bring the broth to a rolling boil over high heat. Add tomatoes and salt. Drop the dumplings into the broth. Reduce the heat and cook 10 minutes or until tender.

Meanwhile, in a small skillet melt the butter over moderate heat. Mash the garlic together with the salt and add to the skillet. Sauté briefly, stirring constantly, until the garlic is lightly browned. Mix in mint and pour the contents of the skillet into the soup. Taste for seasoning. Serve at once.

Serves 6 as a main course

MEAT AND VEGETABLE SOUP

Echmiadzin Bozbash

A robust mélange of meat, vegetables, and herbs—almost a stew.

> 1 pound lean lamb shoulder, cut into 1-inch cubes
> 8 cups water
> 1 small onion, finely chopped
> 2 tablespoons butter
> 2 medium potatoes, peeled and cubed
> 1½ cups cubed eggplant
> 1 cup diced green pepper
> 1½ cups green beans, trimmed and halved
> 1 cup tender okra, washed and trimmed of stem ends (optional)
> 2 medium tomatoes, peeled, seeded, and chopped
> Salt to taste
> 3 tablespoons finely chopped fresh basil or a mixture of basil, coriander, and parsley

Combine the lamb and water in a large, heavy casserole. Cover and simmer until the meat is half done. Skim off any foam or scum that rises to the surface. Remove the meat from the broth. Strain the broth and return it to the casserole.

In a skillet sauté the onion in the butter until soft but not browned. Add the meat and continue to sauté until the meat and onion are lightly browned. Add to the broth with the potatoes, eggplant, green pepper, green beans, and okra. If necessary, more water may be added. Cover and cook until all the vegetables are tender, adding the tomatoes, salt, and basil 15 minutes before the end of the cooking period.

Serves 4

LAMB SOUP WITH APPLE AND QUINCE

Shoushin Bozbash

Practically unknown outside of the Caucasus, this artful and fragrant combination of meat, vegetables, and fruits is one of the private delights of Caucasian Armenians.

> 1 pound lean lamb shoulder, cut into 1-inch cubes
> 8 cups water
> 1 small onion, finely chopped
> 2 tablespoons butter
> 2 tablespoons flour
> 1 medium potato, peeled and diced
> 1 small quince, cored and cut up
> Salt to taste
> 1 medium tart eating apple, peeled, cored, and cut up
> 1 tablespoon sugar or to taste
> ¼ cup finely chopped fresh savory or mint

Combine the lamb and water in a large, heavy casserole. Cover and simmer, adding more water if necessary, until the meat is half done. Skim off any foam or scum that rises to the surface. Remove the meat from the broth. Strain the broth and return it to the casserole.

In a skillet sauté the onion in the butter until soft but not browned. Add the meat and continue to sauté a few minutes more. Sprinkle with the flour and cook, stirring, until lightly browned. Add the meat mixture to the broth with the potato, quince, and salt and cook 10 minutes. Add the apple, sugar, and savory and cook until fruit is just tender.

Serves 4

✿ LAMB SOUP WITH APRICOTS

Missov Dziranabour

Although the combination of meat and fruit is uncommon in American cuisine, its delicate flavor is appreciated by Armenians. This dish will both surprise and delight your guests.

    1 pound lean lamb, cut into 1-inch cubes
    5 cups cold water
    ¼ cup butter
    1 small onion, finely chopped
    2 medium ripe tomatoes, peeled, seeded, and chopped
    4 medium boiling potatoes, peeled and cut into 1-inch cubes
    ½ cup dried apricots, halved
Salt and freshly ground black pepper to taste
    2 tablespoons chopped walnuts
    ¼ cup sugar or to taste
    ½ teaspoon cinnamon
    2 scallions, chopped

In a saucepan combine the lamb and water. Cover and simmer over low heat about 1½ hours or until the meat is very tender. Skim off any foam or scum as it rises to the surface. Remove the meat from the broth. Strain the broth and set aside.

In a large skillet melt the butter over moderate heat. Add the onion and cook until golden brown, stirring frequently. Stir in the tomatoes and cook until they become pulp. Stir 4 cups of the reserved lamb broth into the pan. Add the potatoes, apricots, and salt and pepper and heat to the boiling point. Reduce the heat to moderate, cover, and cook 15 minutes or until the potatoes are tender. Stir in the reserved meat, walnuts, sugar, and cinnamon and cook over low heat 10 minutes. Taste for seasoning. Sprinkle with the chopped scallions and serve at once.

Serves 4

3. Salads

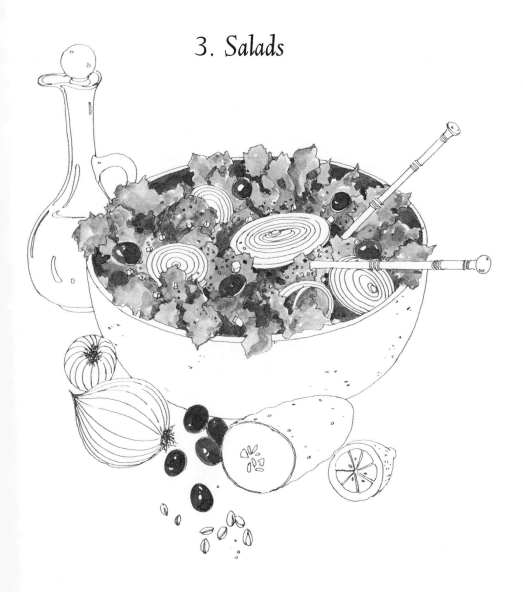

Spinach Salad (page 48)

Salads in one form or another accompany most Armenian meals. They may be presented at the beginning of the meal as *titvash* (pickled vegetables served as appetizers); cooked, dressed, and served chilled as side dishes during the main course; or simply tossed with a dressing of olive oil and lemon juice with a few herbs and seasonings and served raw as an accompaniment to meat, poultry, or fish dishes.

When in season, romaine lettuce is the favorite salad green. It also is a popular snack among some Armenian farmers, who consume a whole head of romaine fresh from the field at one sitting without the usual addition of any dressing except for a light sprinkling of salt on each leaf. The farmers told me that their children, who were also romaine-lovers, owed their rosy cheeks and good health to this and similar eating habits.

Cabbage is another common green used in salads when romaine is out of season. It makes a good accompaniment to beef dishes. Purslane, watercress, and raw spinach are also used, and people who dislike the last usually reappraise it after trying Armenian spinach salad.

Perhaps the most popular of all Armenian salads are those made with tomatoes and cucumbers, the success of which is at least partly dependent upon the quality of the vegetables used. Armenians are fond of sun-ripened, juicy tomatoes that have a rich flavor and fragance, and they prefer the tender, almost seedless variety of firm-textured cucumber. A very refreshing dish made with these cucumbers and yogurt is *jajik*, which can be served as an appetizer or a salad and which goes particularly well with lamb. For a soup version of *jajik*, consult page 27.

The cooked vegetable salads may be served as appetizers or side dishes, or they may constitute a full meal. In the latter case they are

43

arranged decoratively on a large, shallow platter, with the addition of hard-cooked eggs, cheese, olives, tomatoes, onions or scallions, green peppers, radishes, and fresh herbs. Such a platter makes a colorful and appetizing luncheon or buffet dish.

When preparing salads, it is important to use greens and vegetables which have been washed under running cold water, dried thoroughly, and chilled. For the best flavor, serve salads in chilled glass or china dishes, and add dressing just before serving unless the recipe specifically directs otherwise.

COMBINATION SALAD

Haigagan Aghtsan

6 cups torn lettuce leaves (romaine lettuce or a combination of
  romaine, Bibb, chicory, and/or endive)
1 medium tomato, seeded and chopped
1 small cucumber, peeled and sliced (cut out seeds if too large
  and discard)
1 small green pepper, seeded, deribbed, and thinly sliced
¼ cup chopped scallions, including 2 inches of the green tops
2 tablespoons finely chopped fresh mint leaves or basil or to taste
2 tablespoons finely chopped parsley
3 tablespoons olive oil
3 tablespoons freshly squeezed and strained lemon juice
Salt and freshly ground black pepper to taste

Combine the lettuce, tomato, cucumber, green pepper, scallions,
mint, and parsley in a salad bowl. Beat together the olive oil, lemon
juice, and salt and pepper with a fork or whisk until well blended and
pour over greens. Toss gently but thoroughly and serve at once.

Serves 4

NOTE: When made with mint, this salad is sometimes sprinkled with
¼ cup coarsely grated feta cheese or 2 tablespoons chopped fresh dill.

CRACKED WHEAT SALAD

Tabbouleh

This is a favorite salad in Lebanon and Syria and is enjoyed by Armenians from those countries. Certainly no picnic is complete without it.

1 cup fine bulghur
1 medium cucumber, peeled, quartered, and diced
   (cut out seeds if too large and discard)
2 large ripe tomatoes, seeded and chopped
1 small green pepper, seeded, deribbed, and finely chopped
1 cup finely chopped onions or scallions
2 cups finely chopped parsley
½ cup finely chopped fresh mint
½ cup olive oil
½ cup freshly squeezed and strained lemon juice
Salt and freshly ground black pepper to taste
Romaine lettuce leaves

Soak the bulghur in water to cover for 15 to 20 minutes. Drain in a colander lined with a double thickness of dampened cheesecloth, then enclose in the cheesecloth and squeeze dry. Place the bulghur in a mixing bowl, add the remaining ingredients except for the lettuce, and toss gently but thoroughly together with a fork. Taste for seasoning and mound in the center of a serving platter. Surround with romaine lettuce leaves and serve cold.

Serves 6

ROMAINE SALAD

Hazar Aghtsan

8 cups torn romaine lettuce leaves
½ cup peeled and thinly sliced cucumber (cut out seeds if too large and discard)
¼ cup chopped scallions, including 2 inches of the green tops
¼ cup finely chopped fresh mint leaves
¼ cup finely chopped parsley
¼ cup olive oil
¼ cup freshly squeezed and strained lemon juice
Salt and freshly ground black pepper to taste

Combine the lettuce, cucumber, scallions, mint, and parsley in a salad bowl. Beat together the olive oil and lemon juice with a fork or whisk until well blended. Season with salt and pepper and pour over greens. Toss gently but thoroughly and serve at once. This is very good with fish, chicken, and meat dishes.

Serves 4 to 6

CABBAGE SALAD

Gaghamp Aghtsan

2 cups finely shredded white cabbage
½ cup thinly sliced green pepper
¼ cup thinly sliced sweet onion
1 small tomato, seeded and finely chopped
¼ cup finely chopped fresh mint leaves (optional)
¼ cup olive oil
2 tablespoons freshly squeezed and strained lemon juice
Salt to taste

Combine the cabbage, green pepper, onion, tomato, and mint in a salad bowl. Beat together the olive oil and lemon juice with a fork or whisk until well blended. Season with the salt and pour over the vegetables. Toss gently but thoroughly and serve at once. This salad is very good with beef dishes.

Serves 4

✿ SPINACH SALAD

Sbanakh Aghtsan

1 pound spinach, washed, drained, stemmed, and torn into pieces
2 medium cucumbers, peeled, quartered lengthwise, and diced (cut out seeds if too large and discard)
¼ cup sliced black olives
2 tablespoons thinly sliced sweet onion
½ cup finely chopped parsley
2 tablespoons chopped salted and roasted pistachios
¼ cup olive oil
3 tablespoons freshly squeezed and strained lemon juice or 1½ tablespoons red wine vinegar
Salt and freshly ground black pepper to taste

Combine the spinach, cucumbers, olives, onion, parsley, and pistachios in a salad bowl. Beat the olive oil and lemon juice together with a fork or whisk until well blended. Season with the salt and pepper and pour over the vegetables. Toss gently but thoroughly and serve at once.

Serves 4

SPINACH-YOGURT SALAD

Sbanakh yev Madzoon Aghtsan or Borani

⅓ cup water
½ pound spinach, washed, drained, stemmed
 1 small clove garlic
¼ teaspoon salt
 1 tablespoon freshly squeezed and strained lemon juice
 2 tablespoons finely chopped fresh mint leaves or 1 teaspoon
   crushed dried mint
Salt and freshly ground black pepper to taste
1½ cups unflavored yogurt

In a saucepan bring the water to a boil over high heat. Add the spinach and lower the heat. Cover and simmer 10 minutes. Drain and cool the spinach, then squeeze it dry and chop finely. Mash the garlic together with the salt. In a mixing bowl combine the spinach with the lemon juice, mint, garlic and salt, and salt and pepper and blend well. Gradually stir in the yogurt and mix thoroughly. Taste for seasoning. Transfer to a serving dish, cover, and refrigerate until thoroughly chilled.

Serves 4

CUCUMBER AND YOGURT SALAD

Jajik

 2 medium cucumbers, peeled and quartered lengthwise (cut out
   seeds if too large and discard)

1 small clove garlic
¼ teaspoon salt or to taste
2 tablespoons finely chopped fresh mint leaves or 1 teaspoon crushed dried mint
2 cups unflavored yogurt

Slice the cucumbers crosswise into ¼-inch pieces. With a small mortar and pestle mash together the garlic and salt to a smooth paste. Add with the mint to the yogurt and mix well. Stir in the cucumbers, taste for seasoning, and refrigerate. *Jajik* is particularly good in warm weather as a first course or accompaniment to lamb. A recipe for a soup version of this salad is on page 27.

Serves 4

CUCUMBER AND TOMATO SALAD

Varounk yev Lolig Aghtsan

2 medium cucumbers, peeled, quartered lengthwise (cut out seeds if too large and discard), and diced
4 medium tomatoes, seeded and cut into small pieces
4 scallions, chopped, including 2 inches of the green tops
¼ cup finely chopped fresh mint leaves
5 tablespoons olive oil
¼ cup freshly squeezed and strained lemon juice
Salt and freshly ground black pepper to taste
Crusty bread, thickly sliced

Combine the cucumbers with the tomatoes, scallions, and mint in a salad bowl. Add the olive oil, lemon juice, and salt and pepper to the vegetables and toss gently but thoroughly. Taste for seasoning and serve at once with the crusty bread for dipping in the salad juices. This is excellent with fried meatballs, meat loaf, fried or broiled fish, and broiled or roasted poultry and lamb.

Serves 6

NOTE: Finely chopped fresh dill or a combination of basil and parsley are sometimes substituted for the mint. A small green or red pepper, chopped, may be added.

TOMATO AND ONION SALAD

Lolig yev Sokh Aghtsan

4 medium tomatoes, seeded and cut into small pieces
1 medium sweet onion, chopped, or 8 scallions, chopped, including 2 inches of the green tops
3 tablespoons olive oil
2 tablespoons freshly squeezed and strained lemon juice
Salt and freshly ground black pepper to taste
Crusty bread, thickly sliced

Combine the tomatoes and scallions in a salad bowl. Add the olive oil, lemon juice, and salt and pepper to the vegetables and toss gently but thoroughly. Taste for seasoning, cover, and refrigerate 1 hour. Just before serving, carefully stir once more, taste again for seasoning, and serve at once with the crusty bread for dipping in the salad juices.

Serves 4

Variation: 1 small green pepper, thinly sliced, ½ cup chopped parsley, and 2 tablespoons finely chopped fresh mint leaves are sometimes added to this salad. Prepared this way, it is often served with Raw Lamb and Wheat Patties (page 174).

ASPARAGUS AND EGG SALAD

Dznepeg yev Havgit Aghtsan

1 pound asparagus
2 hard-cooked eggs, sliced
2 tablespoons finely chopped parsley
3 tablespoons olive oil
2 tablespoons wine vinegar or to taste
1 small clove garlic, mashed
Salt to taste

Snap off the tough ends of the asparagus. Cut into 1-inch pieces. Cover with boiling salted water and boil, uncovered, 15 to 20 minutes or until tender. Drain, place in a serving bowl, and cool. Combine with the eggs. Sprinkle the top with the parsley. Beat together the olive oil, vinegar, garlic, and salt until well blended. Pour over the asparagus and eggs. Chill.

Serves 4

GREEN BEAN SALAD

Ganach Lupia Aghtsan

2 quarts salted water
1 pound green beans, trimmed and cut into 2-inch pieces
6 tablespoons olive oil
3 tablespoons red wine vinegar
Salt and freshly ground black pepper to taste
1 small onion, thinly sliced
¼ cup finely chopped parsley or fresh dill
1 medium tomato, seeded and chopped

Over high heat bring the salted water to a boil. Drop in the green beans and boil, uncovered, about 10 minutes or until tender but still crisp. Drain the beans and keep them warm. Meanwhile, beat together the olive oil and vinegar with a fork or whisk until well blended. Season with the salt and pepper. Combine the warm beans, onion, and parsley in a salad bowl and pour the dressing over all. Toss gently but thoroughly, taste for seasoning, cover, and refrigerate until chilled. Just before serving, carefully mix in the tomato and taste again for seasoning.

Serves 4

NOTE: Frozen green beans may be substituted for the fresh beans. Cook according to package directions, drain, and proceed as above.

CAULIFLOWER SALAD

Intagaghamp Aghtsan

1 medium head cauliflower, separated into flowerets
1 slice lemon peel
2 scallions, finely chopped
2 tablespoons finely chopped parsley
8 black olives
¼ cup olive oil
¼ cup freshly squeezed and strained lemon juice
Salt to taste

Cover the cauliflower with boiling salted water, add the lemon peel, and boil, uncovered, 10 minutes or until the cauliflower is tender. Drain, place in a salad bowl, and cool. Sprinkle the cauliflower with the scallions and parsley and garnish with the olives. Beat together the olive oil, lemon juice, and salt with a fork or whisk until well blended and pour over the salad. Serve cold.

Serves 4

BEET SALAD WITH TOASTED SESAME SEEDS

Jagintegh Aghtsan

1 sixteen-ounce can julienne or diced beets
3 tablespoons olive oil
1 tablespoon red wine vinegar
1 medium clove garlic, crushed
Salt and freshly ground black pepper to taste
2 tablespoons toasted sesame seeds (see below)
Bibb lettuce leaves

Drain the beets and place in a bowl. Using a fork or whisk, beat together the olive oil, vinegar, garlic, and salt and pepper until well blended. Pour over the beets, taste for seasoning, cover, and refrigerate several hours or overnight. Just before serving, stir gently, taste again for seasoning, and sprinkle with the toasted sesame seeds. Serve on the lettuce leaves. This is tasty with broiled fish and chicken.

Serves 3 or 4

To toast sesame seeds: Spread the seeds in a shallow baking pan and bake in a preheated 350° oven until lightly and evenly toasted, about 15 minutes. Stir the seeds occasionally, watching them closely to prevent burning.

EGGPLANT SALAD

Simpoog Aghtsan

2 eggplants (about 1¼ pounds each)
2 medium tomatoes, cut in eighths and seeded
1 small onion or 2 scallions, finely chopped
¼ cup diced green pepper
½ cup peeled, diced cucumber
¼ cup chopped parsley
1 small clove garlic, crushed (optional)
½ cup olive oil
3 tablespoons red wine vinegar
Salt and freshly ground black pepper to taste

Cut the stem and hull from the top of each eggplant and discard. Bake the eggplants in a preheated 350° oven about 1 hour or until cooked through. When cool enough to handle, peel off the skin and slit the eggplants open. Scoop out the seeds and discard. Dice the flesh and place in a salad bowl. Add the tomatoes, onion, green pepper, cucumber, and parsley. If the garlic is used, combine with the olive oil and stir to extract the garlic flavor, then discard the garlic pieces. Add the olive oil with the vinegar and beat together with a fork or whisk until well blended. Season with the salt and pepper and pour over the vegetables. Toss gently but thoroughly, taste for seasoning, and marinate 1 hour. Stir gently before serving. This is excellent with broiled or fried fish.

Serves 4

VARIATION

Mashed Eggplant Salad

Prick the skin of 1 large eggplant in several places and broil, preferably over charcoal, turning frequently, until the flesh is very soft and the skin charred. (The eggplant must be thoroughly cooked inside; otherwise it will have a bitter taste, rendering the dish inedible.) When cool enough to handle, peel off the skin, remove any badly charred spots, and slit open. Scoop out the seeds and discard. Place the eggplant pulp in a bowl. Immediately pour 3 tablespoons freshly squeezed and strained lemon juice over it and mash thoroughly into a smooth paste. Gradually beat in 2 tablespoons olive oil, 1 small clove garlic, crushed (optional), and salt and pepper to taste. Spread on a serving platter, cover, and chill. Before serving, garnish with tomato, green pepper, and onion slices and black olives. Sprinkle with minced parsley.

KIDNEY BEAN SALAD

Garmir Lupia Aghtsan

1 cup drained canned red kidney beans
2 tablespoons vegetable or olive oil
1 tablespoon wine vinegar
¼ cup finely chopped onion
¼ cup finely chopped parsley
2 tablespoons finely chopped fresh coriander or ½ teaspoon ground coriander
Salt and freshly ground black pepper to taste
Bibb or red-tipped lettuce leaves
2 tablespoons finely chopped fresh dill (optional)
1 medium tomato, cut into eighths
1 small green pepper, seeded, deribbed, and sliced
8 black olives
1 lemon, cut into 4 wedges

Rinse the beans under running cold water and dry with paper towels. In a deep bowl combine the vegetable oil, vinegar, onion, parsley, coriander, and salt and pepper and beat together with a fork or whisk until well blended. Add the beans and toss gently but thoroughly.

Taste for seasoning, cover, and chill. Just before serving, stir gently and taste again for seasoning. Serve on lettuce leaves, sprinkled with the dill and garnished with the tomato, green pepper, olives, and lemon wedges.

Serves 2

WHITE BEAN SALAD

Germag Lupia Aghtsan or Fassoulia Piaz

1 cup dried white beans (preferably, Great Northern)
¼ cup olive oil
¼ cup freshly squeezed and strained lemon juice
1 tablespoon wine vinegar
Salt and freshly ground black pepper to taste
 1 medium clove garlic, crushed (optional)
 2 medium tomatoes, seeded and chopped
 1 small green pepper, seeded, deribbed, and chopped
 ¼ cup chopped scallions, including 2 inches of the green tops
 2 tablespoons chopped parsley

Soak the beans overnight in water to cover. Drain and rinse. Cover with fresh water and bring to a boil over high heat. Reduce the heat to low and simmer, partially covered, until beans are tender but not mushy. Add boiling water if needed to keep beans covered during cooking. When done, drain, place in a salad bowl, and keep warm. Beat together the olive oil, lemon juice, vinegar, salt and pepper, and garlic with a fork or whisk until well blended. Pour over the warm beans and toss gently but thoroughly. Taste for seasoning, cover, and chill. Just before serving, carefully mix in the tomatoes, green pepper, scallions, and parsley. Taste again for seasoning. This can be served either as an appetizer or as a salad.

Serves 4

NOTE: You may substitute lentils or chick-peas for the white beans. You also may add drained canned tuna, quartered hard-cooked eggs, and black olives to the salad to make a pleasant luncheon dish.

POTATO SALAD

Kednakhintzor Aghtsan

6 medium potatoes
1 small cucumber, peeled and sliced
1 tomato, seeded and cut into eighths
1 small onion or 4 scallions, finely chopped
¼ cup finely chopped fresh dill or to taste
¼ cup olive oil
¼ cup freshly squeezed and strained lemon juice
1 tablespoon wine vinegar
Salt and freshly ground black pepper to taste
8 black olives (preferably the Greek variety)
Paprika

Cook the potatoes in boiling salted water until tender but not mushy. Drain and peel. Cube and place on a flat serving dish. Surround with the cucumber and tomato. Sprinkle with the onion and dill. Beat together the olive oil, lemon juice, vinegar, and salt and pepper with a fork or whisk until well blended and spoon over the salad. Garnish with black olives and sprinkle with paprika. This salad goes well with cold cuts as a luncheon or buffet dish.

Serves 4

NOTE: Some Armenians like to eat this salad without the dressing.

POTATO SALAD WITH SOUR CREAM

Titvaserov Kednakhintzor Aghtsan

This salad is enjoyed by Russian Armenians.

   4 medium potatoes
   1 small cucumber, peeled and diced (cut out seeds if too large
      and discard) (optional)
Salt and freshly ground black pepper to taste
   ½ cup sour cream
   2 scallions, finely chopped
   3 tablespoons finely chopped parsley

Cook the potatoes in boiling salted water until tender. Drain and peel. Cut into small pieces and place in a salad bowl with the cucumber. Season with the salt and pepper and toss gently with the sour cream. Serve cold, sprinkled with the scallions and parsley.

Serves 4

EGG SALAD

Havgit Aghtsan

   4 hard-cooked eggs, sliced
   2 tablespoons thinly sliced onion
   1 medium tomato, cut into wedges
   1 small green pepper, seeded, deribbed, and sliced
   8 black olives
   3 tablespoons olive oil
   3 tablespoons freshly squeezed and strained lemon juice

Salt and freshly ground black pepper to taste
1 tablespoon finely chopped fresh mint leaves
1 tablespoon finely chopped parsley
Crusty bread (optional)

Arrange the eggs, onion, tomato, green pepper, and olives in an attractive pattern on a serving platter. Beat together the olive oil and lemon juice with a fork or whisk until well blended. Season with the salt and pepper and mix in the mint and parsley. Spoon over the eggs and vegetables to coat them evenly. Serve at once as a salad or appetizer, accompanied with the crusty bread. This also makes a tasty luncheon dish when served with cold cuts, shellfish, salmon, or tuna.

Serves 4

TONGUE SALAD

Lehzou Aghtsan

1 small fresh beef or veal tongue (about 2 pounds), trimmed
   of fat and gristle
Salt and freshly ground black pepper to taste
Bibb lettuce leaves
½ cup chopped scallions, including 2 inches of the green tops
½ cup chopped parsley
¼ cup olive oil
¼ cup freshly squeezed and strained lemon juice or 2 tablespoons
   red wine vinegar
1 large clove garlic, crushed (optional)
Salt and freshly ground black pepper to taste
2 hard-cooked eggs, quartered
2 medium tomatoes, cut into eighths
8 black olives

Scrub the tongue well and rinse under running cold water. Place in a saucepan and cover with boiling water seasoned with the salt and pepper. Reduce the heat and simmer, uncovered, about 2 hours or until tender. Lift out the tongue from the saucepan and discard the cooking liquid. While the tongue is still hot but cool enough to handle, skin and slice. Place the lettuce leaves on a serving platter and arrange the tongue slices over them. Sprinkle the scallions and parsley over the top. Beat together the olive oil, lemon juice, garlic, and additional salt and pepper with a fork or whisk until well blended. Spoon over the tongue. Garnish with the eggs, tomatoes, and olives. Serve at once as a luncheon or buffet dish.

Serves 4

4. Egg Dishes and Sandwiches

Hard-cooked eggs served with tarragon and Lavash (page 301)

Eggs are an important food in Armenian cuisine and a popular choice for lunch. Most of the following egg dishes, accompanied by a salad of greens and tomatoes, are suitable for a light meal. Some are equally good as a first course.

Green bean or spinach omelets may start the meal, or they may even be served in place of a vegetable in a Western menu featuring roast or fried chicken. Basterma with Eggs is a dish with an unusual taste, often served during the winter. It can be quite strong and is usually accompanied by crusty bread and plenty to drink. Tea goes well with it, and it will quench your thirst afterward. A mystery dish is Fruit Paste Dipped in Egg; its tantalizing taste will keep your guests guessing. Plain omelets are served sprinkled with powdered sugar or with honey or jam on the side. They may also be served with Garlic Yogurt Sauce (page 288).

At Easter a basketful of hard-cooked eggs dyed a deep red decorates the dinner table. In keeping with an old Armenian custom, these eggs are cracked against one another by the diners before being peeled and eaten. The person whose egg is champion wins all the rest!

Since sandwiches do not form an integral part of traditional Armenian cuisine, colorful pictures of them in American magazines held irresistible magic for us as children, much to the chagrin of our elders, who found that even their flaming skewers of shish kebab could not match the imagined delights of a hot dog photographed with mouth-watering realism, an exotic foreign delicacy that we yearned to taste.

This is not to say that Armenian sandwiches do not exist. A popular sandwich with Caucasian Armenians is hard-cooked eggs and fresh tarragon rolled in *lavash*. Also a favorite snack is the Armenian cheese sandwich, made with *lavash*. The baked cheese sandwich is based on the idea of cheese *boereg*. If you suddenly find yourself craving the latter and don't have time to prepare it, try the former instead.

Most of the sandwiches included in this chapter I have improvised from recipes in the meat and vegetable chapters. Broiled Skewered Lamb (shish kebab), Ground Lamb on Skewers (*luleh kebab*), and Cumin Patties (*chamanov keufteh*), all from Chapter 7, are delicious in sandwiches. This is especially true if the sandwiches are made with *lavash*, which can easily be rolled around them, making a leakproof package. Most of the omelets listed in this chapter will also make excellent sandwich fillings.

CHEESE OMELET

Banirov Tzuazegh

4 eggs
Salt and freshly ground black pepper to taste
¼ cup milk
1 tablespoon finely chopped parsley
1 tablespoon finely chopped fresh mint or basil leaves
¼ cup finely chopped scallions, including 2 inches of the
 green tops
½ cup freshly grated Gruyère cheese
2 tablespoons butter

In a mixing bowl beat the eggs with the salt and pepper until frothy, using a large fork or whisk. Beat in the milk, parsley, mint, scallions, and cheese until well blended. Taste for seasoning. In a heavy skillet melt the butter over moderate heat. Pour in the egg mixture and spread it out evenly. Reduce the heat to low, cover, and cook until the edges of the omelet begin to get firm. Uncover and run a spatula around the edges to keep it from sticking to the pan. When the center of the omelet is almost firm, place a plate over the skillet and invert, dropping the omelet onto the plate. Gently slide it back into the pan, cover, and cook a few minutes longer until the underside is lightly browned. Slide out onto a serving plate, cut into wedges, and serve at once.

Serves 2

EGGS WITH TOMATOES

Loligov Havgit

   2 tablespoons olive oil
  ¼ cup finely chopped onion
   1 medium tomato, peeled, seeded, and finely chopped
   4 eggs
Salt and freshly ground black pepper to taste
   2 tablespoons light cream or milk
   1 tablespoon finely chopped parsley
  ¼ teaspoon curry powder or to taste

In a heavy skillet heat the olive oil over moderate heat. Add the onion and sauté until transparent, stirring frequently. Add the tomato, reduce the heat to low, and simmer about 5 minutes, stirring occasionally.

In a mixing bowl beat the eggs with the salt and pepper until frothy, using a large fork or whisk. Beat in the cream, parsley, and curry powder until well blended. Pour the mixture into the skillet and cook, stirring constantly, until the eggs are thick and creamy.

Serves 2

VARIATION

Eggs with Tomatoes and Basil or Mint

In a skillet with an ovenproof handle sauté 2 medium-size tomatoes, peeled, sliced, and seeded, in 2 tablespoons butter. Sprinkle with salt and finely chopped basil or mint leaves to taste and mix gently, being careful not to break the tomatoes. Beat 4 eggs with a pinch of salt and pour into the skillet. Bake in a preheated 350° oven about 4 minutes or until the eggs are firm. Sprinkle with freshly ground black pepper and serve at once.

68

PARSLEY OMELET

Azadkeghov Tzuazegh or Ijjah

This omelet is traditionally served at Easter by some Armenians.

   4 eggs
   ¼ cup finely chopped parsley
   4 scallions, finely chopped, including 2 inches of the green tops
   1 medium clove garlic, finely chopped (optional)
Salt and freshly ground black pepper to taste
   1 cup olive or vegetable oil

   Place the eggs in a mixing bowl and beat until frothy. Add the parsley, scallions, garlic, and salt and pepper and mix well. Heat the oil in a heavy skillet until hot. Drop the egg mixture a tablespoon at a time into the hot oil, being careful not to overcrowd the skillet. When each omelet is golden brown on one side, turn to brown the other side. Serve warm or cold.

Serves 4

ASPARAGUS AND CHEESE OMELET

Dznepegov yev Banirov Tzuazegh

   ½ pound asparagus
   2 tablespoons butter
   ½ cup finely chopped scallions, including 2 inches of the green tops
   2 tablespoons finely chopped parsley
   4 eggs
   3 tablespoons milk
Salt to taste
   ⅓ cup freshly grated Gruyère or Monterey Jack cheese

Snap off the tough ends of the asparagus. Cut the stalks into ¾-inch pieces. Drop into boiling salted water and cook briefly until half tender. Drain in a colander.

In a small skillet with an ovenproof handle melt the butter over moderate heat. Add the scallions and sauté until soft but not browned, stirring frequently. Add the asparagus and sauté, turning to cook on all sides. Stir in the parsley.

In a small bowl beat the eggs with the milk and salt, using a large fork or whisk. Mix in the cheese. Pour over the asparagus mixture and bake in a preheated 350° oven 2 to 3 minutes or until the eggs are firm. Serve at once.

Serves 4

SPINACH OMELET

Sbanakhov Tzuazegh

1 pound spinach, washed and stemmed
4 tablespoons butter
1 small onion, finely chopped
Salt to taste
4 eggs

Place the spinach leaves in a saucepan. Cover and cook 5 minutes over moderate heat. Drain thoroughly and chop coarsely.

In a skillet melt 2 tablespoons of the butter over moderate heat. Add the onion and sauté until soft but not browned, stirring frequently. Add the spinach and salt. Cook until the liquid in the pan has almost completely evaporated. Add the remaining 2 tablespoons butter to the skillet, reduce the heat to low, and cook, stirring frequently, a few minutes longer.

Beat the eggs well. Pour half into a buttered shallow baking dish, about 9 inches in diameter. Using a spatula, spread the spinach mixture in an even layer over this. Pour the remaining eggs on top. Bake in a preheated 375° oven 15 to 20 minutes or until the eggs are firm and a golden crust forms on top. Cut into squares or wedges and serve at once.

Serves 4

70

❀ ZUCCHINI OMELET

Titoumov Tzuazegh

2 tablespoons butter
2 medium zucchini, quartered and cut into ⅜-inch-thick slices
1 cup scallions, chopped, including 2 inches of the green tops
1 medium tomato, peeled, seeded, and chopped
1 medium clove garlic, crushed
1 tablespoon chopped fresh dill
Salt and freshly ground black pepper to taste
4 eggs

In a heavy skillet with an ovenproof handle melt 1 tablespoon of the butter over moderate heat. Add the zucchini and sauté until golden brown on both sides. Transfer to a plate and keep warm.

Place the remaining 1 tablespoon butter in the skillet and heat. Add the scallions and sauté until soft but not browned, stirring frequently. Add the tomato and garlic, stir, and cook until the juice from the tomato has almost completely evaporated.

Return the zucchini to the skillet and mix gently. Stir in the dill and season with the salt and pepper. Using a large fork or whisk, beat eggs well with a pinch of salt and pour over the vegetables in the skillet. Bake in a preheated 450° oven about 6 minutes or until the eggs are set. Serve at once.

Serves 4

❀ LAMB OMELET

Missov Tzuazegh

2 tablespoons butter
1 medium onion, finely chopped

    2 tablespoons pine nuts or chopped walnuts (optional)
½ pound lean ground lamb
    1 small tomato, peeled, seeded, and chopped
    1 medium clove garlic, crushed
½ teaspoon curry powder or to taste
    2 tablespoons finely chopped parsley
Salt and freshly ground black pepper to taste
    4 eggs

In a heavy skillet with an ovenproof handle melt the butter over moderate heat. Add the onion and sauté until soft but not browned, stirring frequently. Stir in the nuts and sauté until golden brown on all sides. Add the lamb and cook until lightly browned, breaking it up with the back of a spoon or fork. Add the tomato, garlic, and curry powder and continue to cook until the tomato juice is absorbed, stirring frequently. Stir in the parsley and salt and pepper.

Using a large fork or whisk, beat the eggs well with a pinch of salt. Pour over the lamb mixture in the skillet. Bake in a preheated 450° oven about 10 minutes or until the eggs are firm. Serve hot or cold, cut into wedges, with a green salad.

Serves 2

LAMB AND GREEN BEANS WITH EGGS

Havgitov yev Missov Ganach Lupia

    1 pound lean boneless lamb, cut into 1-inch cubes
Lamb or beef broth
    1 pound green beans, trimmed and halved
    4 tablespoons butter
    1 small onion, finely chopped
¼ cup finely chopped fresh dill
Salt and freshly ground black pepper to taste
    4 eggs

In a heavy saucepan cover the lamb with the broth. Simmer, covered, about 1 hour or until the lamb is tender, skimming off any foam or scum as it rises to the surface. Drain and set the meat aside. Drop the beans into fresh boiling broth and cook until tender. Drain the beans and reserve.

In a large, heavy skillet with an overproof handle melt 2 tablespoons of the butter over moderate heat. Add the onion and sauté until soft but not browned, stirring frequently. Add the meat and the remaining 2 tablespoons butter. Sauté until the onion and meat are lightly browned. Remove from the heat, add the beans and dill, and toss gently. Sprinkle with the salt and pepper. Beat the eggs well and pour into the skillet. Bake in a preheated 375° oven 4 to 5 minutes or until the eggs are firm. Serve at once.

Serves 4

Plain Green Bean Omelet

Ganach Lupia Tzuazegh

Omit the lamb and broth. Trim the beans and cut lengthwise in half, French style. Drop into 2 quarts boiling salted water and boil, uncovered, 10 minutes or until tender but still somewhat firm. Drain and keep warm. Sauté the onion in the butter as above. Add the remaining butter to the skillet, then the green beans and salt. Reduce the heat to low and cook 5 minutes, stirring occasionally. Remove from the heat, add the dill or basil to taste, and toss gently. Beat the eggs and pour half into a buttered shallow baking dish about 9 inches in diameter. Spread the bean mixture evenly over and pour the remaining eggs on top. Bake as above about 15 minutes or until the eggs are firm and a golden crust forms on top. Cut into squares or wedges and serve at once.

BASTERMA WITH EGGS

Havgitov Basterma

1 tablespoon butter
10 thin slices *basterma* with some fat on it
 4 eggs
Salt and freshly ground black pepper to taste
Crusty bread

In a heavy skillet melt the butter over moderate heat. Cover the bottom of the pan with the *basterma*, reduce the heat to low, and cook 30 seconds on each side. Break the eggs over the *basterma*, keeping them well apart. Sprinkle lightly with the salt and pepper, cover, and cook gently until the eggs set. Serve with the bread.

Serves 2

SAUSAGE WITH EGGS

Havgitov Yershig (Soudjuk)

¼ pound *soudjuk* (or you may substitute garlic-seasoned smoked
   sausage)
 4 eggs
Salt and freshly ground black pepper to taste
 1 tablespoon butter

Remove the casing from the sausage and cut into ¼-inch-thick slices. Using a large fork or whisk, beat the eggs well with the salt and

74

pepper. In a heavy skillet melt the butter over moderate heat. Cover the bottom of the pan with the sausage slices, reduce the heat to low, and cook until the sausage begins to sizzle. Turn the sausage, pour on the beaten eggs, and fry until the eggs are set. Serve at once.

Serves 2

FRUIT PASTE DIPPED IN EGG

Havgitov Bastegh

4 sheets apple, apricot, plum, raspberry, or strawberry fruit roll (page 352)
2 tablespoons butter (approximately), preferably Clarified Butter (page 355)
1 egg, lightly beaten

Cut the fruit roll into 2-inch pieces. In a heavy skillet melt the butter over moderate heat. Dip the pieces of fruit roll in beaten egg to coat thoroughly on both sides. Fry 1 minute or so on each side, a few at a time, regulating the heat as needed. As the pieces are cooked, remove to a serving plate and keep warm. Continue to cook the remaining pieces of fruit roll, adding more butter as necessary. Serve hot.

Serves 6

ARMENIAN CHEESE SANDWICH

Haigagan Banirov Sandvich

I have not given specific amounts here because one usually determines them according to his taste or mood.

Armenian Thin Bread (page 301), rolled to a diameter of about 14 inches
Thinly sliced feta cheese

Thinly sliced, seeded, and drained tomato
Thinly sliced cucumber (use the tiny, almost seedless variety if
    available)
Salt to taste
Fresh mint leaves

Sprinkle the bread (*lavash*) with water to soften as described in the
recipe on pages 301–302. When pliable, arrange the cheese slices in a
straight line 4 inches from the bottom, leaving a 2- to 3-inch border on
each side. Place the tomato slices and then the cucumber slices over the
cheese. Sprinkle with the salt and top with the mint leaves. Fold over
the sides of the bread, then fold the bottom edge over the filling and
roll up tightly like a jelly roll. Serve at once.

Makes 1

NOTE: The above is also delicious as a filling for *pideh* (Armenian
Bread, page 302), French bread, or hard rolls. If desired, you may
substitute imported Bel Paese, brick, Edam, or Muenster cheese for
the feta.

BAKED CHEESE SANDWICH

Yepvadz Banirov Sandvich

Thinly sliced French bread, crusts removed
Melted butter
Grated cheese (brick, Muenster, Havarti [Danish Tilsit], Parme-
    san, or Romano)
Beaten egg
Finely chopped parsley (optional)
Salt to taste

Brush 1 side of the bread slices with the butter. Blend the cheese
with enough of the egg to make a soft paste. Mix in a little parsley
and the salt.

Arrange half the bread slices, buttered sides down, on a baking sheet. Spread the cheese mixture evenly over the surface of each slice and cover with the remaining bread slices, buttered sides up. Bake in a preheated 350° oven about 15 minutes or until toasted. Serve hot.

NOTE: The Cheese Filling (page 18) and Spinach-Cheese Filling (page 19) for *boeregs* may also be used in this sandwich.

VARIATION

Baked Eggplant and Cheese Sandwich

Place slices of Fried Eggplant (page 260) over cheese filling before baking sandwich.

FRIED EGGPLANT AND CHEESE SANDWICH

Dabgvadz Simpoogov yev Banirov Sandvich

Sliced French or Italian bread
Slices of Fried Eggplant (page 260) or Eggplant Fried in Eggs (page 275)
Thinly sliced Havarti (Danish Tilsit), Monterey Jack, brick, or imported Bel Paese cheese
Salt to taste

Place 1 slice each of eggplant and cheese on a bread slice, sprinkle with salt, top with another bread slice, and press together. Cut in half and serve.

Makes 1

VARIATION

Fried Zucchini and Cheese Sandwich

Substitute slices of Fried Zucchini (page 268) or Zucchini Fried in Eggs (page 276) for the eggplant.

✿ EGG AND TOMATO SANDWICHES

Havgitov yev Loligov Sandvichner

1 tablespoon butter
1 tablespoon olive oil
4 eggs, beaten
2 small Armenian Rolls (page 303) or 2 hard rolls, cut lengthwise
   in half
Tomato slices
Fresh mint, basil, or tarragon leaves
Salt and freshly ground black pepper to taste

In a heavy skillet heat the butter and olive oil over low heat. Add the eggs and cook to taste, stirring with a fork as they begin to thicken. Spoon the eggs onto two of the roll halves. Cover with the tomato slices and mint, season to taste, and top with the remaining roll halves. Serve at once.

Makes 2

NOTE: These sandwiches are also good made with French or Italian bread, toasted English muffins, or *lavash* (Armenian Thin Bread, page 301).

5. Fish and Shellfish

Trout on a Spit garnished with pomegranate seeds (page 96)

People who are interested in Armenian cuisine have heard of *boereg, dolma,* shish kebab, and *baklava,* and those who have tasted them appreciate the enthusiasm with which they are acclaimed. Few, however, are aware of the culinary adventure that Armenian fish cookery can provide.

Throughout Armenian history fish has been highly valued. In ancient times fish were kept in large tanks. Then as now trout was considered a delicacy. Ancient ways of preparing fish included brushing with butter and roasting whole on a spit or stuffing and gilding with saffron; *kutap* is a dish that has come down to us virtually unchanged.

The waters of Armenia have yielded a rich harvest since antiquity. At one time she bordered on the Black Sea, which provided her citizens with a bounteous array of fish and shellfish of supreme flavor. The great lakes of Van and Urmia lay within her territory, and smaller Lake Sevan, now in Soviet Armenia, has for many centuries been a source of trout renowned throughout the Caucasus for its flavor and succulence. During the time of the Crusades the kingdom of Cilicia, or Little Armenia, was situated on the Mediterranean coast in what is now southern Turkey and included the cities of Seleucia and Tarsus. Its location enabled Armenians to enjoy seafood in abundance and variety.

The fish industry in modern Soviet Armenia is highly developed. Many different kinds of fish, including bass, carp, salmon, and trout, are harvested from its lakes and rivers. There are several kinds of trout, some weighing over thirty pounds, but the most famous is the *ishkhan,* or "prince," with its silvery scales and reddish flesh.

Trout is a Caucasian Armenian specialty which is cooked in many ways. Eggs, *lavash,* pomegranate seeds, potatoes, dried plums, walnuts, wine, and tarragon are used in the preparation of trout dishes.

In this chapter I have included recipes for stewed, baked, fried, and broiled fish. The popular fish *plaki* as well as Fried Fish Balls are excellent when served cold and make ideal summer meals. These are often served as hors d'oeuvres or featured at buffet dinners. The delightful shellfish pilafs in Chapter 10 are also fine choices for buffets.

Fried fish is particularly appetizing when served with lemon sauce and garnished with cucumbers, tomatoes, scallions, and fresh mint and parsley leaves. For an unusual dish try Fried Fish with Oranges or Fried or Baked Stuffed Mackerel with an exotic filling of pine nuts, scallions, parsley, and curry powder.

A favorite preparation method is to grill fish over a charcoal fire and serve it with plenty of lemon juice or lemon sauce. Sometimes the fish is cubed and marinated in an olive oil and lemon juice dressing, in the same manner as shish kebab, and charcoal broiled on skewers. Broiled whole fish or fish steaks are prepared with a variety of delicious sauces including lemon sauce flavored with scallions, garlic, or curry powder; egg sauce; pomegranate sauce; or the famous *tarator* sauce, made with nuts and flavored with garlic, which is also good with baked fish or Fried Fish Balls.

OYSTER PLAKI

Vosdré Plaki

2 medium onions, cut lengthwise and thinly sliced
4 medium tomatoes, peeled, seeded, and chopped
⅓ cup finely chopped parsley
2 medium cloves garlic, finely chopped
2 tablespoons olive oil
1 tablespoon freshly squeezed and strained lemon juice
⅓ cup hot chicken broth
Salt and freshly ground black pepper to taste
12 large oysters, cleaned and shucked
1 lemon, quartered

Combine the onions, tomatoes, parsley, garlic, olive oil, lemon juice, broth, and salt and pepper in a heavy saucepan. Bring to a boil and reduce the heat to low. Cover and simmer about 30 minutes or until the mixture is reduced to the consistency of a thick sauce. Scatter the oysters on top and continue to simmer about 10 minutes. Remove from the heat and cool. Serve cold, with the lemon wedges.

Serves 4

NOTE: You may substitute clams, mussels, or shrimp for the oysters.

❧ SHRIMP IN WINE SAUCE

6 tablespoons butter
1 pound shrimp, cleaned and deveined
2 medium onions, finely chopped
4 large tomatoes, peeled, seeded, and finely chopped
½ teaspoon dried thyme leaves
½ cup dry white wine
½ cup hot water
Salt and freshly ground black pepper to taste

Melt 2 tablespoons of the butter in a skillet over moderate heat. Add the shrimp and sauté about 3 minutes or just until they turn pink, stirring frequently. Remove to a plate and keep warm.

Place the remaining 4 tablespoons butter in the skillet and heat. Add the onions and sauté until lightly browned, stirring frequently. Add the tomatoes, thyme, wine, and water, reduce the heat to low, and simmer 40 minutes.

Return the shrimp to the skillet and add the salt and pepper. Cook, 8 minutes, stirring several times. Serve hot, over Plain Rice Pilaf (page 219) or spaghetti, and follow with a crisp green salad.

Serves 4

FISH PLAKI

Tsoug Plaki

1 2½- to 3-pound red snapper or any firm whole white-fleshed
   fish, cleaned, split from head to tail, and boned
⅓ to ½ cup olive oil
Salt and freshly ground black pepper to taste
3 medium tomatoes, peeled, seeded, and chopped
¼ cup finely chopped parsley
2 large cloves garlic, finely chopped
¾ cup crushed saltine crumbs
½ cup dry white wine
Romaine lettuce leaves
2 lemons, cut into wedges

Wash the fish well under running cold water. Drain and dry thoroughly with paper towels. Place skin side down in a shallow bake-and-
serve dish brushed with a bit of the olive oil. Sprinkle with the salt and
pepper.

Mix together the remaining olive oil, tomatoes, parsley, and garlic
and spread over fish. Sprinkle the top with the cracker crumbs and
pour the wine around the fish. Bake in a preheated 350° oven 30 to
40 minutes or until just done, basting occasionally with the pan
juices. Do not overcook. Cool and serve on lettuce leaves, accompanied
by the lemon wedges.

Serves 4

VARIATION

Fish and Vegetable Plaki

Omit the saltine crumbs and lettuce. Peel and dice 3 medium potatoes and 2 medium carrots. Combine with 1 stalk celery, diced, and salt
in a large, heavy saucepan with enough water to cover. Bring to a boil

and cook 10 minutes. Drain and set aside. Prepare the fish as above and surround in the pan with the cooked vegetables. If desired, cover the fish with 1 lemon, thinly sliced. Mix together the remaining olive oil, tomatoes, ½ cup parsley, garlic, and salt and pepper and spread over the fish. Add the wine and bake as above. Serve cold, with the lemon wedges.

STUFFED SOLE EN PAPILLOTE

8 sole or flounder fillets of equal size (about 2 pounds)
3 tablespoons olive oil
1 large onion, finely chopped
⅓ cup finely chopped parsley
½ teaspoon curry powder or to taste
Salt and freshly ground black pepper to taste
Olive oil
1 lemon, cut into wedges

Wash the fish under running cold water and dry thoroughly with paper towels. In a small skillet heat the olive oil over moderate heat. Add the onion and sauté until golden brown, stirring frequently. Stir in the parsley, curry powder, and salt and pepper and mix well.

Spoon the onion mixture evenly over 4 of the fillets and cover with the remaining 4 fillets. Brush generously with olive oil. Wrap each "sandwich" separately in a double layer of waxed paper. Place the packages in an oiled ovenproof baking dish, dampen the tops with a little water, and bake in a preheated 350° oven about 30 minutes. Serve hot, with the lemon wedges. This is good with baked or fried potatoes and Combination Salad (page 45).

Serves 4

Variation: Here is the Caucasian Armenian version of this dish. Brush a double layer of waxed paper with butter. Lay cleaned fish fillets in the center and cover with tomato slices, minced scallions, and chopped fresh tarragon. Sprinkle with salt and pepper. Wrap up the waxed

86

paper securely, turning the ends under. (Armenians traditionally used parchment paper and sealed the edges with dough to insure a leak-proof package.) Place in a buttered shallow baking dish and bake about 20 minutes.

BAKED STUFFED BASS

Porov Tsoug

1 3½- to 4-pound striped bass, cleaned and eviscerated but not split
Salt to taste
Stuffing (below)
3 tablespoons butter
1 lemon, cut crosswise into ⅛-inch-thick slices

Wash the fish well under running cold water and dry thoroughly with paper towels. Sprinkle inside and out with the salt and fill with the stuffing. Sew up the opening. Lay the fish in an oiled shallow bake-and-serve dish. Dot with the butter. Bake in a preheated 350° oven 50 to 60 minutes, basting occasionally with the pan juices. Serve hot, garnished with the lemon slices and accompanied by buttered new potatoes, baby carrots, and Cabbage Salad (page 47).

Serves 6

Stuffing for Baked Fish

6 tablespoons olive oil
1 cup finely chopped onions
½ cup pine nuts
1 cup soft fresh bread crumbs
Salt and freshly ground black pepper to taste
½ cup dried currants
⅓ cup finely chopped parsley
¼ cup finely chopped fresh dill or 2 tablespoons dried dill weed

In a large, heavy skillet heat the olive oil over moderate heat. Add the onions and cook until golden brown, stirring frequently. Stir in the pine nuts, reduce the heat to low, and cook a few minutes until the nuts begin to take on color. Add the bread crumbs and salt and pepper. Cook 5 minutes, stirring often. Remove from the heat and stir in the currants, parsley, and dill. Taste for seasoning. Cool to room temperature before stuffing fish.

VARIATION

Baked Unstuffed Fish with Garlic and Nut Sauce

Place the fish in a shallow baking dish and brush with melted butter. Sprinkle with salt and 1 bay leaf, broken up. Pour a little water around the fish and bake in a preheated 350° oven until done. Serve hot, with Garlic and Nut Sauce (page 290) and a side dish of fried sliced vegetables such as eggplant, cauliflower, or zucchini.

✿ FRIED FISH WITH GARNISH

Dabgvadz Tsoug

This dish can provide a colorful and original main course for a summer meal. The vegetables, mint, and lemon sauce give it a garden freshness and fragrance which elicit much praise, even from those who do not ordinarily care for fried fish.

> 2 pounds fish fillets, about ½ inch thick (red snapper, cod, whitefish, or flounder)
> ¼ cup freshly squeezed and strained lemon juice
> 2 large cloves garlic, mashed
> Salt to taste
> ½ cup flour seasoned with salt and pepper to taste
> Olive oil for deep frying
> Romaine lettuce leaves
> 1 medium cucumber, peeled and sliced
> 2 medium tomatoes, sliced
> 24 fresh mint leaves
> Lemon Sauce (page 288)

Wash the fish under running cold water and dry thoroughly with paper towels. Cut into small uniform serving pieces. Dip into the lemon juice, rub evenly with the garlic, and sprinkle lightly with the salt on both sides. Roll in the seasoned flour and deep-fry in hot oil until golden brown. Drain on absorbent paper and arrange over the lettuce on a serving platter. Garnish with the cucumber, tomatoes, and mint leaves. Serve at once, with the Lemon Sauce and French-fried potatoes or homemade potato chips.

Serves 4

✿ FRIED FISH WITH ORANGES

Narinchov Dabgvadz Tsoug

The combination of fish and oranges may seem odd at first glance but is actually very subtle and refreshing, as well as visually appealing. I have served this dish often, and it has always turned out to be a great success.

2 pounds whitefish or red snapper fillets, about ½ inch thick
Salt to taste
Grated rind of 2 oranges
¼ cup flour, seasoned with salt, pepper, and 1 teaspoon paprika
Olive oil for deep frying
Romaine or chicory leaves
  4 medium oranges, peeled and thinly sliced crosswise
  1 small onion, sliced ⅛ inch thick and separated into rings
20 pitted black olives
30 fresh mint leaves (approximately)
½ cup olive oil
¼ cup freshly squeezed and strained lemon juice
½ cup freshly squeezed and strained orange juice
  1 small clove garlic, mashed (optional)

Wash the fish under running cold water and dry thoroughly with paper towels. Cut into small uniform serving pieces. Sprinkle lightly with the salt and rub both sides with the grated orange rind. Roll in the seasoned flour and deep-fry in the hot olive oil until golden brown. Drain on absorbent paper and arrange over the lettuce on a serving platter. Surround with the orange slices topped with the onion rings and olives. Garnish with the mint.

Beat together the oil, lemon juice, orange juice, garlic, and additional salt with a fork or whisk until well blended. Spoon evenly over the fish and oranges. Serve at once, with shoestring potatoes or homemade potato chips.

Serves 4

FRIED STUFFED MACKEREL

Uskumru Dolma

This classic preparation is an example of the stuffed dishes for which Armenians have such a fondness.

    4 mackerel (about 12 ounces each)
    6 tablespoons olive oil
    4 medium onions or 16 scallions, finely chopped
    ⅓ cup pine nuts
    ½ cup finely chopped parsley
    1 teaspoon curry powder or to taste
Salt and freshly ground black pepper to taste
    2 eggs, beaten
    2 tablespoons flour, seasoned with salt and pepper to taste
    1 lemon, cut into 6 wedges

Remove the head and tail from each mackerel, then split lengthwise into 2 fillets. Remove as many bones as possible. Wash under running cold water, drain, and dry thoroughly with paper towels.

In a heavy skillet heat 4 tablespoons of the olive oil over moderate heat. Add the onions and sauté until soft and lightly browned, stirring frequently. Stir in the pine nuts, reduce the heat to low, and cook 2 or 3 minutes until golden brown. Remove from the heat and mix in the parsley, curry powder, and salt and pepper.

Divide the mixture into 4 equal portions and spread over 4 of the fillets. Cover with the remaining 4 fillets and sew up the edges securely. Dip each stuffed fish in the beaten eggs, roll in the seasoned flour, and fry in the remaining 2 tablespoons olive oil about 4 or 5 minutes on each side or until golden brown and tender. Serve at once, with the lemon wedges, accompanied by Fried Eggplant (page 260) or sautéed potatoes and Tomato and Onion Salad (page 51).

Serves 4

VARIATIONS

Omit the eggs and seasoned flour. Instead of frying the stuffed fish, brush with oil, wrap separately in aluminum foil, place in a baking pan, and bake in a preheated 350° oven about 30 minutes or until done.

Kutap

Armenians living in the Caucasus have made a dish with trout similar to Fried Stuffed Mackerel (above) since ancient times. To prepare it, trim off the fins of each trout and break the backbone in several places by bending the tail forward. Roll the fish back and forth on a board until the backbone and flesh are loosened. Cut the fish through the throat behind the gills. With a long-handled spoon, scoop out the viscera through this opening and discard. Rinse the fish thoroughly inside and out, then pull out the backbone. Without breaking the skin, gently press the fish with your thumbs from the tail forward, so that the loosened flesh will come out through the opening behind the gills. Sprinkle the cavity with salt and stuff with a mixture of the chopped flesh, boiled rice, melted butter, raisins, and ginger, using only as much stuffing as the fish will comfortably take. Curve each fish into a ring and insert the tail into the mouth. Place in a buttered shallow baking dish and coat the top lightly with bread crumbs. Sprinkle with melted butter. Bake in a preheated 350° oven about 30 minutes or until tender. Garnish with parsley before serving.

FRIED FISH BALLS

Tsougov Keufteh

2 cups water
1 small onion, cut lengthwise, then thinly sliced
2 sprigs parsley
1 bay leaf
1 tablespoon freshly squeezed and strained lemon juice
Salt to taste
4 peppercorns
1 pound haddock, halibut, mackerel, or sea bass, cleaned and washed
2 thick slices white bread, trimmed of crusts, soaked in water, squeezed dry, and crumbled
1 medium onion, grated
2 eggs
¼ cup finely chopped parsley
¼ cup finely chopped fresh dill (optional)
Freshly ground black pepper to taste
1 egg, beaten
Olive oil for deep-frying

Combine the water, onion, parsley sprigs, bay leaf, lemon juice, salt and peppercorns in a wide saucepan and bring to a boil over high heat. Add the fish and reduce the heat to low. Cover and cook about 15 minutes or until the fish is tender. With a perforated spoon, remove the fish to a platter.

When cool enough to handle, skin, bone, and grind the fish. In a mixing bowl combine the ground fish, bread, onion, 2 eggs, parsley, dill, additional salt, and pepper. Knead thoroughly until smooth. Taste for seasoning. Shape into 1-inch balls, dip in the beaten egg, and fry in the hot olive oil until golden brown, about 2 minutes. Serve hot or cold as an hors d'oeuvre or entrée with Lemon Sauce (page 288), Garlic and Nut Sauce (page 290), or Tomato Sauce (page 293).

Serves 4

Variation: Caucasian Armenians make fish balls with trout. To prepare, clean, wash, and bone 1 pound trout. Cut into pieces and grind twice. Add fresh bread crumbs, beaten egg, 1 clove mashed garlic, ⅛ teaspoon nutmeg, and salt and pepper to taste, and mix well. Form into 1-inch balls and fry in hot oil. Serve with a tomato sauce.

ARMENIAN BROILED FISH

Khorovadz Tsoug

2 pounds whole mackerel, red snapper, bass, flounder, or other
    fish, cleaned, or fish fillets
2 tablespoons olive oil
Salt and freshly ground black pepper to taste
Lemon Sauce (page 288)

Wash the fish under running cold water and dry with paper towels. Brush an ovenproof pan with 1 tablespoon of the olive oil. Place the fish skin side down in the pan, brush with the remaining 1 tablespoon oil, and sprinkle with the salt and pepper. Broil slowly in a preheated broiler 15 to 20 minutes, basting several times with the pan juices. Transfer the fish to a heated platter and spoon the Lemon Sauce over it. Serve with fried eggplant, zucchini, or cauliflower.

Serves 4

NOTE: 1 teaspoon dried oregano leaves may be added, along with parsley. Broiled shrimp or lobster are also delicious with this sauce.

(continued)

Broiled Fish with Egg Sauce

Omit the Lemon Sauce. Serve fish with Egg Sauce (page 289) and a garnish of parsley sprigs, pimientos, and olives.

Broiled Fish with Garlic and Lemon Sauce

Omit the Lemon Sauce. In a small skillet melt 2 tablespoons butter over moderate heat. Stir in 2 tablespoons freshly squeezed and strained lemon juice, 2 cloves garlic, mashed, and ¼ cup minced parsley and remove from heat. When the fish is done, discard the pan juices. Spoon the contents of the skillet over it and place under the broiler for a few minutes. Serve hot, garnished with lemon wedges and accompanied by boiled potatoes and Spinach Salad (page 48).

❀ Broiled Fish with Lemon Curry Sauce

Omit the Lemon Sauce. Substitute 3 tablespoons melted butter for the olive oil. When the fish is done, pour off the excess liquid from the pan. Spoon Lemon Curry Sauce (page 292) over it and broil 1 or 2 minutes longer. Serve hot, accompanied by small boiled potatoes over which some of the sauce has been spooned.

GRILLED FISH ON SKEWERS

Tsougov Shish Kebab

> 2 tablespoons grated onion
> ¼ cup freshly squeezed and strained lemon juice
> 2 tablespoons olive oil
> 1½ teaspoons salt
> ½ teaspoon freshly ground black pepper
> 24 bay leaves
> 2 pounds swordfish or halibut, skinned, boned, and cut into 1-inch cubes

½ cup melted butter

½ cup finely chopped scallions, including 2 inches of the green tops

¼ cup finely chopped parsley

2 medium tomatoes, cut into eighths

2 lemons, cut into wedges

In a large bowl combine the onion, lemon juice, olive oil, salt, pepper, and bay leaves. Add the cubed fish and turn about to coat thoroughly with the marinade. Cover and let stand at room temperature 2 to 3 hours or in the refrigerator 4 to 5 hours, turning the fish from time to time.

Remove the fish and bay leaves from the marinade and thread them alternately on skewers. Broil, preferably over a charcoal fire, 3 inches from heat about 10 minutes, basting frequently with the butter and turning the skewers to allow the fish to brown lightly but evenly on all sides.

Using a fork, push the fish off the skewers onto warm individual plates and sprinkle with the scallions and parsley. Garnish with the tomato and lemon wedges and serve at once with Plain Saffron Rice Pilaf (page 222).

Serves 4

NOTE: 1 teaspoon dried oregano may be added to the marinade.

Variation: Quartered tomatoes, green peppers, and onions may also be strung on the skewers and broiled along with the fish, in which case omit the scallions, parsley, tomatoes, and lemons. Serve instead with Lemon Sauce (page 288).

TROUT ON A SPIT

Khorovadz Ishkhanatsoug

The magic of this simple dish depends largely on the quality and flavor of the fish and the glittering tartness provided by the pomegranate seeds. It tastes best, of course, on the banks of Lake Sevan, made with trout just pulled from the water, and a visit to Armenia can hardly be considered complete without the sampling of Sevan trout.

    4 trout (about 8 to 10 ounces each)
    Salt and paprika to taste
    2 tablespoons butter
    2 lemons, sliced
    Fresh tarragon leaves
    2 cups pomegranate seeds

Clean the fish. Cut down through the throat just behind the gills. With a long-handled spoon, scoop out and discard the viscera. Wash the fish inside and out and dry with paper towels. Carefully make several gashes on the outside with a knife. Sprinkle inside and out with the salt and paprika. Put long skewers lengthwise through the fish and grill over charcoal, brushing the fish with the butter and turning occasionally until golden brown and cooked through.

Slide the fish off the skewers onto a heated serving platter and garnish with the lemon slices, tarragon, and ½ cup of the pomegranate seeds. Serve the remaining pomegranate seeds in a bowl on the side.

Serves 4

6. Poultry and Game

Armenian Fried Chicken (page 105)

Armenia's many mountain streams and lakes furnish ideal settings for outdoor picnics and festivals, where the traditional folklore—in music, dances, games, and foods—comes to life. Some of the most delectable Armenian dishes, prepared on the spot, may include poultry and game birds such as chicken, duck, goose, partridge, pheasant, quail, squab, turkey, and woodcock roasted on a spit over wood embers. The bird is rubbed with melted butter and lemon juice and basted with the drippings until done, when it will have turned a rich golden brown and have a very special flavor of wood smoke. It is then served on a large platter surrounded by a rice pilaf and vegetables or fruits.

For less festive occasions such as a family outing or back-yard cookout one could serve marinated broiled chicken with pilaf and a salad or *titvash* (assorted pickles). Other favorites often reserved for special occasions and holidays include roast turkey, chicken, or goose, which is usually accompanied by saffron, fruited, or almond pilaf.

A winter chicken dish is the traditional Chicken and Wheat Puree, with its souplike consistency, whereas Chicken Casserole with Vegetables would provide an excellent main course in summer suitable for a buffet dinner.

ROAST CHICKEN WITH RICE
OR WHEAT STUFFING

Pilavov Letzvadz Hav

A stuffed chicken is an honored dish among Armenians.

1 3- to 3½-pound chicken
Rice Stuffing or Wheat Stuffing (opposite page)
4 tablespoons melted butter
1 tablespoon vegetable oil
Salt to taste
1 to 2 tablespoons hot chicken broth

Dry the chicken inside and out with paper towels. Loosely fill the body cavity with one of the stuffings. Reserve any leftover stuffing to serve later with chicken. Sew the vent closed and truss the chicken. Combine the melted butter and vegetable oil. Brush the chicken thoroughly with the mixture and place breast side up in a shallow roasting pan just large enough to hold it comfortably.

Put the pan in a preheated 450° oven and reduce the heat to 350°. Roast about 1 hour and 20 to 30 minutes or until cooked through, basting every 15 minutes with the butter and oil mixture, and when this is used up, with the pan juices. Salt the chicken when half done. The chicken is done if the drumstick can be moved easily in its socket and when the juices that run from the fleshiest part of the thigh when it is pierced with the point of a sharp knife are a pale yellow. If you are using a meat thermometer, cook to an internal temperature of 180 to 190°, depending on how well done you like chicken.

Transfer the chicken to a heated serving platter and remove the trussing strings. Let stand 5 to 10 minutes before carving. Reheat any reserved leftover stuffing over low heat, adding the hot chicken broth to moisten. Fluff with a fork and simmer until the broth is absorbed and the mixture is heated through. Serve in a separate bowl for second helpings. This chicken is good with buttered green peas or beans and Tomato and Onion Salad (page 51).

Serves 4

Rice Stuffing

> ¼ cup butter
> ½ cup finely chopped onion or scallions, including 2 inches of the green tops
> The liver and heart of the chicken, coarsely chopped
> 2 tablespoons pine nuts
> 1 cup uncooked long-grain white rice
> 1 medium tomato, peeled, seeded, and puréed
> 1½ cups chicken broth
> 2 tablespoons dried currants
> 1 tablespoon chopped parsley
> ½ teaspoon allspice or cinnamon
> Salt and freshly ground black pepper to taste

In a heavy saucepan melt the butter over moderate heat. Add the onion and sauté until soft, stirring frequently. Add the liver, heart, and pine nuts and cook until lightly browned. Add the rice and cook until the grains are coated with butter, stirring constantly. Add the tomato, broth, currants, parsley, allspice, and salt and pepper. Bring to a boil and reduce the heat to low. Cover and simmer about 20 minutes or until the liquid in the pan is absorbed. Cool to room temperature before stuffing the chicken.

NOTE: You may substitute 3 tablespoons finely chopped fresh dill for the allspice or cinnamon and omit the parsley.

Wheat Stuffing

> 5 tablespoons butter
> The liver and heart of the chicken, coarsely chopped
> Salt and freshly ground black pepper to taste
> 1 medium onion, finely sliced

½ cup thinly sliced celery or green pepper
2 medium tomatoes, peeled, seeded, and finely chopped
1 cup coarse bulghur
2 teaspoons finely chopped fresh mint leaves (optional)
½ cup drained canned chick-peas (optional)
1¼ cups chicken broth

In a skillet melt 1 tablespoon of the butter over moderate heat. Add the liver, heart, and salt and pepper and sauté 2 or 3 minutes, stirring frequently. Remove from the heat and set aside.

In a heavy saucepan melt the remaining 4 tablespoons butter over moderate heat. Add the onion and sauté until it begins to soften, stirring frequently. Add the celery and tomatoes and cook a few minutes more until the vegetables are golden brown on all sides. Add the bulghur and mint and cook until the bulghur grains are coated with butter, stirring constantly. Add the chick-peas, broth, reserved liver and heart, and additional salt and pepper. Bring to a boil and reduce the heat to low. Cover and simmer 20 to 25 minutes or until the liquid in the pan is absorbed. Cool to room temperature before stuffing the chicken.

NOTE: Either of the above stuffings may be used to fill a turkey, capon, Cornish hen, squab, quail, woodcock, pheasant, or grouse.

❧ ROAST CHICKEN WITH APRICOT AND CHESTNUT STUFFING

Dziranov yev Shakanagov Letzvadz Hav

This festive chicken, with an extravagantly rich stuffing, can provide a treat for a special occasion.

1 4-pound roasting chicken
¼ cup melted butter
½ cup pomegranate juice made from fresh pomegranates, sweetened with 1 tablespoon sugar or to taste
Apricot and Chestnut Stuffing (opposite page)

Dry the chicken inside and out with paper towels. Loosely fill the body cavity with the stuffing. (Bake any leftover stuffing in a buttered shallow baking dish, putting it in the oven with the chicken for the last 30 minutes of baking. Serve for second helpings.) Sew up the vent and truss the chicken. Brush thoroughly with the melted butter. Place the chicken breast side up in a shallow roasting pan just large enough to hold it comfortably.

Put the pan in a preheated 450° oven and reduce the heat to 350°. Roast 1 hour and 30 minutes or until cooked through and golden brown, basting every 15 minutes with butter and pomegranate juice, and when these are used up, with pan drippings. The chicken is done if the drumstick can be moved easily in its socket and when the juices that run from the fleshiest part of the thigh when it is pierced with the point of a sharp knife are a pale yellow. If you are using a meat thermometer, cook to an internal temperature of 180 to 190°, depending on how well done you like chicken.

Transfer the chicken to a heated serving platter, and remove the trussing strings. Let stand 5 to 10 minutes before carving. Serve with Plain Rice Pilaf (page 219) and a green salad.

Serves 4 or 5

Apricot and Chestnut Stuffing

½ pound chestnuts
2 tablespoons butter or vegetable oil
1 medium onion, finely chopped
½ pound lean ground or chopped lamb
½ cup dried apricots or pitted prunes, quartered (soak prunes in a bowl of warm water for 10 minutes to soften)
¼ cup chopped walnuts or ¼ cup pine nuts sautéed in butter
¼ teaspoon cinnamon
¼ teaspoon allspice
⅛ teaspoon nutmeg
Salt and freshly ground black pepper to taste
2 cups toasted bread cubes (made from French or homemade white bread) with 2 tablespoons melted butter (optional)
3 to 4 tablespoons pomegranate juice made from fresh pomegranates, sweetened with sugar to taste

With a sharp knife slit the chestnut shells without cutting through the meat. Place in a pan and bake in a preheated 500° oven 15 minutes. Remove the outer shells and peel off the inner skins. Cover the chestnuts with salted water and simmer, covered, 20 minutes. Drain, chop coarsely, and set aside.

In a skillet melt the butter over moderate heat. Add the onion and lamb and sauté until lamb is lightly browned, stirring frequently. Add the apricots and sauté 5 minutes. Remove from the heat and add the nuts, cinnamon, allspice, nutmeg, salt and pepper, and the bread cubes and butter, if used, and reserved chestnuts. Mix well, moisten with the pomegranate juice, and taste for seasoning. Cool to room temperature before stuffing the chicken.

NOTE: The above stuffing may be used to fill a turkey, duck, goose, capon, or Cornish hen.

BROILED CHICKEN

Khorovadz Varyag

2 **two-pound chickens, cut into serving pieces**
6 **tablespoons olive oil**
6 **tablespoons freshly squeezed and strained lemon juice**
2 **large cloves garlic, crushed**
2 **teaspoons dried oregano or thyme**
Salt and freshly ground black pepper to taste

Wipe chicken with damp paper towels. In a large bowl mix together the remaining ingredients until well blended. Add chicken, turning to coat thoroughly with the mixture. Cover and marinate at room temperature 2 hours or in the refrigerator 4 to 5 hours, turning the pieces over occasionally.

Remove chicken from the marinade and broil 20 to 25 minutes, preferably over charcoal, about 3 inches from heat, turning and brushing frequently with the marinade until well browned, crisp, and cooked through. Serve hot, with Plain Saffron Rice Pilaf (page 222) or Plain Cracked Wheat Pilaf (page 231) and Tomato and Onion Salad (page 51).

Serves 4

VARIATION

 Curried Broiled Chicken

Marinate the chicken in a mixture of 1 cup grated onion, ½ cup freshly squeezed and strained lemon juice, and 1½ teaspoons salt. Broil as above, brushing with both the marinade and ½ cup melted butter mixed with 2 teaspoons curry powder or to taste and ¾ teaspoon salt.

ARMENIAN FRIED CHICKEN

Tapaka

2 squab chickens (1 to 1¼ pounds each) or Cornish game hens
Salt and freshly ground black pepper to taste
3 to 4 tablespoons Clarified Butter (page 355)

Dry the chickens thoroughly with paper towels. Beginning at the neck end, cut each bird lengthwise along the backbone. Pull out and discard the backbone. Cover the chickens with waxed paper and flatten by pounding with a cleaver. Rub thoroughly with the salt and pepper.

In a heavy skillet heat the butter over moderate heat. Add the chickens, skin side down, cover, and cook 15 minutes. Lower heat and cook 10 minutes. Turn chickens over, cover, and again cook 15 minutes over medium heat and 10 minutes over reduced heat or until a deep golden brown and very tender.

(continued)

Serve hot, with sautéed tomato, green pepper, and eggplant slices and a bowl of hot chicken bouillon, flavored with puréed garlic, if desired, on the side.

Serves 2

NOTE: For a crisp skin, Caucasian Armenians brush the chicken with sour cream before frying.

BAKED CHICKEN WITH TOMATO SAUCE

2 large chicken breasts, halved
2 tablespoons olive oil
1 tablespoon freshly squeezed and strained lemon juice
Salt to taste
3 tablespoons butter
2 large ripe tomatoes, peeled, seeded, and puréed, or 2 cups canned tomatoes, mashed
1 teaspoon dried oregano
Freshly ground black pepper to taste

Dry the chicken breasts with paper towels. Mix together the olive oil, lemon juice, and salt until well blended and brush over chicken. Place in an oiled baking dish and bake in a preheated 375° oven 30 minutes, turning once.

Meanwhile, in a small skillet melt the butter over moderate heat. Add the tomatoes, oregano, additional salt, and pepper and cook gently about 10 minutes, stirring occasionally. Spoon sauce evenly over chicken breasts. Reduce oven heat to 325° and bake 50 minutes or until tender, basting from time to time with pan drippings. Serve with Plain Rice Pilaf (page 219), Rice Pilaf with Vermicelli (page 220), or spaghetti and Romaine Salad (page 47).

Serves 4

CHICKEN CASSEROLE WITH VEGETABLES

Havov Kchuch (Guevech)

1 medium eggplant
Salt
2 large chicken breasts, halved
½ cup olive oil (approximately)
2 medium zucchini, scraped and sliced 1 inch thick
2 large green peppers, quartered, seeded, and deribbed
2 medium ripe tomatoes, peeled, seeded, and sliced very thinly
2 medium cloves garlic, finely chopped
Freshly ground black pepper to taste
2 tablespoons butter

Remove stem and hull from the eggplant. Peel lengthwise in ½-inch strips, leaving ½-inch strips of skin between, making a striped design. Cut crosswise into 1-inch thick slices. Sprinkle generously with the salt, weigh down with a heavy object, and let stand 20 minutes. Rinse and dry thoroughly with paper towels. Set aside.

Dry the chicken breasts well with paper towels. In a heavy skillet heat 2 tablespoons of the oil over moderate heat. Add the chicken breasts, skin side down, and sauté until golden brown on both sides. Transfer the chicken to a casserole and sprinkle with more salt.

Add the eggplant to the skillet and sauté briefly until the slices are lightly browned on both sides, adding more oil as necessary. Place over the chicken in the casserole. Sauté the zucchini and arrange over the eggplant. Sauté the green peppers and place over the zucchini. Cover with the tomato slices, sprinkle the top with the garlic, more salt, and pepper, and dot with the butter.

Cover and bake in a preheated 350° oven about 1 hour or until chicken and vegetables are tender. Serve hot, with Plain Rice Pilaf (page 219), or serve cold with French bread.

Serves 4

(continued)

Variation: Here is the Caucasian Armenian version of this dish. Place a row of thick tomato slices in the bottom of a casserole rubbed generously with soft butter and sprinkle them with salt. Rub chicken breasts with salt and place over the tomatoes, then cover with a layer each of tomato, eggplant, onion, and green pepper slices, sprinkling each layer with salt, pepper, and cinnamon. Add 4 whole cloves, dot with butter, cover, and simmer until the chicken and vegetables are tender. Sprinkle with chopped fresh dill and serve hot with Plain Rice Pilaf (page 219).

BRAISED CHICKEN WITH VEGETABLES AND WINE

Panjareghenov yev Kiniov Yepvadz Hav

1 3-pound chicken, cut into serving pieces
3 tablespoons olive oil
2 medium onions, halved lengthwise and sliced
2 medium carrots, peeled and sliced crosswise 1 inch thick
4 medium ripe tomatoes, peeled, seeded, and finely chopped
2 medium cloves garlic, finely chopped
¼ cup finely chopped parsley
Salt and freshly ground black pepper to taste
1 cup water
¼ cup sauterne

Dry the chicken thoroughly with paper towels. In a large, heavy skillet heat the olive oil over moderate heat. Add the chicken, skin side down, and sauté, turning to brown evenly on all sides. Remove to a plate and set aside. Add the onions and carrots to the skillet and cook until lightly browned, stirring frequently. Return the chicken to the skillet. Add the tomatoes, garlic, parsley, salt and pepper, and water. Cover and simmer 30 minutes. Add the wine and simmer 10 minutes or until the chicken is tender. Taste for seasoning. Serve with Plain Rice Pilaf (page 219) and Romaine Salad (page 47).

Serves 4

Variation: Omit the carrots and wine. Sauté the chicken as above and transfer to a casserole. Add the onions and ½ pound whole mushrooms to the skillet and sauté until brown. Spoon the mixture over the chicken together with the tomatoes, garlic, parsley, and salt and pepper. Add ¾ cup water, cover, and bake in a preheated 350° oven about 1 hour or until chicken is tender. Serve hot as above, or cold, with French bread.

CHICKEN WITH OKRA

Bamiyov Hav

1 3- to 3½-pound chicken, cut into serving pieces
3 tablespoons butter
1 large onion, finely chopped
4 large ripe tomatoes, peeled, seeded, and chopped, or 1 pound canned plum tomatoes
½ cup water
Salt and freshly ground black pepper to taste
1 pound okra, washed and trimmed of stem ends, or 2 ten-ounce packages frozen whole okra, defrosted
3 tablespoons freshly squeezed and strained lemon juice

Dry the chicken thoroughly with paper towels. In a large, heavy casserole melt the butter over moderate heat. Add the chicken, skin side down, and sauté until barely colored on all sides, turning with tongs and regulating the heat. Add the onion and sauté until golden brown. Add the tomatoes, water, and salt and pepper. Cover and cook over medium heat 15 minutes. Add the okra and lemon juice. Cover and simmer 40 minutes or until the chicken and okra are tender, adding more water if the mixture seems dry. Serve with Rice Pilaf with Vermicelli (page 220) and a green salad.

Serves 4 to 6

(continued)

NOTE: Other vegetables such as green peas, green beans, artichokes, eggplant, zucchini, or potatoes may be substituted for the okra in this recipe. If the vegetable chosen does not require long cooking, it should be added when the chicken is almost tender.

CHICKEN AND WHEAT PUREE

Keshkeg (Herissah)

Keshkeg is a very old dish that was served to pilgrims in the early Armenian monasteries. It is traditionally made with skinless whole-grain wheat that has been soaked in water overnight. The following day it is drained and combined with boiled, boned, and shredded chicken or lamb and broth, cooked for many hours, and beaten for a long time until the mixture is the consistency of porridge. The following recipe is a simplified version, requiring much less time and energy.

> 1 2½-pound chicken, cut into serving pieces
> 2 cups coarse bulghur, soaked overnight in water to cover
> Salt and freshly ground black pepper to taste
> ¼ cup butter
> 1 teaspoon paprika
> 2 teaspoons ground cumin (optional)

In a large, heavy saucepan simmer the chicken in water to cover until tender, about 1½ hours. Remove the bones and discard. Shred the meat as finely as possible and return it to the broth. Drain the bulghur, add to the broth, and cook until the bulghur is tender and most of the liquid in the pan is absorbed, stirring occasionally. If necessary, some chicken broth may be added. Add the salt and pepper and continue to simmer 30 minutes or more, stirring and beating constantly, until the mixture is reduced to a thin porridgelike consistency. (The Armenian cook will rely on a large wooden spoon and plenty of elbow grease for this task. A less authentic but quicker way is to use an electric beater.)

110

In a small skillet melt the butter over moderate heat. Add the paprika and mix well. Divide the *keshkeg* among individual warmed soup bowls. Form a well in the center of each serving and fill with a spoonful of the butter and paprika mixture. Sprinkle lightly with the cumin and serve at once.

Serves 4 to 6

NOTE: Instead of cumin, sprinkle the top of the *keshkeg* with cinnamon or curry powder to taste. For *keshkeg* made with lamb, consult page 145.

❀ CHICKEN WITH WHITE SAUCE

Ararat Hav

This dish, in which the chicken is cooked in a fragrant wine sauce tasting of walnuts and tarragon, seems to appeal to every palate and never fails to elicit considerable admiration.

1 2½ to 3 pound chicken, cut into serving pieces
6 tablespoons butter
1 bunch scallions, chopped, including 2 inches of the green tops
½ pound mushrooms, quartered
2 cups chicken broth
½ cup dry sherry
Salt and freshly ground black pepper to taste
2 tablespoons flour
1 cup light cream
¼ cup finely chopped fresh tarragon or 1 teaspoon dried tarragon
⅓ cup chopped walnuts

Dry the chicken thoroughly with paper towels. In a large, heavy skillet heat 4 tablespoons of the butter over moderate heat. Add the chicken, skin side down, and sauté, turning to brown evenly on all sides. Remove to a plate and set aside.

Add the scallions and mushrooms to the skillet and cook until vegetables are lightly browned, stirring frequently. Return the chicken to the skillet. Add the broth, sherry, and salt and pepper. Cover and simmer until tender. Transfer the chicken and vegetables to a serving platter and keep warm. Reserve the cooking liquid in the skillet.

In a small saucepan melt the remaining 2 tablespoons butter over low heat. Add the flour and cook 3 or 4 minutes, stirring constantly. Gradually add the cream and the reserved cooking liquid from the chicken, stirring constantly with a wire whisk. Simmer until the sauce is smooth, thickened, and hot. Stir in the tarragon and walnuts, taste for seasoning, and pour over the chicken. Serve with buttered noodles and buttered green peas or asparagus tips.

Serves 4

CHICKEN WITH APRICOTS, PRUNES, AND RAISINS

Bdoughov Hav

Here is an irresistible Caucasian Armenian combination which is a perfect balance of bland and vivid tastes, all delicately mingled.

4 medium chicken breasts, halved
4 tablespoons butter, preferably Clarified Butter (page 355)
Salt to taste
1 teaspoon cinnamon
1½ cups hot water
1 cup dried apricots
1 cup prunes
1 cup seedless golden raisins
2 tablespoons sugar or to taste

Dry the chicken with paper towels. In a heavy saucepan melt 2 tablespoons of the butter over moderate heat. Add the chicken, skin side

112

down, and sauté, turning to brown evenly on both sides. Sprinkle with the salt and cinnamon and pour in the water. Cover and simmer 15 minutes.

Meanwhile, in a small skillet melt the remaining 2 tablespoons butter. Add the dried fruits and sauté briefly over low heat, stirring frequently. Add to the chicken and stir in the sugar. Continue to cook until the chicken is tender, adding more water if necessary. Serve hot, with Plain Rice Pilaf (page 219).

Serves 4

TURKEY WITH APPLES

Khintzorov Hintgahav

The delectable apples found everywhere in Armenia probably inspired this fragrant and subtly-flavored creation, which is a specialty of Caucasian Armenians.

1 6-pound turkey
Salt to taste
6 tablespoons melted butter
2 cups hot water
6 medium tart apples, peeled and cored
2 tablespoons sugar
Cinnamon
Parsley or fresh mint

Dry the turkey inside and out with paper towels. Sprinkle with the salt and place breast side up in a shallow roasting pan just large enough to hold the bird comfortably. Brush with the melted butter and add the water to the pan. Bake in a preheated 325° oven about 25 minutes per pound, basting occasionally with the pan juices. When done, remove the turkey to a heated serving platter and keep warm. Add the apples to the roasting pan and sprinkle with the sugar and cinnamon. Bake about 1 hour or until tender but not mushy, basting often with pan juices. Surround the turkey with the baked apples and garnish with the parsley. Spoon the pan juices over the turkey and serve.

Serves 8

ROAST GOOSE WITH APRICOTS IN WINE

Khorovadz Saq

This can be the *pièce de résistance* of a holiday dinner.

1 teaspoon salt
1 9-pound goose, trimmed of exposed fat
1 apple, cored and quartered
1 large onion, quartered
½ cup hot chicken broth
¼ cup medium-dry sherry or port
Freshly ground black pepper to taste
Apricots in Wine (opposite page)

Salt the cavity of the goose. Stuff with the apple and onion. Prick the skin to allow excess fat to escape during cooking. Dry thoroughly with paper towels and place breast side up on a rack in a shallow roasting pan just large enough to hold the goose comfortably. Roast in a preheated 425° oven 15 minutes. Reduce heat to 350° and roast about 1 hour and 45 minutes, removing the excess fat as it accumulates in the pan. To test for doneness prick the thigh. If the juices that run out are a pale yellow, the goose is done. If not, cook a little longer, being careful not to overcook; otherwise the meat will dry out. When done, transfer the goose to a heated platter. Tilt the roasting pan and remove the fat, leaving the juices. Add the broth and wine and cook over high heat, stirring and scraping up the solidified juices in the pan, until the mixture is reduced to a smooth gravy. Season to taste with additional salt and the pepper. Serve the goose with this gravy, the apricots, and Plain Rice Pilaf (page 219), buttered green peas, and sautéed pearl onions.

Serves 6 to 8

NOTE: When roasting a fat goose, Armenian cooks brush the bird with lemon juice during the cooking.

❦ Apricots in Wine

    1 pound dried apricots
    ½ cup sugar or to taste
    ½ cup medium-dry sherry or port
    18 toasted blanched almonds (below)

In a saucepan combine the apricots with cold water to cover and bring to a boil. Reduce the heat to low and simmer 10 minutes. Gently stir in the sugar until dissolved and cook 5 minutes. Remove from the heat and add the wine. Place in a glass jar, cover, and refrigerate. Serve chilled, in individual glass compotes, garnished with the almonds.

Serves 6 to 8

Toasted blanched almonds: Toast the almonds on a baking sheet in a preheated 300° oven until golden brown, about 15 minutes, stirring occasionally. Be careful not to let them burn.

PHEASANT IN WINE

Kiniov Pasean

    1 2½- to 3-pound pheasant
    Salt to taste
    Clarified Butter (page 355)
    1 cup dry white wine
    Fried potatoes
    Sliced pickled cucumbers
    2 tablespoons finely chopped parsley

Dry the pheasant inside and out with paper towels. Sprinkle with the salt and fry in the butter in a deep, heavy casserole until evenly browned

POULTRY AND GAME   115

on all sides. Pour the wine over the bird and cover. Simmer over low heat about 45 minutes or until tender, adding a little broth if the pan becomes dry. Transfer the pheasant to a heated serving platter and cut into serving pieces. Spoon the cooking juices over it and surround with the fried potatoes and pickled cucumbers. Garnish with the parsley and serve at once.

Serves 3

PARTRIDGES ON A SPIT

Khorovadz Gakav

4 tender young partridges
Salt to taste
Melted butter
Wine vinegar or freshly squeezed and strained lemon juice
Parsley
Pickled fruits (grapes, peaches, pears, or plums), preferably home-
    made

Dry the partridges with paper towels. Sprinkle with the salt. With the point of a sharp knife, make 2 or 3 gashes in the breasts. Combine equal parts butter and vinegar. Put the birds on a spit and grill over glowing coals until browned on all sides and cooked through, turning occasionally and brushing with the butter mixture. Arrange the partridges on a heated serving platter, garnish with the parsley, and serve with the pickled fruits on the side. Or serve surrounded with grilled whole tomatoes and green peppers.

Serves 4

ROAST RABBIT

Khorovadz Nabasdag

1 2½- to 3-pound rabbit, cut up into serving pieces
¼ cup melted butter
Salt and freshly ground black pepper to taste
2 tablespoons freshly squeezed and strained lemon juice

Dry the rabbit with paper towels. Place in a buttered shallow oven-proof dish just large enough to hold the pieces comfortably and brush generously with butter on all sides. Roast in a preheated 425° oven 15 minutes. Reduce the heat to 325° and roast 1 hour or until tender, basting every 15 minutes with the remaining butter, mixed with the salt and pepper. During the last 15 minutes of cooking add the lemon juice to the basting liquid. When the rabbit is done, place the dish briefly under the broiler. Serve at once, with Plain Rice Pilaf (page 219), buttered peas, and sautéed apple or quince slices.

Serves 4

NOTE: A whole rabbit or hare may be roasted in the same way. The Armenians also barbecue rabbit over an open fire. Brush it liberally with butter seasoned as above. Turn and baste frequently with additional butter, adding the lemon juice, as above, until done.

7. Meats

Broiled Skewered Lamb (page 124)

For Meat Pilafs consult Chapter 10.

In Armenian cuisine lamb is the most widely used meat. Although beef, veal, and pork are also used, lamb is preferred for the majority of meat dishes.

Whole baby lamb rubbed with olive oil, garlic, various seasonings, and herbs, roasted on a spit over a charcoal fire, and served on a platter surrounded with pilaf and vegetables is a favorite at outdoor feasts. Armenian roast lamb is seasoned simply but thoroughly with salt, pepper, and slivers of garlic. It may be stuffed with a mixture of rice or bulghur, pine nuts, currants, and herbs. It is roasted until the meat is very tender and moist. Sometimes a few sliced onions or scallions and a little broth are added to the pan, producing a tasty gravy.

When some of the less tender cuts of meat are used, the roast is marinated overnight in a mixture of olive oil, vinegar, sliced onions, and seasonings before cooking. This results in a moist and flavorful roast.

A characteristic feature of Armenian meat cookery is the cutting of meat into small cubes or squares, which are then broiled, stewed, or baked, according to the particular recipe. Shish kebab is the best-known example of the numerous dishes that use cubed pieces of meat. Cubed meat is also used in a great variety of imaginative stews, skillfully seasoned, that incorporate many different kinds of vegetables and sometimes fruits, which Armenians have combined with meat and fish since ancient times.

Another feature of Armenian cuisine is the seemingly endless variety of dishes using ground meat. *Luleh kebab* is a ground meat version of shish kebab and is almost as popular. Ground meat is also essential in various meat and vegetable casseroles. *Moussaka* is one such favorite; others are raw and cooked meat patties such as *chee keufteh* (Raw

122

Lamb and Wheat Patties, see Chapter 8) and *Izmir keufteh* (Meatballs Smyrna) and the many stuffed vegetables and fruits (see Chapter 9), as well as meat *boeregs* and pastries (see Chapters 1 and 11).

An unusual ground meat dish is *Ashtarak kololik,* a large meatball, enclosing a small whole boiled chicken, which in turn has been stuffed with a hard-cooked egg! It is then wrapped in cheesecloth, cooked in broth, and served with rice soup flavored with fried onion and tarragon.

A NOTE ON BUYING LAMB: Since some meat markets do not like to fill small lamb orders, it is best to buy a whole leg or shoulder of lamb and have it divided for use in several recipes. The unused packages may be frozen and used as needed. A leg of lamb prepared this way offers enough meat for several shish kebab and *keufteh* recipes. A shoulder of lamb, even after having been trimmed of most fat and bone, will still provide sufficient meat for a number of stew or *dolma* recipes.

BROILED SKEWERED LAMB

Khorovadz or Shish Kebab (Shashlik)

Shish kebab, or "meat on a skewer," has been a favorite dish throughout the Caucasus, Central Asia, and the eastern Mediterranean for at least three thousand years. The specific location of its origin is lost in antiquity, when soldiers on the battlefield would gather around a fire and roast wild game impaled on their swords. As the dish became "domesticated," the sword gave way to the skewer, and wild game was supplanted by pieces of meat.

Although shish kebab can be made with beef, pork, chicken, or fish, it is usually made with lamb, the basic meat of the entire region. It is ideally grilled over wood embers or charcoal, but it may also be broiled. The liver, heart, and kidney of lamb may also be used. The meat is usually marinated, and many arguments rage back and forth about how to marinate it or whether it should be marinated at all. Fresh, tender young lamb need not be marinated.

Rice pilaf is the most popular accompaniment for shish kebab, although crusty bread is also satisfying. As the meat is cooked, the bread slices are gently squeezed around the skewer to soak up the succulent juices.

A famous Armenian dish, *Karski shashlik*, although impractical to make in an American home, should be described here because of the interesting manner in which it is prepared. Large round slices of boneless lamb from the hind leg and pieces of *kyurdyuk* (fat from fat-tailed sheep) are marinated for 6 or 7 hours in a mixture of salt, pepper, ground onion, wine vinegar or lemon juice, parsley, and perhaps Cognac and fresh dill or tarragon. The lamb slices, alternated with the pieces of *kyurdyuk*, are threaded tightly together on a large spit and grilled vertically, rotating slowly in front of a special tiered charcoal broiler. As the meat cooks on the outside, it is cut off in thin slices and falls into a pan at the bottom of the spit. This process is continued, the freshly exposed meat being cooked and then sliced, until the center is reached. The meat is served sprinkled with chopped onion and fresh dill, coriander, and parsley. *Karski shashlik* is probably named after the Armenian city of Kars, located in what is now northeastern Turkey, close to the Soviet Armenian border, near the ruins of the medieval Armenian fortress capital of Ani.

> 2 pounds boneless leg of lamb, trimmed of excess fat and cut into 1½- to 2-inch cubes
> 2 large onions, quartered and separated
> 2 large tomatoes, quartered
> 2 medium green peppers, quartered, seeded, and deribbed
> ¼ cup olive oil
> 2 tablespoons dry red wine
> 1½ tablespoons freshly squeezed and strained lemon juice
> 1 large clove garlic, finely chopped
> 1 teaspoon dried oregano leaves
> 1 bay leaf
> 1½ teaspoons salt
> ½ teaspoon freshly ground black pepper

Place the lamb, onions, tomatoes, and green peppers in a deep bowl. Combine the remaining ingredients and pour over the lamb and vegetables. Turn the pieces about to coat them thoroughly with the marinade. Cover and let stand at room temperature 2 to 3 hours or in the refrigerator 5 to 6 hours, turning the meat and vegetables from time to time.

Remove the lamb from the marinade and thread the cubes on long skewers, leaving a few inches bare at each end. String the vegetables on separate skewers, since the cooking time for them varies. If you are broiling in the oven, place the skewers next to one another across the length of a deep roasting pan. Broil in the oven or over charcoal 3 to 4 inches from heat until the vegetables and meat brown evenly on all sides, turning frequently and basting with the marinade. Broil about 15 to 20 minutes, depending on how well done you like the meat to be. Armenians as a rule like shish kebab that is well done but still juicy and not overcooked. Since the vegetables will cook more quickly than the lamb, remove and keep them warm until the lamb is ready. Using a fork, push the kebabs off skewers onto warmed individual plates and serve with rice or bulghur pilaf and the broiled vegetables.

Serves 4

(continued)

NOTE: Chunks of unpeeled eggplant and whole mushrooms, brushed with melted butter or olive oil, may also be strung on skewers and broiled with the vegetables. Small whole green peppers, onions, and tomatoes are sometimes substituted for the cut-up vegetables. For variety, you may use cherry tomatoes and small white boiling onions, adjusting the broiling time accordingly.

Variation: Combine the lamb with 1 large onion, grated, 1 teaspoon salt, and ¼ teaspoon black pepper. Marinate and broil as above. Garnish with parsley sprigs and/or fresh dill and lemon wedges. Serve hot, with 2 medium-size tomatoes, cut into eighths, and 8 scallions, trimmed. Or serve the lamb with grilled cubes of eggplant, tomato, and green pepper. Caucasian Armenians slit baby eggplants lengthwise without cutting them through and stuff them with pieces of *kyurdyuk* before grilling.

MARINATED BROILED LAMB CHOPS

6 shoulder lamb chops, about ½ inch thick, trimmed of fat and
   skin
¼ cup olive oil
¼ cup freshly squeezed and strained lemon juice
 1 large clove garlic, crushed, or 2 tablespoons grated onion
½ teaspoon dried oregano or thyme leaves
Salt and freshly ground black pepper to taste

If desired, you may pound the chops until about ⅜ inch thick. Combine the remaining ingredients in a shallow dish large enough to hold the chops comfortably in 1 layer. Add the chops, turning them about to coat thoroughly with the marinade. Cover and refrigerate 5 to 6 hours, turning occasionally.

Remove the chops from the marinade and broil, preferably over a charcoal fire, about 3 inches from the source of heat, 5 to 6 minutes on each side, depending on the thickness of the chops and on how well

126

done you like the meat to be. Baste often with the marinade during broiling. Serve at once, with sautéed potatoes or fried eggplant and a salad.

Serves 3

Broiled Spiced Lamb Chops or Beef Steaks

Omit the lemon juice and oregano. Blend together 4 medium cloves garlic, mashed, 1 teaspoon curry powder, ½ teaspoon olive oil, and salt and pepper to taste to form a smooth paste. Coat 2 pounds lamb chops or beef steaks thoroughly with the mixture. Cover and refrigerate 2 hours. Broil 5 to 6 minutes on each side or to taste. Remove the meat to a serving platter and keep warm. Pour off the excess fat from the pan juices, add 2 tablespoons dry red wine, heat, and pour over the meat. Serve at once with French bread and homemade spiced peaches or apricots if you like. This will serve 4.

✿ LAMB CHOPS IN WINE SAUCE

    4 large lamb chops, trimmed of excess fat
    3 tablespoons butter
 ½ pound fresh mushrooms, sliced
    1 medium green pepper, thinly sliced lengthwise (discard the
        seeds and white membrane)
    1 large clove garlic, finely chopped
Salt and freshly ground black pepper to taste
 ½ teaspoon dried oregano leaves
    2 large ripe tomatoes, peeled, seeded, and chopped
 ⅓ cup dry sherry

Wipe the chops with paper towels. In a large, hot, heavy skillet cook the chops in their own fat until lightly browned on both sides. Remove to a plate and set aside.

(continued)

Pour off the fat from the skillet and add the butter. Add the mushrooms, green pepper, and garlic and sauté until golden brown, stirring frequently. Return the chops to the skillet and sprinkle with the salt and pepper and oregano. Cover with the tomatoes. Pour in the sherry. Cover and simmer 45 minutes or until the chops are tender. Serve hot, with the sauce, over Plain Rice Pilaf (page 219).

Serves 4

FRIED LAMB RIBS WITH APPLES

In this Caucasian Armenian specialty the lamb, apples, and cinnamon interact harmoniously to create an original and memorable dish.

2 pounds lean lamb ribs, cut into small pieces
Vegetable oil
4 cooking apples
Salt and pepper to taste
Cinnamon and sugar to taste

Sauté the lamb ribs in a little of the vegetable oil until browned on all sides. Remove to a plate and keep warm. Pour off the excess fat from the pan. Add the apples and sauté on all sides. Return the ribs to the pan, placing the apples over them. Season with the salt and pepper. Cover and cook over low heat 20 minutes. Sprinkle with the cinnamon and sugar and cook, uncovered, until the meat and apples are tender.

Serves 4

VARIATION

Fried Lamb Ribs with Vegetables

Sprinkle the ribs with salt and sauté as above. Remove to a serving platter and surround with slices of eggplant, potatoes, tomatoes, and green pepper which have been fried separately in Clarified Butter (page 355). Serve hot, sprinkled with ¼ cup minced fresh dill.

STEWED LAMB SHANKS

Khash or Pacha

4 lean lamb shanks (about ¾ pound each)
2 slices lemon with the peel
3 medium cloves garlic, crushed
Salt to taste
2 tablespoons butter
½ teaspoon paprika
2 tablespoons finely chopped fresh mint leaves or parsley
1½ tablespoons freshly squeezed and strained lemon juice
Freshly ground black pepper to taste

Place the lamb shanks in a heavy pot. Cover with cold water, bring to a boil over high heat, and boil 1 minute. Drain and rinse under running cold water to remove any scum. Wash the pot, return the lamb to it, and add enough water to cover the meat by 2 or 3 inches. Bring to a boil over high heat and remove the scum that rises to the top. Reduce the heat to low. Add the lemon slices, 1 clove of the garlic, and salt. Partially cover and simmer 2 to 2½ hours or until tender, skimming off any scum as it forms. Remove the meat from the bones. Return to the pan and keep warm. Discard the bones and lemon.

In a small skillet melt the butter over moderate heat. Add the remaining 2 cloves garlic and sauté briefly. Stir in the remaining ingredients. Mix well and pour over the lamb.

Serves 4

LAMB SHANKS WITH TOMATOES
AND POTATOES

Kouzou Kzartma

4 lean lamb shanks (about ¾ pound each)
8 medium ripe tomatoes, peeled, seeded, and finely chopped
8 small peeled whole potatoes or 4 medium peeled and
  quartered potatoes
2 medium cloves garlic, finely chopped
¼ teaspoon dried rosemary leaves
½ teaspoon paprika
Salt and freshly ground black pepper to taste
2 to 3 cups water

Place the lamb shanks in an oiled flameproof dish large enough to hold them easily in one layer. Bake in a preheated 450° oven 30 minutes, turning the pieces from time to time to brown evenly on all sides.

Remove the dish from the oven and spread the tomatoes and potatoes over the lamb. Sprinkle with the garlic, rosemary, paprika, and salt and pepper. Add the water and bring to a boil on top of the stove. Return to the oven and bake 1 hour or until done. Serve with a green salad.

Serves 4

ROAST LEG OF LAMB

1 5½- to 6-pound leg of lamb, trimmed of excess fat but with the fell (outer skin) left on
¼ cup butter, softened
2 large cloves garlic, mashed
1 tablespoon finely chopped fresh mint leaves
1½ teaspoons salt
¼ teaspoon freshly ground black pepper

With the tip of a sharp knife, make 1-inch-deep incisions in various spots on both sides of the lamb. Combine the remaining ingredients and blend well. Stuff some of this mixture into the slits and rub the rest all over the lamb. Insert a meat thermometer into the thickest part of the meat, making sure that the tip does not touch any bone or fat. Place the lamb, fat side up, on a rack in a shallow roasting pan. Roast, uncovered, in a preheated 450° oven 15 minutes. Reduce the heat to 350° and continue to roast about 20 to 25 minutes per pound or until the meat thermometer registers 160 to 170°, depending on how well done you like lamb. When done, transfer the lamb to a warmed large serving platter and let stand at room temperature 10 minutes before carving. Serve with rice pilaf and a green vegetable.

Serves 8

ROAST RACK OF LAMB WITH STUFFING

Kabourga

Kabourga is a great favorite with Armenians and a flavorful way of preparing lamb.

 3 tablespoons butter
 1 cup finely chopped onion
 ½ cup finely chopped green pepper
 1 cup uncooked long-grain white rice
 2 tablespoons pine nuts
 2 tablespoons finely chopped parsley
 2 tablespoons dried currants
 ½ teaspoon allspice
 ¼ teaspoon cinnamon
 1 teaspoon salt
 ¼ teaspoon freshly ground black pepper
 1 cup hot water or meat broth
 1 4-pound lean rack of lamb together with the breast, with a
   pocket cut in the breast for stuffing
Salt and freshly ground black pepper to taste
 ½ cup canned tomato sauce

In a heavy skillet melt the butter over moderate heat. Add the onion and green pepper and sauté until soft but not browned, stirring frequently. Add the rice and pine nuts and sauté until the grains are coated with butter and the pine nuts and vegetables are golden brown, stirring constantly. Stir in the parsley, currants, allspice, cinnamon, salt, and pepper. Add the hot water and bring to a boil. Reduce the heat to low, cover, and simmer until the liquid in the pan is absorbed and the rice is partially cooked.

Wipe the meat with a damp cloth. Sprinkle lightly inside and out with the salt and pepper. Loosely fill the pocket with the rice stuffing and sew the opening closed with a large needle and strong thread. Place the stuffed lamb in a roasting pan, fat side up. With the tip of a pointed knife, make several incisions in the top of the meat and pour the tomato sauce over. Cover the pan with aluminum foil and bake in a preheated 350° oven 1 hour. Remove the foil and bake 30 to 45 minutes or until the meat is done to taste, removing the excess fat as it accumulates in the pan. Transfer the lamb to a heated serving platter and let stand 5 minutes before carving. Remove strings and spoon out stuffing into a heated serving bowl. Slice meat and serve with stuffing and a vegetable.

Serves 6

Variation: Substitute coarse bulghur for the rice and add finely chopped fresh basil or mint with the parsley. Omit the pine nuts, currants, allspice, and cinnamon.

MARINATED BEEF ON SKEWERS

Basterma Shashlik

One of the better-known Caucasian specialties.

   1 cup finely grated onion
   1 teaspoon salt
   ¼ teaspoon freshly ground black pepper
   ¼ cup red wine vinegar
   2 pounds beef fillet or boneless sirloin, cut into 1½-inch cubes
   2 medium ripe, firm tomatoes, halved
   2 medium green peppers, halved, seeded, and deribbed
   8 scallions, chopped, including 2 inches of the green tops
Chopped fresh coriander or parsley

   In a large bowl combine the onion, salt, pepper, and vinegar. Add the meat and toss to coat thoroughly with the marinade. Cover and let stand at room temperature about 6 hours, turning the pieces of meat about in the marinade from time to time.

Remove the meat from the marinade and thread on long skewers, leaving a few inches bare at each end. String the tomatoes and green peppers on separate skewers, since cooking time for them varies. Broil, preferably over charcoal, 3 to 4 inches from the heat, turning frequently, until the vegetables and meat are browned evenly on all sides. For rare meat broil about 10 to 15 minutes; for well-done meat allow 15 to 20 minutes. The vegetables cook more quickly, so remove them when they are done and keep warm. Using a fork, push the meat off skewers onto warmed individual plates and garnish with the scallions and coriander. Serve at once, with the broiled vegetables.

Serves 4

FILLET OF BEEF ON SKEWERS

4 six-ounce fillet steaks, trimmed of fat and gristle
Salt and freshly ground black pepper to taste
Melted butter
Wine vinegar or freshly squeezed and strained lemon juice
2 medium firm tomatoes, quartered
2 medium green peppers, seeded, deribbed, and quartered
1 small onion, sliced ¼ inch thick and separated into rings
1 lemon, sliced

Sprinkle the steaks with the salt and pepper and put on skewers. Broil over glowing coals until done to taste, turning occasionally and basting with a mixture of equal parts butter and vinegar. Meanwhile, string the tomatoes and green peppers onto separate skewers and grill, turning to cook evenly on all sides.

Using a fork, push the shashlik off the skewers onto a warmed serving platter and surround with the tomatoes and green peppers. Garnish with the onion rings and lemon slices. Serve with Rice Pilaf with Vermicelli (page 220).

Serves 4

Broiled Fillet of Beef

Place steaks between sheets of waxed paper and pound slightly. Sprinkle with salt and pepper and broil to taste, preferably over charcoal. Do not overcook. Place on warmed individual serving plates. Top each steak with a pat of butter. Sprinkle with chopped parsley and garnish with lemon slices. Serve hot, accompanied by sautéed potatoes and a green vegetable.

SAUTÉED FILLET OF BEEF
WITH VEGETABLES

4 six-ounce fillet steaks, trimmed of fat and gristle
Salt and freshly ground black pepper to taste
6 tablespoons Clarified Butter (page 355) (approximately)
1 ¾-pound eggplant, sliced crosswise ½ inch thick
3 medium tomatoes, quartered
1½ tablespoons flour
2 cups beef broth
⅓ cup dry red wine

Place the steaks between sheets of waxed paper and pound slightly. Sprinkle with the salt and pepper.

In a heavy skillet heat 2 tablespoons of the clarified butter over moderately high heat. Add the steaks and sauté quickly on both sides until browned and done to taste. Transfer to a heated serving platter and keep warm.

Separately sauté the eggplant and tomatoes in the remaining 4 tablespoons clarified butter until golden brown on all sides, adding more butter if necessary. Cook the flour in a small pan over low heat until lightly browned, stirring constantly. Add to the vegetables with the broth, wine, and additional salt and pepper. Mix well and bring to a boil once. Serve the fillets with the vegetables and Plain Rice Pilaf (page 219) or Plain Cracked Wheat Pilaf (page 231).

Serves 4

(continued)

Plain Sautéed Fillet of Beef

Prepare the steaks as above. Transfer to a heated serving platter and spoon the pan drippings over them. Serve with onion rings and potatoes sautéed in butter and a green salad or pickled cucumbers on the side.

FILLET OF BEEF WITH SOUR CREAM

Serve this dish with rice or potato balls sautéed in butter, or with homemade pickled grapes as Armenians living in the Caucasus do.

  2 pounds fillet of beef, trimmed of fat and gristle
  Salt and freshly ground black pepper to taste
  3 tablespoons Clarified Butter (approximately) (page 355)
  ½ teaspoon ground cloves or to taste
  1½ cups sour cream

Cut the meat into ½-inch slices and pound with a mallet until thin. Sprinkle with the salt and pepper. In a skillet heat the clarified butter over moderately high heat. Sauté the meat quickly, turning to brown evenly on both sides, adding more butter if necessary. Sprinkle with the cloves and add the sour cream. Cover and simmer over low heat 10 minutes. Do not allow to boil. Serve hot.

Serves 4

BROILED SKEWERED PORK
WITH POMEGRANATE SAUCE

Khorovadz Khozi Miss

Unlike most Middle Easterners, who do not eat pork, Armenians have developed some original and outstanding dishes using this flavorful meat. The following is a simple yet glorious example of Caucasian Armenian cooking which, unlike its counterpart in lamb, the world-famous shish kebab, is little known outside the Caucasus. The pomegranate sauce adds a touch of splendor and unexpected piquancy.

2 pounds boneless lean loin of pork, cut into 1½-inch cubes
Salt and freshly ground black pepper to taste
8 scallions, chopped, including 2 inches of the green tops
Spiced pears, peaches, grapes, or apricots (preferably homemade)
    or 3 medium tomatoes, cut in eighths
Pomegranate Sauce (page 291)

Rub the pork cubes with the salt and pepper and thread on long skewers. Broil, preferably over charcoal, 3 to 4 inches from heat, turning frequently until cooked through and evenly browned on all sides, about 15 to 20 minutes. Slide the meat off the skewers onto warmed individual plates. Garnish with the scallions and spiced fruits. Serve with the Pomegranate Sauce on the side.

Serves 4

FRIED PORK WITH QUINCE

Sergevilov Dabgvadz Khozi Miss

Quince, a delicately flavored and fragrant fruit, has greatly captured the imagination of Armenians, who esteem it highly and cook it in many fascinating ways. In the following recipe it is combined with pork, for which it seems to have a special affinity. The result is a simple yet extraordinary dish with a subtly exciting taste and aroma.

> 3 pounds lean pork ribs, cut into serving pieces and pounded slightly
> Salt and freshly ground black pepper to taste
> 6 tablespoons Clarified Butter (page 355)
> 2 pounds unpeeled quinces, washed, cored, and cut lengthwise into thick pieces
> 6 whole cloves
> Cinnamon and sugar to taste
> 2 tablespoons finely chopped parsley

Sprinkle the pork ribs with the salt and pepper and fry in 3 tablespoons of the clarified butter until browned on all sides. In a flameproof baking dish sauté the quinces in the remaining 3 tablespoons butter until half done. Add the cloves, cinnamon and sugar, and fried pork. Cover and bake in a preheated 350° oven about 15 minutes, until meat and fruit are tender. Serve hot, sprinkled with the parsley.

Serves 4

NOTE: Peeled, cored, and sliced apples may be substituted for the quinces.

Fried Pork with Spiced Fruits

Omit the quinces, cloves, sugar, and parsley. Sprinkle the pork with salt, pepper, and cinnamon and fry in 3 tablespoons clarified butter until browned on all sides. Serve hot, with homemade spiced grapes, peaches, or pears.

VEAL IN TOMATO SAUCE

4 tablespoons butter
1 pound boneless veal, cut into 1-inch cubes
1 small onion, finely chopped
¼ cup tomato puree
1 tablespoon flour
Salt and paprika to taste
½ cup dry red wine
Chopped fresh dill

In a heavy saucepan melt 2 tablespoons butter over moderate heat. Add the veal and sauté until evenly browned on all sides, stirring frequently. Add just enough water to cover the meat and cook, covered, over low heat until tender.

In a small skillet sauté the onion in 1 tablespoon butter and stir in the tomato puree. Remove from the heat and set aside. Separately fry the flour in 1 tablespoon butter until lightly browned. Gradually stir in some of the meat broth, then the onion and tomato mixture, and the salt and paprika. Bring to a boil. Add the veal to the skillet, along with the wine. Cover and simmer 10 to 15 minutes. Serve sprinkled with the dill.

Serves 4

GRILLED LIVER WITH GREEN PEPPER AND TOMATOES

Khorovadz Giger

3 tablespoons butter
1 large clove garlic
¼ teaspoon salt
1 tablespoon crushed dried mint
1 pound calf's or lamb's liver, cut into 1-inch squares
1 large green pepper, seeded, deribbed, and sliced lengthwise ⅓ inch thick
2 medium tomatoes, cut into eighths
Salt and freshly ground black pepper to taste
1 lemon, cut into wedges

In a shallow flameproof pan just large enough to hold the liver, green pepper, and tomatoes in one layer, melt the butter. Mash the garlic with the salt to a puree. Stir into the butter along with the mint and mix well. Add the liver, green pepper, and tomatoes, turning them about to coat thoroughly with the butter mixture.

Broil about 5 inches from the source of heat 10 minutes or until done to taste, stirring occasionally. Season with the salt and pepper and serve with the lemon wedges. This is good with Cracked Wheat Pilaf with Vermicelli (page 232).

Serves 4

POTTED LAMB

Tas Kebab

This popular dish, which varies somewhat from cook to cook, is one of the classics of the Armenian repertoire and is easy to prepare.

> 2 tablespoons butter
> 1 pound boneless lean leg of lamb, trimmed of excess fat and cut into 1-inch cubes
> 1 large onion, finely chopped
> ½ teaspoon paprika
> Salt and freshly ground black pepper to taste
> 2 medium tomatoes, peeled, seeded, and chopped
> ½ cup warm water
> ¼ cup dry white wine
> 1 tablespoon finely chopped parsley

In a heavy casserole melt the butter over moderate heat. Add the lamb and onion and sauté until browned on all sides, stirring occasionally. Add the paprika, salt and pepper, and the tomatoes and cook a few minutes. Add the water and reduce the heat to low. Cover and simmer about 1 hour or until the meat is tender, adding the wine 15 minutes before the end of cooking. Spoon the meat into the middle of a heated round serving platter and sprinkle with the parsley. Surround with Plain Rice Pilaf (page 219), or Eggplant Puree (page 273), and serve at once.

Serves 4

SHASHLIK IN A PAN

Cheop Kebab

1 pound boneless lean leg of lamb, trimmed of excess fat and cut
   into 1-inch cubes
1 medium eggplant, peeled and cut into 1-inch cubes
¼ cup butter
Salt and freshly ground black pepper to taste
3 medium ripe tomatoes, peeled, seeded, and thinly sliced

Thread the meat and eggplant cubes alternately on short skewers. In
a heavy skillet melt the butter over moderate heat. Add the skewered
lamb and eggplant and fry, turning to brown evenly on all sides. Transfer
to a baking dish, arranging the skewers side by side. Sprinkle with the
salt and pepper and cover with the tomato slices. Bake in a preheated
350° oven 40 minutes or until the meat is tender. Using a fork, push
the kebabs off the skewers onto warmed individual plates and serve
with Plain Rice Pilaf (page 219) or Plain Cracked Wheat Pilaf (page
231).

Serves 4

Variation: Caucasian Armenians season lean lamb ribs with salt and
pepper and fry in butter until tender, adding 1 onion, cut into rings,
5 minutes before the end of cooking. They drain off the fat, mix in ¼
cup fresh pomegranate juice, and then serve the shashlik with pomegranate seeds and parsley on the side.

LAMB WITH EGGPLANT AND GREEN PEPPER

    2 medium eggplants
Salt
    2 tablespoons butter
    1 pound boneless lean leg or shoulder of lamb, trimmed of
       excess fat and cut into 1-inch cubes
    1 medium onion, finely chopped
    1 medium ripe tomato, peeled, seeded, and chopped
1½ cups hot water
Freshly ground black pepper to taste
    2 cups olive oil
    4 medium green peppers, quartered, seeded, and deribbed
    1 large ripe tomato, peeled, seeded, and thinly sliced

Remove the stems and hulls from the eggplants. Peel and cut length-wise into ½-inch thick slices. Lay on paper towels, sprinkle generously with the salt, weigh down with a heavy object, and let stand 30 minutes. Rinse and dry thoroughly with fresh paper towels. Set aside.

In a heavy casserole melt the butter over moderate heat. Add the lamb and onion and sauté until browned on all sides, stirring frequently. Add the chopped tomato and cook 10 minutes more, stirring occasionally. Add the water, additional salt, and pepper. Reduce the heat to low, cover, and simmer about 1 hour and 15 minutes or until the meat is tender and most of the liquid in the casserole is absorbed. Remove from the heat and set aside.

In a heavy skillet heat the olive oil over moderate heat. Add the eggplant slices and fry until cooked and golden brown on both sides. Drain on absorbent paper. Add the green peppers to the skillet and fry until they are cooked and golden brown on both sides.

Lay half the eggplant slices side by side in an oiled baking dish. Spread the meat cubes over them and spoon the remaining pan liquid over the meat. Cover with the remaining eggplant slices and top with the green peppers and tomato slices. Cover the dish with aluminum foil and bake in a preheated 375° oven 25 minutes. Serve with Armenian Bread (page 302) or crusty French or Italian bread. Delicious hot, this is even better cold.

Serves 4

LAMB AND MIXED VEGETABLE CASSEROLE

Kchuch or Tourlou Guevech

The Armenian cook is certain to make this country stew during the summer, when there is a bounteous choice of vegetables. Where most fresh vegetables are plentiful throughout the year, as in America, it can be enjoyed at any time.

> 6 tablespoons butter
> 1 cup finely chopped onion
> 2 pounds boneless lean leg or shoulder of lamb, cut into 1-inch cubes
> ½ cup water
> Salt to taste
> ½ pound green beans, trimmed and halved crosswise
> 2 medium zucchini, scraped and sliced crosswise 1½ inches thick
> 1 medium eggplant, stemmed, peeled, and cut into 2-inch pieces
> ¼ pound okra, trimmed of stem ends (optional)
> 1 pound boiling potatoes, peeled and cut into 2-inch cubes
> 4 medium ripe tomatoes, peeled, seeded, and sliced ¼ inch thick
> 2 green peppers, quartered, seeded, and deribbed
> ¼ cup chopped fresh mint leaves or dill
> ¼ cup chopped parsley (optional)
> Freshly ground black pepper to taste
> 1½ cups hot water

In a heavy casserole melt the butter over moderate heat. Add the onion and sauté until soft but not browned, stirring frequently. Add the

144

meat and continue to sauté, turning to brown lightly and evenly on all sides. Add the water and salt and lower the heat. Cover and simmer 30 minutes or until the meat is almost tender. Remove from the heat. Spread the green beans in a layer over the meat, then follow with layers of the zucchini, eggplant, okra, potatoes, tomatoes, and green peppers. Sprinkle with the mint, parsley, additional salt, and pepper. Add the hot water and bring to a boil on top of the stove. Cover and bake in a preheated 350° oven 1 hour or until the meat and vegetables are tender and have absorbed most of the liquid in the casserole. Serve with Plain Rice Pilaf (page 219) or Plain Cracked Wheat Pilaf (page 231).

Serves 6

Variation: Here is a Caucasian Armenian version of *kchuch* which uses apricots. In an earthenware casserole (or use small individual casseroles) combine 1½ pounds potatoes, peeled and sliced; 1 medium onion, thinly sliced; 1 large green pepper, sliced; 6 ounces dried apricots; 3 medium tomatoes, peeled and sliced; and ¾ pound tender green beans, trimmed and halved. Place 2 pounds boneless lean lamb, cut into 1-inch cubes, on top, sprinkle with minced fresh parsley or mint and salt to taste, and add enough water to cover the vegetables and meat. Bake in a preheated 350° oven 1½ hours or until the meat and vegetables are tender, adding more water if necessary.

LAMB AND WHEAT PUREE

Keshkeg (Herissah)

A difficult dish to categorize, this is really a porridge rather than a casserole.

Follow the directions given for Chicken and Wheat Puree on page 110, substituting for the chicken 2 pounds boneless lean lamb, cut in small pieces. Cook the meat until very tender and proceed as the recipe directs.

Serves 4 to 6

LAMB AND ARTICHOKE STEW

Missov Gangar or Gangar Shokep

4 large artichokes
Juice of 1 lemon
3 tablespoons butter
1 medium onion, finely chopped
1 pound boneless lean leg or shoulder of lamb, cut into
    1-inch cubes
2 medium tomatoes, peeled, seeded, and chopped
Salt and freshly ground black pepper to taste
2 cups water

Prepare each artichoke as follows: Peel the tough outer skin from the stem and trim off ⅛ inch of the stem end. Remove any coarse or discolored outer leaves and cut 1 inch off the tops of the remaining leaves. Cut the artichoke into quarters. Remove the fuzzy choke and thorny pinkish leaves from the center. Drop the artichoke into a large bowl of salted cold water, mixed with the lemon juice.

In a heavy saucepan or casserole melt the butter over moderate heat. Add the onion and meat and sauté until lightly browned, stirring frequently. Add the tomatoes, salt and pepper, and water and bring to a boil. Lower the heat, cover, and simmer 40 minutes. Add the drained artichokes and taste for seasoning. Cover and simmer 35 minutes or until the meat and artichokes are tender. Serve with Plain Rice Pilaf (page 219).

Serves 4

NOTE: You may sauté the artichokes in ¼ cup butter before adding them to the meat.

146

LAMB AND CABBAGE STEW

Missov Gaghamp or Gaghamp Shokep

½ cup butter
1 pound boneless lean lamb or beef, cut into 1-inch cubes
1 large onion, finely chopped
½ cup tomato juice
2 cups hot water or beef broth (approximately)
Salt paprika, and cayenne to taste
1 white cabbage (about 3 pounds), quartered, cored, and
    coarsely shredded
¼ to ½ cup finely chopped fresh dill

In a heavy saucepan or casserole melt the butter over moderate heat. Add the lamb and onion. Cover and cook 25 minutes, stirring occasionally. Add the tomato juice, 1 cup of the hot water, and the salt, paprika, and cayenne. Cover and cook 30 minutes. Add the cabbage, the remaining 1 cup hot water, and the dill. Cover and cook 30 minutes or until the meat and cabbage are tender, adding more water or broth if necessary. Taste for seasoning and serve with Plain Rice Pilaf (page 219).

Serves 4

LAMB AND CAULIFLOWER STEW

Missov Intagaghamp or Intagaghamp Shokep

2 tablespoons butter
1 pound boneless lean leg or shoulder of lamb, cut into
    1-inch cubes
1 medium onion, finely chopped
½ teaspoon paprika
Salt and freshly ground black pepper to taste
2 cups hot water
1 large head cauliflower, separated into flowerets
1 tablespoon freshly squeezed and strained lemon juice
    (optional)

In a heavy saucepan or casserole melt the butter over moderate heat. Add the lamb and onion and sauté until evenly browned on all sides, stirring frequently. Add the paprika, salt and pepper, and water. Bring to a boil and reduce the heat to low. Cover and simmer 1 hour or until tender.

Meanwhile, in another saucepan add the cauliflower to boiling salted water and cook over moderate heat until almost tender. Drain and combine with the meat. Add the lemon juice and simmer 15 minutes. Serve with Plain Rice Pilaf (page 219).

Serves 4

LAMB AND GREEN BEAN STEW

Missov Ganach Lupia or Ganach Lupia Shokep

3 tablespoons butter
1 medium onion, finely chopped
1 pound boneless lean lamb, trimmed of excess fat and cut into
    1-inch cubes
3 medium cloves garlic, finely chopped
4 medium tomatoes, peeled, seeded, and finely chopped
Salt and freshly ground black pepper to taste
2 cups hot water
1 pound green beans, trimmed and halved lengthwise and then
    crosswise, or 1 ten-ounce package frozen French-cut beans, de-
    frosted
1 medium tomato, peeled, seeded, and finely chopped

In a heavy casserole melt the butter over moderate heat. Add the
onion and sauté until soft but not browned, stirring frequently. Add the
meat and cook until evenly browned on all sides. Stir in the garlic,
tomatoes, salt and pepper, and water. Bring to a boil and reduce the
heat to low. Cover and simmer 30 minutes. Stir in the beans, tomato,
and additional salt and pepper. Cover and simmer about 1 hour or until
the meat and beans are tender. Serve with Plain Rice Pilaf (page 219)
or Plain Cracked Wheat Pilaf (page 231).

Serves 4

VARIATION

Lamb and Fava Bean Stew

Missov Paglah

Omit the garlic. Sauté the lamb and onion in 2 tablespoons butter.
Add 1 pound shelled fava beans (broad beans); 2 tomatoes, peeled,

seeded, and chopped; 2 tablespoons minced fresh dill, salt, pepper, and 1 cup water. Bring to a boil. Cover and simmer 1½ hours or until the meat and beans are tender, adding more water if necessary.

LAMB AND LEEK STEW

Missov Bras or Bras Shokep

2 tablespoons butter
1 pound boneless lean lamb, trimmed of excess fat and cut into 1-inch cubes
2 medium onions, finely chopped
2 bunches leeks, washed, trimmed, and cut crosswise into 2-inch pieces
2 medium ripe tomatoes, peeled, seeded, and chopped
2 cups boiling broth or water
Salt and freshly ground black pepper to taste

In a heavy casserole or saucepan melt the butter over moderate heat. Add the lamb and sauté until lightly browned, stirring frequently. Stir in the onions and leeks and sauté 5 minutes. Add the tomatoes, broth, and salt and pepper. Reduce the heat to low. Cover and simmer 45 minutes to 1 hour or until the meat and leeks are tender.

Serves 4

Variation: Omit the tomatoes. When the stew is done, keep it warm over a very low flame while you make an egg and lemon sauce. To prepare, beat 2 eggs with 3 tablespoons freshly squeezed and strained lemon juice. Slowly add 1 cup of the liquid from the stew to the mixture, stirring constantly. Gradually stir into the stew until well blended and heated, being careful not to allow it to boil. Serve at once.

LAMB AND LENTIL STEW

Missov Vosb or Vosb Shokep

1 cup dried lentils
5 cups water
2 tablespoons butter
1 pound boneless lean lamb, trimmed of excess fat and cut into
    1-inch cubes
1 large onion, finely chopped
2 large tomatoes, peeled, seeded, and chopped
1 tablespoon tomato paste
2 cups beef broth (approximately)
Salt and freshly ground black pepper to taste
2 tablespoons freshly squeezed and strained lemon juice

Combine the lentils and water in a saucepan and boil 10 minutes. Drain and set aside.

In a heavy saucepan or casserole heat the butter over moderate heat. Add the lamb and onion and sauté until evenly browned on all sides, stirring frequently. Add the tomatoes, tomato paste, broth, and salt and pepper and bring to a boil. Cover and cook over moderate heat until the meat is almost tender. Add the lentils and more broth if necessary and cook until the meat and lentils are done. Just before serving, stir in the lemon juice. Serve with Rice Pilaf with Vermicelli or Noodles (page 220).

Serves 4

LAMB AND OKRA STEW

Missov Bami or Bami Shokep

3 tablespoons butter
1 pound boneless lean lamb, trimmed of excess fat and cut into 1-inch cubes
2 medium onions, finely chopped
4 medium ripe tomatoes, peeled, seeded, and chopped
Salt and freshly ground black pepper to taste
2 cups hot water or beef broth (approximately)
1 pound tender okra, washed and trimmed of stem ends, or 2 ten-ounce packages frozen okra, defrosted
2 to 3 tablespoons freshly squeezed and strained lemon juice

In a heavy casserole melt the butter over moderate heat. Add the lamb and sauté until lightly browned on all sides, stirring frequently. Add the onions and sauté 5 minutes more, stirring. Add the tomatoes, salt and pepper, and water. Cover and cook over low heat 45 minutes or until the meat is almost tender, adding more broth or water if necessary. Stir in the okra. Cover and simmer 30 minutes or until the meat and okra are tender. Add the lemon juice 15 minutes before the end of cooking. Serve with Plain Rice Pilaf (page 219).

Serves 4

LAMB AND ONION STEW

Missov Sokh or Sokh Shokep

2 tablespoons butter
1 pound boneless lean lamb, trimmed of excess fat and cut into
  1-inch cubes
1 cup water (approximately)
¼ teaspoon ground cumin or to taste
Salt and freshly ground black pepper to taste
2 medium ripe tomatoes, peeled, seeded, and chopped
12 small white boiling onions
1 teaspoon paprika

In a heavy saucepan or casserole melt the butter over moderate heat. Add the lamb and sauté until evenly browned on all sides, stirring frequently. Add the water, cumin, and salt and pepper. Bring to a boil and reduce the heat to low. Cover and simmer 45 minutes, adding more water if necessary. Add the tomatoes, onions, and paprika. Cook, covered, 45 minutes or until the lamb and onions are tender. Serve with Plain Cracked Wheat Pilaf (page 231).

Serves 4

LAMB AND PEA STEW

Missov Volorn or Volorn Shokep

4 tablespoons butter
1 pound boneless lean lamb, trimmed of excess fat and cut into
   1-inch cubes
1 large onion, finely chopped
1 tablespoon dried tarragon leaves
2 cups hot water or broth (approximately)
Salt and freshly ground black pepper to taste
2 ten-ounce packages frozen peas, defrosted

In a heavy saucepan or casserole melt 2 tablespoons of the butter over moderate heat. Add the lamb, onion, and tarragon. Cover and cook 25 minutes, stirring occasionally. Add the water and salt and pepper. Cover and cook 45 minutes or until the meat is tender. Stir in the peas and the remaining 2 tablespoons butter. Cover and cook until the peas are tender, adding more water if necessary. Taste for seasoning. Serve with Rice Pilaf with Vermicelli (page 220) and a green salad.

Serves 4

LAMB AND SPINACH STEW

Missov Sbanakh or Sbanakh Shokep

2 tablespoons butter
1 medium onion, finely chopped
1 pound boneless lean lamb, trimmed of excess fat and cut into
   1-inch cubes

2 medium ripe tomatoes, chopped, or 2 tablespoons tomato paste diluted with ½ cup water
1 cup water (approximately)
Salt and freshly ground black pepper to taste
2 pounds spinach, washed, drained, and stemmed

In a heavy saucepan or casserole melt the butter over moderate heat. Add the onion and sauté until soft but not browned, stirring frequently. Add the lamb and sauté, stirring, until evenly browned on all sides. Stir in the tomatoes, water, and salt and pepper. Bring to a boil and reduce the heat to low. Cover and simmer 50 minutes, adding more water if necessary. Add the spinach to the meat and simmer 15 minutes. Serve with Plain Rice Pilaf (page 219).

Serves 4

Variation: Brown the meat and onion as above. Add the tomatoes, water, and salt and pepper. Cover and simmer 45 minutes. Add ½ cup chopped parsley, ½ cup chopped fresh coriander or 1 teaspoon ground coriander, 4 scallions, chopped, and 2 tablespoons uncooked long-grain white rice. Simmer 15 minutes, adding more water if necessary. Stir in the spinach and 1½ tablespoons freshly squeezed and strained lemon juice. Cover and simmer 15 minutes.

LAMB AND ZUCCHINI STEW

Missov Titoum or Titoum Shokep

2 tablespoons butter
1 pound boneless lean lamb, trimmed of excess fat and cut into 1-inch cubes
Salt and freshly ground black pepper to taste
1½ cups hot water or chicken broth
1 small green pepper, seeded, deribbed, and cut into 1-inch squares
2 large tomatoes, peeled, seeded, and chopped

2 medium cloves garlic, finely chopped

2 medium zucchini, cut lengthwise in half and then into 1-inch lengths

3 tablespoons freshly squeezed and strained lemon juice (optional)

In a heavy casserole or saucepan melt the butter over moderate heat. Add the lamb and sauté, turning to brown evenly on all sides. Add the salt and pepper and water. Cover and simmer 30 minutes. Add the green pepper, tomatoes, and garlic. Cover and simmer 30 minutes or until the lamb is almost tender. Stir in the zucchini and lemon juice. Cover and simmer until the lamb and zucchini are tender. Serve hot with Plain Rice Pilaf (page 219).

Serves 4

NOTE: ¼ cup finely chopped fresh dill or a combination of dill and mint may be added with the zucchini.

VARIATION

Lamb and Pumpkin Stew

To prepare, combine the lamb, 4 cups water, and salt to taste in a heavy saucepan. Bring to a boil, removing the scum that rises to the top. Add the garlic, tomatoes, 1 tablespoon tomato paste, and 2 tablespoons freshly squeezed and strained lemon juice. Cover and simmer 1 hour. Stir in 1 pound peeled pumpkin, cut into 1-inch cubes, and the green pepper. Cover and simmer about 45 minutes or until the meat and pumpkin are tender. Stir in 1 tablespoon dried crushed mint leaves. Taste for seasoning.

CURRIED LAMB STEW

¼ cup butter
1 pound boneless lean lamb, trimmed of excess fat and cut into
  1-inch cubes
2 medium onions, halved lengthwise and thinly sliced
2 cups water
2 medium tomatoes, peeled, seeded, and chopped
1 teaspoon curry powder or to taste
Salt and freshly ground black pepper to taste
3 tablespoons freshly squeezed and strained lemon juice

In a heavy casserole melt the butter over moderate heat. Add the lamb and onions and sauté until lightly browned on all sides, stirring frequently. Add the water. Bring to a boil and reduce the heat to low. Cover and simmer 30 minutes. Stir in the tomatoes, curry powder, salt and pepper, and lemon juice. Cover and simmer 45 minutes or until the meat is tender. Serve with Plain Cracked Wheat Pilaf (page 231) and a green salad.

Serves 4

NOTE: Chicken may be substituted for the lamb.

VARIATION

Lamb with Potatoes

Arrange the lamb, 4 medium potatoes, sliced ¼ inch thick, and 3 onions, thinly sliced, in layers in an oiled casserole. Season each layer with a mixture of 4 tomatoes, peeled, seeded, and chopped, curry powder to taste, salt, and pepper. Top with the lemon juice, dot with 3 tablespoons butter, and add ¼ cup warm water. Bake, covered, in a preheated 350° oven about 1 hour or until done. Pickled apricots go well with this.

LAMB AND APRICOT STEW

Missov Dziran or Dziran Shokep

As winter approaches and fresh fruits and vegetables become scarce, the Armenian cook makes use of nuts and dried fruits, which are often artistically combined with meat, as the following recipe eloquently demonstrates.

    2 tablespoons butter
    1 medium onion, finely chopped
    1 medium clove garlic, finely chopped
    1 pound boneless lean lamb, trimmed of excess fat and cut into
       1-inch cubes
    2 cups water
    1 tablespoon freshly squeezed and strained lemon juice
    ½ teaspoon ginger
    Salt and freshly ground black pepper to taste
    1 cup dried apricots
    2 tablespoons chopped walnuts
    2 tablespoons sugar or to taste

In a heavy saucepan or casserole melt the butter over moderate heat. Add the onion and garlic and sauté until soft but not browned, stirring frequently. Add the lamb and sauté until browned on all sides. Add the water, lemon juice, ginger, and salt and pepper. Cover and simmer 1 hour. Add the apricots, nuts, and sugar, stirring well to dissolve the sugar. Cover and simmer 15 minutes or until the meat and fruit are tender. Serve with Plain Rice Pilaf (page 219).

Serves 4

LAMB AND PRUNE STEW

Missov Salor or Salor Shokep

Follow the directions given above for Lamb and Apricot Stew, omitting the garlic and substituting cinnamon for the ginger, 3 to 4 cups fresh or 2 cups dried prunes for the apricots, and 2 tablespoons pine nuts for the walnuts. Increase the lemon juice to 2 tablespoons.

Serves 4

LAMB AND QUINCE STEW

Missov Sergevil or Sergevil Shokep

Follow the directions given above for Lamb and Apricot Stew, omitting the garlic and substituting ½ teaspoon cinnamon and ¼ teaspoon nutmeg for the ginger; 3 unpeeled quinces, washed, cored, sliced, and sautéed in butter, for the apricots; and 2 tablespoons pine nuts for the walnuts. Increase the lemon juice to 2 tablespoons. This dish may also be made with pork or beef.

Serves 4

GROUND LAMB ON SKEWERS

Luleh (Lyulya) Kebab or Keyma Kebab

The word *luleh*, meaning "rolled," refers to the shape of the meat, which is formed into long rolls or rolled around a skewer. Traditionally, *luleh kebab* is broiled over wood embers or charcoal.

  2 pounds lean ground lamb
  1 cup very finely chopped onion
  1¼ cups finely chopped parsley
  1½ teaspoons salt or to taste
  ½ teaspoon freshly ground black pepper
  1 teaspoon ground coriander (optional)
  8 scallions, finely chopped, including 2 inches of the green tops
  1 cup finely chopped fresh mint leaves
  2 medium tomatoes, cut into eighths

In a large mixing bowl combine the lamb, onion, ¼ cup of the parsley, salt, pepper, and coriander. Mix and knead until the mixture is well blended and smooth. With hands dipped in cold water, form portions of the meat mixture into the shape of frankfurters 1 inch in diameter and 4 inches long and thread lengthwise on skewers.

If broiling in the oven, place skewers next to one another across the length of a deep roasting pan. Broil in the oven or preferably over charcoal, 3 inches from the heat. Broil 10 to 13 minutes, depending on how well done you like the meat to be, turning the skewers frequently so the meat browns evenly on all sides. Armenians like *luleh kebab* that is well done but still juicy and not overcooked. Using a fork, push the kebabs off the skewers onto warmed individual plates. Sprinkle with the scallions mixed with the remaining 1 cup parsley and mint. Garnish with the tomato wedges. Serve with Armenian Bread (page 302) or French bread.

Serves 4 or 5

NOTE: You may omit the tomato garnish and instead serve the kebabs with quartered tomatoes, quartered green peppers, quartered onions, and chunks of buttered unpeeled eggplant, all broiled on skewers, and Rice Pilaf with Vermicelli (page 220) or Cracked Wheat Pilaf with Vermicelli (page 232).

VARIATION

Armenian Lamburgers

Combine 1 pound lean ground lamb, 1 medium onion, grated, 1 large clove garlic, crushed, ¼ cup minced parsley, and salt and pepper to taste. Knead until well blended and smooth. Form the mixture into sausage shapes or round patties. Broil, preferably over charcoal, 5 to 8 minutes on each side. Serve with corn on the cob and a salad. This will serve 3.

FRIED MEAT PATTIES

Dabgvadz Keufteh

1 pound lean lamb or beef, ground twice
1 medium onion, grated
2 thick slices white bread, trimmed of crusts, soaked in water, squeezed dry, and crumbled
1 egg or egg yolk
¼ cup finely chopped parsley
2 tablespoons finely chopped fresh mint leaves or 2 teaspoons crumbled dried mint
1 large clove garlic, finely chopped
1 teaspoon salt or to taste
¼ teaspoon freshly ground black pepper
¼ cup flour
1 tablespoon olive oil
1 tablespoon butter (approximately)

Combine all but the last 3 ingredients in a deep bowl and knead well until thoroughly blended and smooth. With hands moistened in water, shape the mixture into flat round patties about 2 inches in diameter. Roll lightly in the flour.

In a heavy skillet heat the olive oil and butter over moderate heat. Add the meat patties and fry until evenly browned on both sides, adding more butter if needed. Serve with sautéed or French-fried potatoes and Combination Salad (page 45).

Serves 4

Variation: Omit the parsley, mint, and garlic. Add 4 tablespoons finely chopped fresh dill, and if desired, ½ teaspoon cinnamon to the meat mixture.

 Fried Meat Sandwich

Spread slices of French bread with butter. Place the chilled meat patties, tomato slices or canned pimientos, sliced green olives or cucumber pickles, thin onion rings (optional), and romaine lettuce leaves between the bread slices. Salt to taste and press together. Cut in half and serve.

CUMIN PATTIES

Chamanov (Kimionov) Keufteh

Follow the directions given for Cumin Fingers (page 14), but form the mixture into large hamburger-size patties. Serve with French-fried potatoes or Rice Pilaf with Vermicelli (page 220) or Cracked Wheat Pilaf with Vermicelli (page 232) and a salad.

Serves 4

VARIATION

Cumin Meat Sandwich

Cut hard rolls in half lengthwise and spread with butter. Place the chilled meat patties, sliced tomatoes, fresh mint leaves, scallions if

162

desired, and Bibb lettuce leaves between roll halves. Salt to taste and press together. Cut in half and serve.

MEATBALLS SMYRNA

Izmir Keufteh

1 pound lean lamb or beef, ground twice
3 slices white bread, trimmed of crusts, soaked in water, squeezed
  dry, and crumbled
1 egg, beaten
1 large clove garlic, crushed
¼ to ½ teaspoon ground cumin
¼ teaspoon cinnamon
¼ teaspoon paprika
1 teaspoon salt or to taste
¼ teaspoon freshly ground black pepper or to taste
2 tablespoons flour
2 tablespoons butter, preferably Clarified Butter (page 355)
4 medium ripe tomatoes, peeled, seeded, and chopped
1 green pepper, seeded, deribbed, and chopped
Salt and freshly ground black pepper to taste
1 cup water

Combine the meat, bread, egg, garlic, cumin, cinnamon, paprika, salt, and pepper in a deep bowl. Knead well until thoroughly blended and smooth. With hands moistened in water, shape the mixture into flat round patties about 2 inches in diameter or form into egg-shaped ovals. Roll lightly in the flour.

In a heavy skillet heat the butter over moderate heat. Add the meatballs and sauté until evenly browned on all sides. Transfer to a plate and keep warm. Add the tomatoes, green pepper, salt and pepper, and water to the skillet. Cover and cook over low heat 15 minutes. Return the meatballs to the skillet and cook 15 minutes. Serve over spaghetti or egg noodles, with a dish of freshly grated Parmesan cheese on the side, or serve with Rice Pilaf with Vermicelli (page 220) or Cracked Wheat Pilaf with Vermicelli (page 232).

Serves 4

BAKED EGGPLANT, GROUND MEAT, AND TOMATO CASSEROLE

Simpoog Moussaka

Armenian cuisine abounds in excellent and numerous dishes made with eggplant, but this one is outstanding and certainly deserves the international status it has achieved. *Moussaka* is a favorite throughout the Middle East and exists in many different versions.

  2 medium eggplants
Salt
½ cup Clarified Butter (page 355) (approximately)
  1 large onion, finely chopped
  1 pound lean ground lamb or beef
  2 medium ripe tomatoes, peeled, seeded, and finely chopped
  1 teaspoon cinnamon
Salt and freshly ground black pepper to taste
  3 eggs

Remove the stems and hulls from the eggplants and cut crosswise into ½-inch-thick slices. Layer on paper towels and sprinkle with the salt. Place a heavy weight on the slices and let stand 30 minutes.

Meanwhile, in a heavy skillet heat 2 tablespoons of the clarified butter over moderate heat. Add the onion and sauté until soft but not browned, stirring frequently. Add the meat and cook until lightly browned, breaking it up with the back of a spoon. Stir in the tomatoes, cinnamon, and salt and pepper. Cook 5 minutes.

Dry the eggplant slices with fresh paper towels. Sauté in the remaining 6 tablespoons clarified butter until golden brown on both sides.

164

Arrange half the eggplant slices in the bottom of a buttered baking dish. Spread the meat mixture evenly over them and cover with the remaining eggplant slices. Cover and bake in a preheated 375° oven 35 minutes.

Beat the eggs until frothy. Uncover the dish, pour the beaten eggs over the top, and bake 15 minutes. Serve with Plain Rice Pilaf (page 219) or Rice Pilaf with Tomatoes (page 221).

Serves 4

Variation: Omit the cinnamon. Add 2 tablespoons each finely chopped parsley and dill or 2 teaspoons fresh basil or mint leaves with the tomatoes. You may sprinkle the casserole with ½ cup grated Parmesan or Romano cheese and paprika after adding the beaten eggs.

ZUCCHINI, GROUND MEAT, AND TOMATO CASSEROLE

Titoum Moussaka

5 tablespoons butter
4 medium zucchini, scraped and halved lengthwise
1 pound lean ground lamb or beef
2 medium onions, grated
4 medium ripe tomatoes, peeled, seeded, and finely chopped
¼ cup chopped fresh mint leaves
¼ cup chopped fresh dill
2 large cloves garlic, crushed
Salt and freshly ground black pepper to taste

In a heavy skillet heat 2 tablespoons of the butter over moderate heat. Add the zucchini slices and sauté until golden brown on both sides. Remove to a plate and set aside.

Add the remaining 3 tablespoons butter, meat, and onions to the skillet and sauté until meat is browned, stirring frequently. Add the remaining ingredients and cook 5 minutes. Return the zucchini to the skillet. Cover and simmer 15 minutes. Serve with Plain Rice Pilaf (page 219), mashed potatoes, or egg noodles.

Serves 4

NOTE: Armenians also make *moussaka* with pumpkin.

BAKED POTATO, GROUND MEAT, AND TOMATO CASSEROLE

Kednakhintzor Moussaka

½ cup vegetable oil (approximately)
8 medium potatoes, peeled and sliced ¼ inch thick
3 tablespoons butter
1 pound lean ground lamb or beef
1 medium onion, finely chopped
2 large ripe tomatoes, peeled, seeded, and finely chopped
1 large clove garlic, mashed
¼ cup finely chopped parsley
¼ cup finely chopped fresh mint leaves, or fresh basil to taste
Salt and freshly ground black pepper to taste
3 eggs
½ cup freshly grated Parmesan or Romano cheese
Paprika

In a heavy skillet heat the vegetable oil over moderate heat. Add the potatoes and fry until lightly browned on both sides. Remove to a plate and set aside.

In another skillet heat the butter over moderate heat. Add the meat and onion and sauté until lightly browned, stirring frequently. Add the tomatoes, garlic, parsley, mint, and salt and pepper and cook 5 minutes.

Arrange half the potatoes in an oiled baking dish. Spread meat mixture

166

over them. Spread the remaining potato slices over the meat. Cover and bake in a preheated 350° oven 35 minutes.

In a small bowl beat the eggs until frothy. Uncover the dish and pour the beaten eggs over the potatoes. Sprinkle with the cheese and paprika. Bake uncovered about 15 minutes. Serve with a green salad.

Serves 4

GROUND LAMB WITH GREEN BEANS

Keymayov Ganach Lupia

¼ cup butter
2 medium onions, finely chopped
1 pound lean ground lamb
3 pounds green beans, trimmed and halved lengthwise, or 3 ten-ounce packages frozen French-cut beans, defrosted
4 medium ripe tomatoes, peeled, seeded, and finely chopped
2 large cloves garlic, crushed, or 1 teaspoon garlic salt (optional)
Salt and freshly ground black pepper to taste
2 cups water

In a heavy saucepan or casserole heat the butter over moderate heat. Add the onions and sauté until soft but not browned, stirring fre-quently. Add the lamb and cook until lightly browned, breaking it up with the back of a spoon. Add the remaining ingredients. Cover and cook until the beans are tender, about 40 minutes. (Frozen beans will take less time.) Serve with Plain Rice Pilaf (page 219), mashed potatoes, or egg noodles.

Serves 4

BAKED STUFFED EGGPLANT

Karni Yarik

12 6-by-2-inch eggplants
½ cup vegetable oil (approximately)
2 tablespoons butter
1 large onion, finely chopped
½ pound lean ground lamb
1 medium tomato, peeled, seeded, and finely chopped
1 small green pepper, seeded, deribbed, and finely chopped
2 tablespoons finely chopped parsley
Salt and freshly ground black pepper to taste
1 large clove garlic, finely chopped
1 large tomato, peeled, seeded, and chopped
½ cup water or broth
1 tablespoon freshly squeezed and strained lemon juice

Remove the stems and hulls from the eggplants and discard. Peel each eggplant lengthwise in ½-inch strips, leaving ½-inch strips of skin between, making a striped design.

In a heavy skillet heat the oil over moderate heat. Add the eggplants and sauté until soft on all sides, adding more oil if necessary. Arrange in a single layer in a shallow flameproof or ovenproof pan.

Add the butter to the skillet and heat. Add the onion and sauté until soft but not browned, stirring frequently. Add the lamb and cook until lightly browned, breaking it up with the back of a spoon or fork. Stir in the tomato and green pepper and cook 5 minutes. Add the parsley, salt and pepper, and garlic, mix well, and remove from the heat.

Transfer each eggplant to a plate, leaving the oil in the pan. Slit lengthwise to within 1 inch of both ends on one side only. Stuff the pocket with several spoonfuls of the meat mixture. Return the eggplants to the pan, arranging them next to one another, slashed sides up. Place the tomato over the eggplants, sprinkle with additional salt and

168

pepper, and pour in the water. Cover and cook over medium heat 30 minutes or bake in a preheated 350° oven 30 minutes. Add the lemon juice and cook 10 minutes. Serve with a pilaf or crusty bread and a green salad.

Serves 4

NOTE: You may prepare this dish with 2 large eggplants, quartered lengthwise. Lay them on paper towels and sprinkle with salt. Place a heavy weight on them and let stand 30 minutes. Dry the pieces with fresh paper towels and sauté them in oil until golden brown on both sides. Cut a lengthwise slit or pocket in each piece and stuff with the meat mixture. Arrange the pieces side by side in a flameproof or oven-proof pan and proceed as above.

8. Wheat Keuftehs

Left: Raw Lamb and Wheat Patties (page 174) and, right: Stuffed Lamb and Wheat Balls Harput (page 179)

A versatile dish with many variations throughout the Middle East, wheat *keufteh* is one of the highlights of Armenian cuisine. *Keufteh* (the name and pronunciation vary, depending on the country) is based on bulghur (Armenian *tzavar*), cracked wheat. It may be prepared with or without meat and may incorporate vegetables, nuts, currants, herbs and seasonings, and even fish. Meat *keufteh* is traditionally made with lamb.

Bulghur is a basic cereal in Armenian cuisine and is served regularly in a variety of dishes in addition to *keufteh*. It has been known since very ancient times and was produced in great quantity in Mesopotamia. Traditionally bulghur is made by boiling whole grains of wheat outdoors in huge cauldrons until they begin to soften. They are then dried in the hot sun. This process both preserves the flavor of the wheat and prevents it from spoiling for years. It is then cracked into one of three different textures: fine, medium, or coarse. The first two are used mainly for making *keufteh*; coarse bulghur is usually used for the various bulghur pilafs (Chapter 10) and stuffed vegetables (Chapter 9). Although today bulghur is made commercially in the United States under modern conditions, the process adheres to the same general steps that have been followed in the Middle East for thousands of years.

Keufteh may be eaten raw or cooked, hot or cold. It may be molded into various shapes, filled with a stuffing, broiled, fried, boiled, or baked in a pan, and served as an appetizer, soup, side dish, or main dish.

RAW LAMB AND WHEAT PATTIES

Chee Keufteh

This great Armenian favorite, a version of steak *tartare*, has a very refreshing taste and is especially good as a summertime first course. It is important to use very lean meat that has been finely ground.

> 1 cup fine bulghur
> ½ pound very lean boneless leg of lamb, ground 3 times
> 1 small onion, finely chopped
> Pinch cayenne
> Salt and freshly ground black pepper to taste
> ½ cup finely chopped parsley
> ¼ cup finely chopped scallions, including 2 inches of the green tops
> ¼ cup finely chopped green pepper
> 2 tomatoes, cut into eighths

Soak the bulghur in cold water to cover about 10 minutes. Drain in a colander lined with a double thickness of dampened cheesecloth. Enclose the bulghur in the cheesecloth and squeeze dry. Place in a mixing bowl and add the lamb, onion, cayenne, and salt and pepper. Knead the mixture about 8 minutes with hands moistened by occasionally dipping them into a bowl of lightly salted ice water. Add 2 tablespoons each of the parsley, scallions, and green pepper. Knead 1 or 2 minutes longer until the mixture is well blended and smooth. Taste for seasoning. Keeping hands moist, form the mixture into patties and arrange on a serving platter. Season the remaining chopped parsley, scallions, and green pepper with additional salt and sprinkle over the *keufteh*. Garnish with the tomatoes. Serve immediately.

Serves 4

Omit the parsley, scallions, green pepper, and tomatoes. Serve the *keufteh* for lunch with Tomato and Onion Salad (page 51).

Omit the parsley, scallions, green pepper, and tomatoes. Spread the *keufteh* mixture 1 inch thick on individual plates. Make a well in the center of each serving and fill with Meat Sauce (page 293). Serve immediately as a luncheon dish.

You may blend 2 to 3 teaspoons tomato paste with the *keufteh* mixture. Finely chopped fresh basil or mint leaves may be added with the chopped parsley, scallions, and green pepper.

BAKED LAMB AND WHEAT WITH STUFFING

Sini Keufteh

An excellent dish for entertaining, *sini keufteh* may be prepared and baked in advance, frozen well-covered, and warmed in the oven just before serving. It is also delicious eaten cold.

STUFFING

> 6 tablespoons butter
> 3 medium onions, finely chopped
> 1 pound ground leg or shoulder of lamb (not too lean)
> ½ cup pine nuts sautéed in 1 tablespoon butter until golden brown (optional)
> Salt and freshly ground black pepper to taste

KEYMA

> 3 cups fine bulghur
> 2 pounds very lean boneless leg of lamb, ground 3 times
> Salt and freshly ground black pepper to taste
> 6 tablespoons Clarified Butter (page 355)
> ¼ cup water

To make the stuffing, in a heavy skillet melt the butter over moderate heat. Add the onions and sauté until they begin to soften, stirring frequently. Add the lamb and cook until lightly browned, breaking it up with the back of a spoon. Pour off the excess fat from the pan. Stir in the pine nuts and salt and pepper and mix well. Remove from the heat and set aside.

To make the *keyma*, soak the bulghur in water to cover 10 minutes. Drain in a colander lined with a double thickness of dampened cheese-cloth. Enclose the bulghur in the cheesecloth and squeeze dry. Place in a mixing bowl and add the lamb and salt and pepper. Moistening your hands now and then by dipping into a bowl of ice water, knead the mixture about 15 minutes or until smooth. Taste for seasoning.

Divide the *keyma* into 2 equal parts. Keeping your hands moistened, press down one part smoothly over the bottom of a 9-by-13-by-1½-inch baking dish. Spread the stuffing evenly over it. Cover with the remaining *keyma* mixture by flattening small portions between your palms and placing them over the stuffing, patting them down firmly and covering it completely. Smooth the top with moist hands. With a knife dipped frequently into cold water, cut the *keufteh* into diamond-shaped pieces or squares. Place a small dab of butter on each diamond or square, sprinkle with the water, and bake in a preheated 375° oven about 50 to 60 minutes or until lightly browned. Serve hot or cold, with Armenian Green Beans (page 256) and Combination Salad (page 45).

Serves 8 to 10

Baked Lamb and Wheat without Stuffing

Prepare the *keyma* as above, using 1½ cups fine bulghur, 1 pound very lean boneless leg of lamb, ground 3 times, 1 small onion, ground, salt, and pepper. Spread the mixture evenly about ¾ inch thick in a buttered shallow baking dish. Smooth the top and dot with butter. Bake in a preheated 375° oven about 45 minutes or until done. Serve hot as is or with Meat Sauce (page 293), spooned over each serving. If desired, 15 minutes before the *keufteh* is done, spoon the Meat Sauce over the surface. This will serve 4.

176

FRIED LAMB AND WHEAT PATTIES

Dabgvadz Keufteh

Delicious hot or cold, this *keufteh* is a perfect picnic food, as well as an excellent appetizer.

1 recipe *keyma* of Stuffed Lamb and Wheat Balls Harput (page 179)
Clarified Butter (page 355) or olive oil

Prepare the *keyma* as described in the recipe on pages 179–81, forming the mixture into small hamburger-shaped patties.

In a heavy skillet heat the clarified butter over moderate heat. Add the *keufteh* patties and fry until evenly browned on both sides. Serve with Combination Salad (page 45), Cucumber and Tomato Salad (page 50), or Tomato and Onion Salad (page 51).

Serves 4

Variation: The *keyma* may be flavored with ½ teaspoon curry powder or a mixture of ½ teaspoon curry powder, ¼ teaspoon allspice, ⅛ teaspoon cinnamon, and ½ teaspoon paprika. Reduce the amount of bulghur to ¾ cup and mix in 1 egg, beaten. Form the mixture into small sausage shapes and fry as above. Serve as an appetizer. Or place the fried *keuftehs* in a saucepan. Add ½ cup chicken broth. Cover and simmer about 10 minutes or until all the broth is absorbed. Serve with Plain Cracked Wheat Pilaf (page 231) and a green salad.

FRIED STUFFED LAMB AND WHEAT BALLS

Dabgvadz Porov Keufteh

This is a delightful choice for a buffet or picnic.

1 recipe Stuffed Lamb and Wheat Balls Harput (page 179)
   (omit the tomato broth)
Olive oil for deep frying

Prepare the stuffing and *keyma* as described in the recipe on pages 179–181. After stuffing, form the mixture into either egg shapes or balls. Fry in the hot olive oil until golden brown on all sides.

Serves 4

VARIATIONS

Brush the stuffed *keuftehs* with 4 tablespoons Clarified Butter (page 355), coating them thoroughly on all sides. Arrange them side by side in an oiled shallow baking dish. Bake in a preheated 375° oven about 30 minutes. Place briefly directly under the broiler flame to brown the tops.

Broiled Stuffed Lamb and Wheat Balls

Brush the stuffed *keuftehs* with olive oil and broil, preferably over charcoal, until evenly browned on all sides and cooked through, turning occasionally.

BROILED LAMB AND WHEAT ON SKEWERS

Khorovadz Keufteh

Here is an ideal *keufteh* for an outdoor barbecue.

**1 recipe *keyma* of Stuffed Lamb and Wheat Balls Harput
(below)
Olive oil**

Prepare the *keyma* as described in the recipe below. With hands dipped in cold water, form portions of the *keyma* into frankfurter-shaped rolls, 1 inch in diameter and 4 inches long. Thread lengthwise on skewers. Brush with the olive oil. Broil, preferably over a charcoal fire, about 15 to 20 minutes, turning to brown evenly on all sides, brushing frequently with olive oil.

Serves 4

STUFFED LAMB AND WHEAT BALLS HARPUT

Harput Keufteh, Porov Keufteh, or Ichli Keufteh

The Armenian version of this dish is said to have come from the town of Harput (Armenian *Kharpert*). The Kharpertsiner are justifiably proud of their *keufteh,* and many an Armenian cook's reputation has been made or unmade by the way he prepares it. *Harput keufteh* should be served hot and is a good choice for a winter meal.

  2 tablespoons butter
  1 large onion, finely chopped
  ½ pound ground lamb (not too lean)
  2 tablespoons chopped green pepper
  1 tablespoon chopped parsley
  1 teaspoon chopped fresh basil or ½ teaspoon dried basil
Salt and freshly ground black pepper to taste
  ½ teaspoon cinnamon
  ¼ cup chopped walnuts or pine nuts

KEYMA

  1½ cups fine bulghur
  1 pound very lean boneless leg of lamb, ground 3 times
  1 small onion, ground
Salt and freshly ground black pepper to taste

TOMATO BROTH

  8 cups lamb, beef, or chicken broth
  4 ripe tomatoes, seeded and puréed, or 3 tablespoons tomato paste
Salt to taste

Make the stuffing: In a heavy skillet melt the butter over moderate heat. Add the onion and sauté until soft but not browned, stirring frequently. Add the lamb and cook until no longer pink, breaking it up with the back of a spoon. Add the green pepper and cook 10 minutes or until the meat is lightly browned and the vegetables are soft. Drain off any excess fat. Stir in the parsley, basil, salt and pepper, cinnamon, and nuts. Taste for seasoning. Remove from heat and cool. Chill, covered, several hours or overnight.

Make the *keyma*: Soak the bulghur in water to cover about 10 minutes. Drain off the excess water by squeezing the bulghur in a double thickness of dampened cheesecloth.

Place the bulghur in a mixing bowl and add the lamb, onion, and salt and pepper. Moistening your hands now and then by dipping

180

them into a bowl of ice water, knead the mixture about 15 minutes or until smooth. Taste for seasoning.

Keeping your hands moist, shape the mixture into 1½-inch balls. Stuff each as follows: Hold a ball in the palm of your left hand. Place your right thumb in the center and press to make an opening. Continue pressing gently but firmly with your thumb all around the inside wall while rotating the ball in the palm of your left hand until you have a hollowed ball about 2½ inches in diameter and as thin as possible without its falling apart. This is necessary because the wheat will swell in cooking, thickening the walls. Place a spoonful of the stuffing in the opening and with moistened hands reshape the *keyma* around the stuffing to enclose it securely. Pat smooth the surface of the ball with ice water. Flatten it slightly by gently pressing your cupped hands around the ball. Repeat this procedure with the remaining *keyma* and stuffing.

Make the tomato broth: In a large, heavy pot bring the broth and tomatoes to a boil over moderate heat. Salt rather generously.

Lower the *keuftehs* gently into the boiling broth and reduce the heat to low. Simmer about 10 minutes or until the *keuftehs* rise to the surface. Using a perforated spoon, transfer the *keuftehs* into individual soup bowls. Serve with a little broth spooned over them. Green Beans with Tomatoes (page 270) and Combination Salad (page 45) or Romaine Salad (page 47) make good accompaniments.

Serves 4 to 6

NOTE: Any leftover *keyma* mixture may be shaped into small patties and cooked along with the stuffed *keuftehs*. These may be eaten hot or removed from the broth and chilled, then dipped in beaten egg and fried in butter.

VARIATION

Lamb and Wheat Ball Soup

For a soup version of this dish, prepare the *keyma* as above, shaping the mixture into 1-inch balls. Cook as above, adding 1 cup drained canned chick-peas to the broth if desired. Meanwhile, in a skillet sauté 1 small onion, minced, in 4 tablespoons butter until golden brown. Mix in 1 tablespoon crushed dried mint and pour the contents of the skillet into the soup. (Or instead of mint, add ½ pound spinach leaves, washed, drained, and stemmed, to the soup with the sautéed onion.) Simmer 2 to 3 minutes. Taste for seasoning. This will serve 8.

STUFFED LAMB AND WHEAT BALLS IN YOGURT SAUCE

Madzoonov Keufteh

This is a particularly satisfying dish for a winter meal and should be served piping hot.

STUFFING

> ½ cup butter, softened
> ¼ teaspoon cinnamon or curry powder or a mixture of cinnamon, allspice, and freshly ground coriander
> Salt and freshly ground black pepper to taste
> ⅓ cup chopped walnuts or pistachio nuts

KEYMA

> 1½ to 2 cups fine bulghur
> 1 pound very lean boneless leg of lamb, ground 3 times
> 1 small onion, ground
> 1 teaspoon paprika
> Salt and cayenne to taste

    8 cups lamb or beef broth
Salt to taste
    4 cups unflavored yogurt
    1 small egg
  ¼ cup butter
    1 medium onion, finely chopped
    2 tablespoons crushed dried mint leaves

Prepare the stuffing by placing the butter in a small bowl. Add the cinnamon and salt and pepper and blend well. Mix in the nuts. Chill thoroughly.

To make the *keyma*, soak the bulghur in water to cover about 10 minutes. Drain in a colander lined with a double thickness of dampened cheesecloth. Enclose the bulghur in the cheesecloth and squeeze dry. Place in a mixing bowl and add the lamb, onion, paprika, and salt and cayenne. Moistening your hands now and then by dipping them into a bowl of ice water, knead the mixture about 15 minutes or until smooth. Taste for seasoning.

Shape the *keyma* into 1½-inch balls as described in the recipe for Stuffed Lamb and Wheat Balls Harput (page 179), filling each ball with about 1 teaspoon of the stuffing. (Any leftover *keyma* mixture may be shaped into small balls and cooked along with the stuffed *keuftehs*.)

Make the yogurt sauce: In a large, heavy pot bring the broth to a boil over high heat. Salt rather generously. Gently lower the *keuftehs* into the boiling broth and reduce the heat to low. Simmer about 7 minutes.

Meanwhile, pour the yogurt into a deep bowl and stir with a large wooden spoon. Add the egg and beat until smooth. Gradually stir a little broth from the pot into the yogurt. Slowly pour the yogurt mixture into the pot and cook about 2 to 3 minutes or until the *keuftehs* are done and the sauce is heated through. Do not let it boil. Remove from the heat and keep warm.

Heat the butter in a small skillet. Add the onion and sauté until golden brown, stirring frequently. Add the mint and stir well. Pour the contents of the skillet over the *keuftehs* and mix in. Simmer over low heat 1 to 2 minutes longer. Taste for seasoning.

Using a perforated spoon, transfer the *keuftehs* into individual soup bowls. Serve with the yogurt sauce spooned over them.

Serves 4 to 6

NOTE: You may substitute 1 large clove garlic, finely chopped, for the onion in the sauce, or both garlic and onion may be eliminated entirely.

The broth for this *keufteh* is traditionally made with bone-in lamb, and the finished dish is served with the boned meat. To prepare, cover 3 pounds bone-in lamb (or 1 chicken) with water, season with salt, and bring to a boil. Remove the scum as it rises. Simmer until the meat is tender. Remove the meat from the bones and reserve. Strain the broth and chill. Remove the fat that solidifies on top. Use the broth for cooking the *keuftehs*. Reheat the reserved meat in the yogurt sauce just before serving. Top each individual bowl of *keufteh* with a portion of the lamb (or chicken).

STUFFED LAMB AND WHEAT BALLS WITH LIVER IN BROTH

Gigerov Keufteh

Liver enthusiasts will appreciate this unusual and little-known *keufteh*, which may also be served as a soup.

KEUFTEHS

> 1 recipe Stuffed Lamb and Wheat Balls in Yogurt Sauce (page 182) (omit the yogurt sauce)

LIVER BROTH

> 10 tablespoons butter
> 1 pound lamb's or calf's liver

184

12 scallions, chopped, including 2 inches of the green tops
2 large ripe tomatoes, peeled, seeded, and puréed
8 cups chicken or beef broth
Salt and freshly ground black pepper to taste
2 medium cloves garlic, crushed
1 teaspoon paprika or to taste

Prepare the *keuftehs* (stuffing and *keyma*) as described in the recipe on pages 179–181.

Make the liver broth: In a skillet melt 4 tablespoons of the butter over moderate heat. Add the liver and sauté briefly on both sides. Remove from the heat and cut into 1-inch-long strips.

In a large, heavy pot melt 4 tablespoons of the butter over moderate heat. Add the scallions and sauté until golden brown, stirring frequently. Add the tomatoes, broth, and salt and pepper and slowly bring to a boil. Stir in the garlic and sautéed liver. Reduce the heat and simmer 15 minutes.

Gently lower the *keuftehs* into the broth, which should cover them completely. Simmer about 10 minutes or until cooked through.

Meanwhile, in a small skillet heat the remaining 2 tablespoons butter over moderate heat. Add the paprika and mix well. Carefully stir into the liver broth when the *keuftehs* are cooked.

Using a perforated spoon, transfer the *keuftehs* into individual soup bowls and spoon the liver broth over them.

Serves 4 to 6

VARIATION

Lamb and Wheat Ball Soup with Liver

To prepare a soup version of this dish, omit the *keufteh* stuffing. Shape the *keyma* into 1-inch balls and cook as above. This will serve 8.

BAKED PORK AND BEEF WITH WHEAT

This is a Caucasian Armenian *keufteh* which is practically unknown elsewhere.

STUFFING

> ½ pound lean ground beef
> 1 small onion, grated
> Salt and freshly ground black pepper to taste

KEYMA

> 1 cup fine bulghur
> 1 pound lean pork, ground twice
> ½ cup finely chopped onion
> Salt and freshly ground black pepper to taste
> ¼ cup Clarified Butter (page 355)

Combine the stuffing ingredients in a deep bowl and knead well until thoroughly blended and smooth.

Prepare the *keyma* by soaking the bulghur in water to cover 10 minutes. Drain in a colander lined with a double thickness of dampened cheesecloth. Enclose the bulghur in the cheesecloth and squeeze dry. Place in a mixing bowl and add the pork, onion, and salt and pepper. Moistening your hands now and then by dipping them into a bowl of ice water, knead the mixture until well blended and smooth. Taste for seasoning.

Divide the *keyma* into 2 equal parts. Keeping your hands moistened, press one part smoothly over the bottom of a buttered shallow baking dish. Spread the stuffing evenly over it. Cover with the remaining *keyma*. Smooth the top with moist hands. Dot with the clarified butter.

186

Bake in a preheated 350° oven about 40 minutes or until lightly browned and cooked through. Serve with lemon wedges or warm Apricot Soup (page 345).

Serves 4

FRIED ONION AND WHEAT PATTIES

Dabgvadz Sokhov Keufteh

    6 tablespoons olive oil or butter
    ¼ cup finely chopped onion
    ⅔ cup canned tomatoes, drained and mashed (reserve the liquid)
    2 tablespoons tomato paste
    ½ teaspoon paprika
   Salt and cayenne to taste
    1½ cups fine bulghur
    ⅓ cup finely chopped green pepper
    ⅓ cup finely chopped scallions, including 2 inches of the
       green tops
    ⅓ cup finely chopped parsley
    ⅓ cup finely chopped fresh mint leaves

In a saucepan or casserole heat the olive oil over moderate heat. Add the onion and sauté until golden brown, stirring frequently. Add the tomatoes, tomato paste, paprika, and salt and cayenne. Bring to a boil and remove from the heat. Add the bulghur, mix well, and let stand 15 minutes.

Turn the mixture into a mixing bowl. Moistening your hands now and then by dipping them into a bowl of salted lukewarm water, knead the mixture about 8 minutes, occasionally adding a little of the tomato juice if it seems dry. Add ¼ cup each of the green pepper, scallions, parsley, and mint. Knead 1 to 2 minutes or until the mixture is well blended and smooth. Taste for seasoning.

(continued)

Keeping your hands moist, form the mixture into patties or smooth onto a serving platter. Season the remaining green pepper, scallions, parsley, and mint with additional salt and sprinkle over the *keufteh*. Serve at once, with Mixed Pickles (page 8) or a green salad and Chilled Yogurt Drink (page 364) if desired.

Serves 4

NOTE: This *keufteh* is also good served cold. Cover and refrigerate until thoroughly chilled. Sprinkle with the green pepper, scallions, parsley, and mint just before serving.

WHEAT PATTIES WITH BUTTER

Garakov Keufteh

⅔ cup canned tomatoes, drained and mashed (reserve the liquid)
2 cups fine bulghur
⅓ cup finely chopped onion
½ cup butter
2 tablespoons tomato paste
½ teaspoon paprika
Salt and cayenne to taste
⅓ cup finely chopped green pepper
⅓ cup finely chopped scallions, including 2 inches of the green tops
⅓ cup finely chopped parsley
⅓ cup finely chopped fresh mint leaves

Combine the tomatoes and bulghur in a deep bowl. Mix well with your hands and let stand 10 minutes.

Add the onion, butter, tomato paste, paprika, and salt and cayenne. Moistening your hands now and then by dipping them into a bowl of

188

salted cold water, knead the mixture about 8 minutes, occasionally adding a little of the tomato juice if it seems dry. Add ¼ cup each of the green pepper, scallions, parsley, and mint. Knead 2 minutes or until the mixture is well blended and smooth. Taste for seasoning.

Keeping your hands moist, form the mixture into patties or smooth onto a serving platter. Season the remaining green pepper, scallions, parsley, and mint with additional salt and sprinkle over the *keufteh.* Serve cold, with Mixed Pickles (page 8) or a green salad and Chilled Yogurt Drink (page 364) if desired.

Serves 4

LENTIL AND WHEAT PATTIES

Vosbov Keufteh

  1 cup dried lentils, washed and drained
  3 cups water (approximately)
Salt to taste
12 tablespoons butter
¾ cup fine bulghur
  1 medium onion, finely chopped
¼ cup finely chopped green or red pepper
¼ cup finely chopped scallions, including 2 inches of the
    green tops
¼ cup finely chopped parsley
¼ cup finely chopped fresh mint leaves
Paprika

Combine the lentils, water, and salt in a heavy saucepan. Bring to a boil over high heat, stirring to dissolve the salt. Reduce the heat and simmer 20 minutes or until the lentils are tender, adding more hot water if necessary. Stir in 8 tablespoons of the butter and the bulghur. Simmer 2 to 3 minutes. Remove from the heat, cover, and set aside 15 minutes.

(continued)

Meanwhile, in a heavy skillet melt the remaining 4 tablespoons butter over moderate heat. Add the onion and sauté until golden brown, stirring frequently. Combine the lentil and bulghur mixture with the contents of the skillet in a large mixing bowl. Dipping your hands occasionally into a bowl of warm water, knead the mixture 2 to 3 minutes or until well blended. Add 3 tablespoons each of the green pepper, scallions, parsley, and mint and mix well. Taste for seasoning.

Keeping your hands moist, form the mixture into patties. Arrange on a serving dish and sprinkle with the paprika and the remaining green pepper, scallions, parsley, and mint. Serve with Cucumber and Tomato Salad (page 50) or Mixed Pickles (page 8).

Serves 4

STUFFED CHICK-PEA AND WHEAT BALLS

Topig

This is a traditional Lenten *keufteh* with an exotic filling which may be served either as an appetizer or main dish.

STUFFING

> 3 tablespoons olive oil
> 2 cups finely chopped onions
> 2 tablespoons flour
> 3 tablespoons chopped walnuts or pine nuts
> 3 tablespoons dried currants
> 2 tablespoons finely chopped parsley
> 1 tablespoon finely chopped fresh mint leaves (optional)
> ¼ teaspoon sugar
> ⅛ teaspoon allspice
> ⅛ teaspoon cinnamon
> Salt and freshly ground black pepper to taste
> ¼ cup *tahini*

KEYMA

¼ pound skinless whole-grain wheat
2 cups water
½ pound chick-peas
2 cups water
¼ pound fine bulghur
¼ cup cold water
3 tablespoons finely chopped onion
1 egg
½ teaspoon paprika
Salt and cayenne to taste

4 cups water
2 teaspoons salt
Paprika
Olive oil
Lemon wedges

Prepare the stuffing: In a heavy skillet heat the olive oil over moderate heat. Add the onions and sauté until soft, stirring constantly. Stir in the flour and sauté 2 to 3 minutes. Remove from the heat and add the nuts, currants, parsley, mint, sugar, allspice, cinnamon, salt and pepper, and *tahini*. Mix well. Transfer into a covered container and refrigerate several hours or overnight until thoroughly chilled.

To make the *keyma*, combine the wheat and water in a small saucepan and bring to a boil over high heat. Remove from the heat and let soak 2 hours. Drain.

In another saucepan combine the chick-peas and water and bring to a boil over high heat. Remove from the heat and let stand 1½ hours. Then cook gently about 30 minutes or until tender but still firm, not mushy. Drain the chick-peas. Remove and discard the skins.

Soak the bulghur in the water 10 minutes. Meanwhile, grind the wheat and chick-peas, using the finest blade of a meat grinder.

In a large mixing bowl combine the wheat and chick-pea mixture with the soaked bulghur. Add the onion, egg, paprika, and salt and cayenne. Moistening your hands now and then by dipping them into a bowl of salted ice water, knead the mixture until well blended and smooth, occasionally adding a little water. Taste for seasoning.

(continued)

Keeping your hands moist, shape the *keyma* mixture into 1½-inch balls as described in the recipe for Stuffed Lamb and Wheat Balls Harput (page 179), filling each ball with 1 to 1½ teaspoons of the stuffing. In a heavy saucepan bring the water and salt to a boil over moderate heat, stirring to dissolve the salt. Lower 6 or 7 *keuftehs* at a time into the boiling water. Reduce the heat and simmer about 10 minutes or until done. Repeat until all the *keuftehs* are cooked.

Using a perforated spoon, transfer the *keuftehs* to a double thickness of paper towels to drain. Sprinkle evenly on all sides with the paprika. Cool. Refrigerate in a covered container several hours, preferably overnight, until thoroughly chilled. Serve cold, as an appetizer or main dish, with the olive oil and lemon wedges on the side to be sprinkled over the *keuftehs* before eating.

Serves 4 or 5

NOTE: Ground cumin or curry powder may also be sprinkled over the *keuftehs* before eating.

9. Stuffed Vegetables and Fruits

Peppers, Quinces, Eggplants, Apples, and Tomatoes Stuffed with Meat
(pages 199–205)

The Armenians' enthusiasm for stuffing foods reaches its zeniths with vegetables and fruits, upon which they have lavished considerable ingenuity. *Dolma* and *sarma* are favorite dishes throughout the Middle East and the Caucasus. *Dolmas* are stuffed vegetables or fruits, simmered in broth or water flavored with lemon juice and sometimes tomatoes. *Sarmas* are stuffed leaves (grapevine, cabbage, and chard being the most common) cooked the same way. Both may be prepared with or without meat. *Sarmas* are sometimes referred to as *dolmas*; for example, stuffed grapevine leaves may be called *yalanchi dolma*.

Meat *dolmas* incorporate ground lamb or beef, rice or coarse bulghur, tomatoes, onions, herbs, seasonings, and occasionally nuts and currants. They are served hot as main dishes. Any leftover meat stuffing from *dolmas* may be shaped into small balls and cooked along with them.

Meatless *dolmas* are based on olive oil and are filled with a mixture of rice, tomatoes, onions, herbs, seasonings, nuts, and currants. They are served cold as appetizers or side or main dishes.

Served with crusty bread and a green salad, *dolmas* and *sarmas* make excellent luncheon and summer dishes.

ARTICHOKES STUFFED WITH MEAT

Missov Gangari Dolma

8 medium artichokes
Juice of 1 lemon
3 tablespoons butter
1 large onion, finely chopped
1 pound lean ground lamb
1 tablespoon pine nuts
1 medium ripe tomato, peeled, seeded, and finely chopped
1 tablespoon dried currants (optional)
2 tablespoons finely chopped parsley
Salt and freshly ground black pepper to taste
Juice of 1 lemon, strained
2 tablespoons butter
2 cups hot water

Prepare each artichoke as follows: Remove any coarse or discolored outer leaves and cut 1 inch off the tops of the remaining leaves. Separate the top leaves and pull out the thorny pinkish leaves from the center. With a spoon, scrape out the fuzzy choke underneath, being careful not to puncture the meaty part. Peel the tough outer skin from the stem and trim off ⅛ inch of the stem end. Cut off the stem and drop along with the artichoke into a bowl of salted water mixed with the lemon juice. Let soak while you prepare the stuffing.

In a heavy skillet melt the butter over moderate heat. Add the onion and sauté until it begins to soften, stirring frequently. Add the meat and nuts and cook until lightly browned. Stir in the tomato and cook a few minutes. Add the currants, parsley, and salt and pepper. Mix well and remove from the heat.

Drain the artichokes. Fill the centers with the meat mixture. Arrange in a heavy pan with the stems. Sprinkle with additional salt and the lemon juice and dot with the butter. Place an inverted plate over the artichokes to keep them in place while cooking. Add the hot water. Cover and bake in a preheated 350° oven or cook on top of the stove 1 to 1½ hours or until tender.

Carefully transfer the artichokes to a heated serving platter and spoon the cooking juices over them. Serve with Plain Rice Pilaf (page 219) or Plain Saffron Rice Pilaf (page 222) and Cucumber and Tomato Salad (page 50).

Serves 4

NOTE: The meat stuffing may be flavored with ¼ teaspoon allspice or 2 tablespoons finely chopped fresh dill.

CABBAGE LEAVES STUFFED WITH MEAT

Missov Gaghampi Dolma (Sarma)

Use the stuffing in the recipe for Grapevine Leaves Stuffed with Meat (page 200), substituting 1 3½-pound head white cabbage for the grapevine leaves. Prepare the cabbage as follows: Remove the thick core from the cabbage, loosening the leaves without detaching them. Drop the cabbage into a large pot of boiling salted water and boil 6 to 7 minutes or until the leaves are softened. Transfer the cabbage to a plate. Using a long fork, loosen the outer leaves and remove them, being careful not to break them. Place the leaves in a colander to drain and cool. Return the cabbage to the boiling water, cook a few minutes more, and again remove the softened outer leaves. Continue this process until you come to the heart of the cabbage. Reserve the inner leaves.

Stuff each of the remaining leaves as follows: Remove the hard rib end and spread the leaf on a plate, cut end toward you. Place about 1 tablespoon (more for larger leaves) of the meat mixture near the cut end. Fold over the sides to enclose the stuffing securely. Beginning at the cut end, roll the leaf firmly away from you toward the tip, forming a cylinder.

Cover the bottom of a heavy casserole with the reserved inner leaves. Layer the stuffed leaves, seam sides down and close together, in neat rows over them. Sprinkle with salt and lemon juice. Gently place an inverted plate over the top to keep the stuffed leaves in place while cooking. Add enough broth to reach the plate. Bring to a boil and cover. Lower the heat and simmer about 1 hour or until tender. Serve with a bowl of unflavored yogurt or Garlic Yogurt Sauce (page 288) on the side.

Serves 4

CHARD LEAVES STUFFED WITH MEAT

Missov Panjarapatat or Panjari Dolma (Sarma)

Follow the recipe for Grapevine Leaves Stuffed with Meat (page 200), substituting Swiss chard leaves for the grapevine leaves. Remove the stems and dip the leaves, a few at a time, in boiling salted water for 1 minute or less until they soften. Then proceed as directed in the recipe.

Serves 6

EGGPLANTS STUFFED WITH MEAT

Missov Simpoogi Dolma

1 pound lean ground lamb or beef

¾ to 1 cup uncooked long-grain white rice, washed and drained, or ¾ to 1 cup coarse bulghur

2 medium onions, finely chopped

¼ cup finely chopped parsley plus 2 tablespoons finely chopped fresh mint leaves, or 3 tablespoons finely chopped green pepper plus 1 tablespoon chopped fresh basil or 1 teaspoon dried basil

⅓ cup tomato juice

Salt and freshly ground black pepper to taste

Cayenne and paprika to taste

10 small eggplants, or as many as needed (approximately 6 by 2 inches each)

2 cups tomato juice; or 2 large ripe tomatoes, peeled, seeded, and puréed, plus 1½ cups water

1½ tablespoons freshly squeezed and strained lemon juice

Combine the meat, rice, onions, parsley and mint, tomato juice, salt and pepper, and cayenne and paprika in a bowl. Knead thoroughly until the mixture is well blended and smooth. Taste for seasoning.

Cut about ½ inch off the stem ends of the eggplants. Shape these into cork-like lids by cutting a little off all around the bottom of the "lid." Using an apple-corer (the Middle Eastern cook uses a special squash-corer for this purpose), scoop out the eggplant pulp and discard, leaving a ¼-inch-thick shell all around. Spoon the stuffing into the eggplants. Cover the filled eggplants with the reserved stem ends.

Place the eggplants side by side in a heavy flameproof casserole large enough to hold them comfortably. Pour the tomato juice around them and sprinkle with the lemon juice and additional salt. Bring to a boil and cover. Lower the heat and cook about 1 hour or until the eggplants are tender, adding more water if necessary. Carefully transfer the eggplants to a heated serving platter and spoon some of the cooking liquid over them. Serve with crusty bread.

Serves 4

NOTE: The stuffing used in this recipe is a basic *dolma* mixture that may also be used to stuff grapevine, cabbage, or chard leaves; zucchini; or green peppers.

GRAPEVINE LEAVES STUFFED WITH MEAT

Missov Derevapatat or Derevi Dolma (Sarma)

1 pound lean ground lamb
½ cup uncooked long-grain white rice, washed and drained
1 large onion, finely chopped or grated
½ cup finely chopped parsley
2 tablespoons finely chopped fresh mint leaves
1½ cups canned tomatoes with juice, chopped, or fresh tomatoes, peeled, seeded, and chopped
Salt and freshly ground black pepper or cayenne to taste
1 16-ounce jar preserved grapevine leaves or about 60 fresh grapevine leaves
¼ cup freshly squeezed and strained lemon juice
Boiling meat broth

Combine the lamb, rice, onion, parsley, mint, tomatoes, and salt and pepper in a bowl. Knead well until the mixture is blended and smooth. Taste for seasoning.

Prepare and stuff the grapevine leaves according to the directions given in the recipe for Grapevine Leaves Stuffed with Rice and Olive Oil (page 9), using 1 tablespoon of the meat mixture (or a little more or less, depending on the size of the leaf) for each leaf.

Cover the bottom of a heavy casserole with 10 of the leaves to prevent the stuffed leaves from burning during cooking. Layer the stuffed leaves, seam sides down and close together, in neat rows in the casserole. Sprinkle additional salt and the lemon juice over them. Gently place an inverted plate over the top to keep them in place while they cook. Add enough of the broth to reach the plate. Bring to a boil and cover. Lower the heat and simmer 50 to 60 minutes, adding a little more hot broth if necessary. Serve with a bowl of Cinnamon Yogurt Sauce (page 287) or Garlic Yogurt Sauce (page 288) on the side.

Serves 6

Variation: Caucasian Armenians stuff the grapevine leaves with a mixture of 1 pound ground lamb, ⅓ cup rice, 1 medium onion, finely chopped, ½ cup minced fresh herbs (a mixture of savory, coriander, mint, basil, and marjoram or a combination of parsley, dill, and coriander), and salt and pepper to taste. The stuffed leaves are covered with boiling meat stock, cooked, and served as above.

GREEN PEPPERS AND TOMATOES STUFFED WITH MEAT

Missov Bighbeghi yev Loligi Dolma

5 medium square-shaped green peppers
5 medium firm tomatoes
Freshly squeezed and strained lemon juice
Salt
1 pound lean ground lamb or beef
1 cup uncooked long-grain white rice, washed and drained, or 1 cup coarse bulghur
1 large onion, finely chopped
2 tablespoons each finely chopped parsley and fresh mint leaves or 3 tablespoons finely chopped green pepper plus 1 tablespoon chopped fresh basil or 1 teaspoon dried basil
Freshly ground black pepper to taste
Cayenne and paprika to taste
2 cups beef broth or water (approximately)
2 tablespoons freshly squeezed and strained lemon juice
1 tablespoon crushed dried mint

Cut about ½ inch off the stem ends of the green peppers and re-serve. These will later be used as lids. Remove the seeds and white membranes. Cut almost through the stem ends of the tomatoes, leaving them attached at one side. These will also later serve as lids. Using a spoon, scoop out the insides of each tomato, leaving a ¼-inch-thick shell all around. Chop the pulp finely and set aside.

Sprinkle the cavities of the tomatoes with a few drops of the lemon juice and a pinch of salt. Combine the meat, rice, onion, parsley and mint, additional salt, pepper, cayenne and paprika, and ½ the reserved chopped tomato pulp in a bowl. Knead thoroughly until the mixture is well blended and smooth. Taste for seasoning.

Spoon the stuffing into the green peppers and tomatoes and cover with the reserved tops. Arrange the peppers side by side in a heavy flameproof casserole large enough to hold them comfortably. Place the tomatoes over them. Sprinkle with additional salt. Pour in the broth, remaining tomato pulp, and lemon juice. Bring to a boil and cover. Lower the heat and simmer about 1 hour, adding a little more hot broth if necessary. Sprinkle with the mint and cook 5 minutes.

Carefully transfer the green peppers and tomatoes to a heated serving platter and spoon the sauce over them. Serve with crusty bread and a green salad.

Serves 5

Combination Dolma

Armenians often make a *dolma* using green peppers, tomatoes, zucchini, and eggplants. To prepare, choose small firm vegetables and cook them according to this recipe, placing the peppers in the casserole first, the eggplants and zucchini next, and the tomatoes on top.

Echmiadzin Dolma

Caucasian Armenians make a combination *dolma* with green peppers, eggplants, tomatoes, apples, and quinces, using the stuffing given in the Caucasian variation under Grapevine Leaves Stuffed with Meat (page 200).

ZUCCHINI STUFFED WITH MEAT

Missov Titoumi Dolma

1 pound lean ground lamb or beef
1 large onion, finely chopped or grated
½ cup uncooked long-grain white rice, washed and drained, or
  ½ cup coarse bulghur
⅓ cup tomato juice
3 tablespoons finely chopped fresh dill
3 tablespoons finely chopped fresh mint leaves
Salt and freshly ground black pepper to taste
10 zucchini, or as many as needed (6 by 2 inches each)
2 tablespoons butter
2 cups broth or water (approximately)

Combine the meat, onion, rice, tomato juice, dill, mint, and salt and pepper in a bowl. Knead thoroughly until the mixture is well blended and smooth. Taste for seasoning.

Cut about ½ inch off the stem ends of the zucchini, shape into cork-like lids, and reserve. These will later serve as covers.

Using an apple-corer (the Middle Eastern cook uses a special squash-corer for this task), scoop out the pulp of each zucchini and discard, leaving a ¼-inch-thick shell all around. Lightly sprinkle the insides with additional salt and spoon the stuffing into the zucchini. Cover with the reserved lids and place side by side in a heavy flameproof casserole just large enough to hold them comfortably. Dot with the butter, sprinkle with additional salt, and pour in the broth. Bring to a boil and cover. Lower the heat and cook 1 hour or until tender, adding a little more hot broth if necessary.

Carefully transfer the zucchini to a heated serving platter and spoon the pan juices over them. Serve with unflavored yogurt or Garlic Yogurt Sauce (page 288) on the side.

Serves 4

ONIONS STUFFED WITH MEAT

Missov Sokhi Dolma

    8 large onions
Boiling salted water or beef broth
    1 pound lean ground lamb
    1 cup finely chopped or grated onion
    1 cup coarse bulghur, washed and drained
    ¼ cup finely chopped parsley
    2½ cups tomato juice
Salt and freshly ground black pepper to taste
Paprika to taste

Make a lengthwise slit on one side of each peeled onion, cutting all the way to the center. Cook the onions in boiling salted water about 5 minutes or until soft enough for the layers to be separated. As each layer becomes softened, gently loosen it with a fork, being careful not to break it, and remove it to a colander to drain and cool.

Meanwhile, combine the lamb, onion, bulghur, parsley, ½ cup of the tomato juice, and salt and pepper in a bowl. Knead thoroughly until the mixture is well blended and smooth. Taste for seasoning.

Place 1 tablespoon of the meat mixture on each layer of onion (or more or less, depending on its size) and roll firmly, following its natural curl to form an oval.

Cover the bottom of a heavy casserole with any leftover pieces of onion. Layer the stuffed onions close together in neat rows over them. Pour in the remaining 2 cups tomato juice and sprinkle with additional salt and the paprika. Cover and cook over low heat about 40 minutes or until done.

Serves 4

NOTE: The stuffing in this recipe may also be used to stuff baby eggplants and grapevine leaves.

204

Variation: Here is another popular stuffing for onion *dolma*. Sauté 1 pound ground lamb and ½ cup finely chopped onion in 2 tablespoons butter. Add 3 tablespoons half-boiled rice, 1 egg, salt, pepper, and minced fresh parsley or coriander to taste and mix well. Stuff the onions and layer in the casserole as above. Scatter around them 12 dried prunes. Add 2 cups beef broth and ½ cup tomato sauce. Cover and simmer until tender, about 40 minutes, or until done.

APPLES STUFFED WITH MEAT

Missov Khintzori Dolma

  6 large tart apples
  2 tablespoons butter
½ pound lean ground lamb or beef
½ cup finely chopped onion
½ cup uncooked long-grain white rice
¼ cup pine nuts
¼ cup dried currants
¼ teaspoon cinnamon
Salt to taste
  1 teaspoon freshly squeezed and strained lemon juice
  3 cups water
1¼ cups sugar

Cut about ½ inch off the stem ends of the apples and reserve. These will later be used as lids. Scoop out the cores and pulp, leaving a ⅓-inch-thick shell all around. Discard the cores and finely chop the pulp.

In a heavy skillet heat the butter over moderate heat. Add the meat and onion and sauté until golden brown, stirring frequently. Stir in the rice, pine nuts, currants, cinnamon, salt, lemon juice, 1 cup of the water, the apple pulp, and ½ cup of the sugar. Cover and cook until the water is absorbed and the rice is almost tender. Taste for seasoning. Remove from the heat and cool to room temperature.

Sprinkle the apple shells with 2 tablespoons of the sugar and spoon the meat mixture into them. Cover with the reserved tops. Arrange them side by side in a shallow baking dish just large enough to hold them comfortably in one layer. Sprinkle evenly with 2 tablespoons of the sugar.

In a small saucepan bring the remaining 2 cups water and ½ cup sugar to a boil, stirring constantly. Pour around the stuffed apples. Cover and bake in a preheated 350° oven about 45 minutes or until the apples are soft, basting occasionally with the liquid in the pan. Remove the cover during the last 10 minutes of baking. Carefully transfer the apples to a heated serving platter and spoon pan juices over them.

Serves 4

VARIATION

Ashtarak Dolma

Caucasian Armenians also make a combination apple and quince *dolma*. To prepare, choose 4 medium apples and 4 quinces. Wash, cut off the tops, and reserve. Scoop out the insides as above. Cook the quinces in beef broth until half tender. Add the apples and 3 tablespoons sugar to the pot and cook until the apples begin to soften. Combine 1 pound lean ground lamb; ¼ cup partly boiled rice; ½ cup minced onion; minced fresh mint, savory, coriander, and marjoram; salt, and pepper and knead until well blended. Stuff the fruit with this mixture and cover with the tops. Place first the quinces and then the apples in the pot. Scatter ¼ cup each dried apricots and dried prunes around them. Pour in some broth, cover, and simmer over low heat until tender. Serve the *dolma* with the pan juices and sprinkle with minced fresh parsley, savory, or mint.

STUFFED MELON

Missov Sekhi Dolma

The exquisitely delicate flavor and aroma of this unique dish will linger in your memory.

1 large cantaloupe
2 tablespoons butter
½ pound lean ground lamb or beef
1 small onion, finely chopped
½ cup uncooked long-grain white rice
¼ cup pine nuts
¼ cup dried currants
⅓ cup plus 2 tablespoons sugar
¼ teaspoon cinnamon
Salt to taste
1 cup water

Cut about 1 inch off the top of the melon and reserve. This will later serve as a lid. Clean out the inside of the melon and discard the seeds. With a long-handled spoon, scoop out 1 cup of the center pulp and chop.

In a heavy skillet heat the butter over moderate heat. Add the meat and onion and sauté until browned, stirring frequently. Add the rice, pine nuts, currants, ⅓ cup of the sugar, cinnamon, salt, chopped melon pulp, and water and mix well. Cook until the liquid in the pan is absorbed, stirring occasionally. Remove from the heat and cool to room temperature.

Sprinkle the inside of the melon with the remaining 2 tablespoons sugar and spoon the meat stuffing into it. Cover with the reserved top and secure with wooden picks. Place in an oiled baking pan just large enough to hold the melon comfortably. Bake in a preheated 350° oven 1 hour or until tender.

Serves 2

CABBAGE LEAVES STUFFED WITH RICE AND OLIVE OIL

Tzitayoughov Gaghampi Dolma (Sarma)

⅔ cup olive oil
4 medium onions, finely chopped
1 cup uncooked long-grain white rice
¼ cup pine nuts
¼ cup dried currants
1 medium tomato, peeled, seeded, and finely chopped
½ teaspoon allspice
¼ teaspoon cinnamon
¼ teaspoon paprika
Salt and freshly ground black pepper to taste
1 cup beef broth or water
3 tablespoons freshly squeezed and strained lemon juice
1 3½-pound head white cabbage
1½ cups water
2 lemons, cut into wedges

In a heavy skillet heat the olive oil over moderate heat. Add the onions and sauté until soft but not browned, stirring frequently. Add the rice and pine nuts and sauté until onions and nuts turn golden brown, stirring almost constantly. Add the currants, tomato, allspice, cinnamon, paprika, salt and pepper, and broth. Bring to a boil, stirring. Reduce the heat to low and cover. Simmer until liquid is absorbed. Remove from the heat, stir in 1½ tablespoons of the lemon juice, and set aside.

Prepare the cabbage and stuff the leaves with the rice mixture as directed in the recipe for Cabbage Leaves Stuffed with Meat (page 197).

Cover the bottom of a heavy casserole with the reserved inner cabbage leaves. Layer the stuffed leaves, seam sides down and close together, in neat rows over them. Sprinkle with the remaining 1½ tablespoons lemon juice and add the water. Gently place an inverted plate over the top to keep the stuffed leaves in place while they cook. Bring to a boil over moderate heat and reduce the heat to low. Cover and simmer about 1 hour or until tender.

Remove from the heat and cool to room temperature. Remove the plate and arrange the *dolmas* on a serving platter. Cover and chill. Garnish with the lemon wedges. Serve as an appetizer or buffet dish.

Serves 8

NOTE: The filling given for Grapevine Leaves Stuffed with Rice and Olive Oil (page 9) may also be used to stuff the cabbage leaves.

CHARD LEAVES STUFFED WITH RICE AND OLIVE OIL

Tzitayoughov Panjarapatat or Tzitayoughov Panjari Dolma (Sarma)

Follow the recipe for Grapevine Leaves Stuffed with Rice and Olive Oil (page 9), substituting Swiss chard leaves for the grapevine leaves. Remove the stems and dip the leaves, a few at a time, in boiling salted water for 1 minute or less until they soften, then proceed as directed in the recipe.

Makes 50 (serves 10 to 12)

EGGPLANTS STUFFED WITH
RICE AND OLIVE OIL

Tzitayoughov Simpoogi Dolma

6 eggplants (about 6 by 2 inches each), or as many as needed
Salt
½ cup olive oil
2 large onions, finely chopped
½ cup uncooked long-grain white rice
2 medium tomatoes, peeled, seeded, and chopped
2 tablespoons finely chopped parsley
1 tablespoon finely chopped fresh dill or mint leaves (optional)
½ teaspoon cinnamon
Salt and freshly ground black pepper to taste
1½ cups warm water
1 lemon, cut into wedges

Cut about ½ inch off the stem ends of the eggplants, shape into cork-like lids, and reserve. These will later serve as covers. Using an apple-corer (the Middle Eastern cook uses a special squash-corer for this operation), scoop out the pulp and reserve, leaving a ¼-inch-thick shell all around. Sprinkle the eggplant pulp with salt and let stand.

In a heavy skillet heat the olive oil over moderate heat. Add the onions and sauté until soft but not browned, stirring frequently. Wash the eggplant pulp in a bowl of cold water, discard the seeds, and squeeze dry. Add to the onions and sauté a few minutes. Add the rice, tomatoes, parsley, dill, cinnamon, and salt and pepper. Cook 5 minutes, stirring almost continuously. Remove from the heat and taste for seasoning.

Spoon the stuffing into the eggplants and cover with the reserved stem ends. Place side by side in a heavy casserole large enough to hold them comfortably. Add the water and sprinkle with additional salt.

Cover and cook over low heat about 1 hour and 15 minutes or until tender.

Remove from the heat and cool to room temperature. Transfer the *dolmas* to a serving platter. Cover and chill. Garnish with the lemon wedges. Serve as an appetizer or as a luncheon dish with salad.

Serves 6 as an appetizer, 3 for lunch

GREEN PEPPERS STUFFED WITH RICE AND OLIVE OIL

Tzitayoughov Bighbeghi Dolma

½ cup olive oil
2 large onions, finely chopped
½ cup uncooked long-grain white rice
2 tablespoons pine nuts (optional)
1 medium tomato, peeled, seeded, and chopped
2 tablespoons dried currants (optional)
½ teaspoon allspice or cinnamon
¼ teaspoon paprika
Salt and freshly ground black pepper to taste
½ cup beef broth or water
¼ cup finely chopped parsley
1 tablespoon finely chopped fresh mint leaves (optional)
1 tablespoon freshly squeezed and strained lemon juice
4 medium green peppers
1½ cups water or tomato juice
1 lemon, cut into wedges

In a heavy skillet heat the olive oil over moderate heat. Add the onions and sauté until soft but not browned, stirring frequently. Add the rice and pine nuts and sauté until onions and nuts turn golden brown, stirring constantly. Add the tomato, currants, allspice, paprika, salt and pepper, and broth and bring to a boil, stirring. Reduce the heat to low. Cover and simmer until the liquid is absorbed. Remove from the heat. Stir in the parsley, mint, and lemon juice and set aside.

Cut about ½ inch off the stem ends of the green peppers and reserve. Remove the seeds and white membranes. Spoon the rice mixture into the peppers and cover with the reserved tops. Place side by side in a heavy casserole large enough to hold them comfortably. Sprinkle with additional salt. Pour the water around them. Cover and cook over moderate heat or bake in a preheated 350° oven 50 to 60 minutes or until tender.

Remove from the heat and cool to room temperature. Transfer the *dolmas* to a serving platter, cover, and chill. Garnish with the lemon wedges. Serve as an appetizer or as a luncheon dish, with crusty bread and a green salad.

Serves 4 as an appetizer, 2 for lunch

NOTE: You may use 2 green peppers and 2 tomatoes instead of 4 green peppers, in which case the scooped-out tomato pulp may be substituted for the whole tomato called for in the recipe.

ZUCCHINI STUFFED WITH RICE AND OLIVE OIL

Tzitayoughov Titoumi Dolma

½ cup olive oil
½ cup uncooked long-grain white rice
8 scallions, chopped, including 2 inches of the green tops
1 large tomato, peeled, seeded, and chopped
Salt to taste
½ cup water
3 tablespoons finely chopped parsley
3 tablespoons finely chopped fresh dill
2 tablespoons finely chopped fresh mint leaves (optional)
8 zucchini (about 6 by 2 inches each), or as many as needed
1½ cups water

In a heavy skillet heat the olive oil over moderate heat. Add the rice and sauté 5 minutes, stirring frequently. Add the scallions and sauté until soft but not browned. Add the tomato and sauté 2 to 3 minutes, stirring almost continuously. Sprinkle with the salt, pour in the water, and bring to a boil, stirring. Reduce the heat to low. Cover and simmer until all the liquid is absorbed. Remove from the heat and stir in the parsley, dill, and mint.

Cut about ½ inch off the stem ends of the zucchini, shape into cork-like lids, and reserve. Using an apple-corer (the Middle Eastern cook uses a special squash-corer for this task), scoop out the pulp and discard, leaving a ¼-inch-thick shell all around. Spoon the rice mixture into the zucchini, cover with the reserved lids, and place side by side in a heavy casserole just large enough to hold them comfortably. Sprinkle with additional salt and add the water. Cover and cook over moderate heat 1 hour or until the zucchini are tender and cooked through. Remove from the heat and cool to room temperature.

Transfer the *dolmas* to a serving platter, cover, and chill. Serve as an appetizer or as a luncheon course, with crusty bread and Cucumber and Tomato Salad (page 50) that has been sprinkled with 1 tablespoon finely chopped fresh dill.

Serves 8 as an appetizer, 4 for lunch

10. Pilafs

Wedding Pilaf with apricots, prunes, currants, and almonds (page 222)

Rice is one of the staple ingredients in Middle Eastern cookery and appears frequently on the dinner table. It is essential in the preparation of stuffings for various *dolmas*, fish, fowl, and meat dishes, and it is the principal ingredient of the versatile pilafs.

In Armenian cuisine the preparation of pilaf is considered an art, one which a cook tries to perfect. The quality of rice is important, the preferred kind being long-grain rice; if properly handled with a gentle touch, it will produce a light and fluffy pilaf with a firm texture, not a gummy or mashed consistency. The amount of liquid used in cooking rice is also crucial in determining the final outcome. Too much liquid will produce a soggy result. Not enough will produce a pilaf that is not fully cooked, in which each individual grain of rice has not been given a chance to absorb all the liquid necessary to enable it to swell up to capacity and stand out on its own. As one cooks pilaf, he gradually develops the ability to determine the exact amount of liquid needed. Roughly, for each cup of rice one should use 2 cups of liquid. The amount of butter used depends on the richness of the liquid. If water is being used, more butter is usually needed. If a rich meat or poultry stock is being used, less butter is needed. When pilaf is cooked, the lid may be removed, a dish towel place over the saucepan to absorb excess moisture, the lid replaced, and the pan allowed to stand in a warm place about 15 minutes before serving.

A bed of pilaf is the perfect accompaniment to all the kebabs and stews, which can be appreciated to the fullest when served with their sauces over it. Plain rice pilaf complements almost any of the meat courses. It is often served with yogurt. Rice pilaf with vermicelli is equally popular and is used interchangeably with plain rice pilaf. It is especially good with chicken and lamb stews. As a youngster I used to be fascinated by the speed and expertise with which the women, using their thumbs and forefingers, would manipulate portions of dough into perfectly uniform threads (*tel*) that were about one inch long and no thicker than vermicelli. These threads were thoroughly dried and stored to be used in the preparation of pilaf with vermicelli. With roast turkey or chicken, Armenians like to serve rice pilaf with almonds or rice pilaf with chicken livers and scallions. On festive occasions a saffron rice pilaf often accompanies roast fowl or meat. Rice pilafs with vegetables, incorporating tomatoes, mushrooms, green pepper, and onions, are delicious with roast or grilled chicken. Rice pilaf with fruits is a wonderful accompaniment to roast or barbecued pork, as well as poultry. Armenians also make rice pilaf with brains, caraway seeds, eggs, ground meat and pomegranate seeds, kidney beans, *lavash*, and trout. Pilafs in which the rice is cooked together with shellfish, chicken, or meat are ideal dishes for buffets.

The various bulghur pilafs often substitute for the rice pilafs, adding variety and interest to menus. Bulghur pilaf goes well with meat and vegetable stews, particularly with curried lamb. It also combines beautifully with lamb, tomatoes, and chick-peas to produce delicious casseroles. Bulghur pilaf may be served with yogurt, tomato sauce, or lemon curry sauce, provided such a sauce does not clash with the rest of the meal.

Pilaf should not be cooked in advance but is best prepared close to serving time. If you must reheat leftover pilaf, moisten it with a few tablespoons of broth or water, cover, and heat in a 350° oven or simmer over very low heat until heated through.

218

PLAIN RICE PILAF

Printz Pilav

¼ cup butter
1 cup uncooked long-grain white rice
2 cups chicken or beef broth
Salt to taste

In a heavy saucepan or casserole melt the butter over moderate heat. Add the rice and cook 2 minutes or until the grains are thoroughly coated with butter but not browned, stirring constantly. Pour in the broth, sprinkle with the salt, and bring to a boil, stirring. Reduce the heat to low. Cover and simmer about 20 minutes or until all the liquid has been absorbed and the rice is tender but still firm to the bite, not mushy. Gently fluff the rice with a fork. Spoon onto a heated serving platter, being careful not to mash it.

Serves 4

NOTE: You may simmer the rice 15 minutes or until just tender, then stir gently with a fork and place, uncovered, in a preheated 325° oven 30 minutes or until the grains are dry and separate. Fluff with a fork every 10 minutes.

Although it is not typical, the pilaf may be flavored with onion or garlic. A small onion, finely chopped, may be sautéed in the butter before you add the rice, or a crushed garlic clove may be added to the sautéed rice before adding the broth. The pilaf may also be sprinkled with finely chopped parsley or paprika to taste just before serving.

RICE PILAF WITH VERMICELLI

Telahaysov (Tel Shehrieyov) Printz Pilav

Follow the recipe for Plain Rice Pilaf (page 219), sautéing ½ cup vermicelli, broken into 1-inch pieces, in the butter until lightly browned. Add the rice and proceed as above.

Serves 4

RICE PILAF WITH NOODLES

Arishtah Pilav

Follow the recipe for Plain Rice Pilaf (page 219), sautéing ½ cup ½ cup fine egg noodles for the vermicelli.

Serves 4

RICE PILAF WITH ALMONDS

Noushov Printz Pilav

  1½ teaspoons butter
  ¼ cup blanched almonds
Salt to taste
  1 recipe Plain Rice Pilaf (page 219)

In a small skillet melt the butter over moderate heat. Add the almonds and sauté until golden brown on both sides, stirring frequently.

220

Drain on absorbent paper and sprinkle with the salt. Serve the hot pilaf on a heated platter, topped with the sautéed almonds.

Serves 4

RICE PILAF WITH TOMATOES

Loligov Printz Pilav

Follow the recipe for Plain Rice Pilaf (page 219), sautéing in the butter 1 small onion, finely sliced, until soft but not browned. Add 2 large tomatoes, peeled, seeded, and minced; ½ teaspoon dried basil (optional); 1 clove garlic, crushed, (optional); and 2 tablespoons minced parsley and cook 2 minutes. Add the rice and proceed as directed in the recipe, reducing the amount of broth to about 1½ cups, depending on how juicy the tomatoes are, and using salt and pepper to taste.

Serves 4

✿ RICE PILAF WITH MUSHROOMS

Soungov Printz Pilav

Follow the recipe for Plain Rice Pilaf (page 219), sautéing in the butter 1 medium onion, minced; 1 cup thickly sliced fresh mushrooms; and 1 small green pepper, thinly sliced, until they begin to soften. Stir in 1 medium tomato, peeled, seeded, and minced, and 1 large clove garlic, crushed, and cook 2 minutes. Add the rice and ¼ teaspoon powdered saffron or to taste and proceed as directed in the recipe, reducing the amount of broth to about 1¾ cups and using salt and pepper to taste. Sprinkle the pilaf with 2 tablespoons minced parsley if you like.

Serves 4

❀ SAFFRON RICE PILAF WITH TOASTED ALMONDS AND SESAME SEEDS

Kirkoumov Printz Pilav

The toasted almonds and sesame seeds add a delightful texture to this golden pilaf with the distinctive flavor of saffron.

Follow the recipe for Plain Rice Pilaf (page 219), adding ¼ teaspoon powdered saffron or to taste with the broth. Toast ¼ cup each sliced almonds and sesame seeds on separate baking sheets in a preheated 300° oven until golden brown, stirring occasionally and watching closely to prevent burning. When the pilaf is done, fluff gently with a fork, stir in the toasted almonds and sesame seeds, and mix thoroughly.

Serves 4

VARIATION

Plain Saffron Rice Pilaf

Omit the toasted almonds and sesame seeds.

WEDDING PILAF

Harsanik Pilav

The color, romance, and splendor of the East are expressed in this magnificent and opulent pilaf, which Caucasian Armenians reserve for great occasions.

¼ cup butter
⅓ cup dried apricots

⅓ cup dried prunes
⅓ cup dried currants
⅓ cup finely chopped blanched almonds
2 tablespoons honey
1 tablespoon hot water
1 recipe Plain Rice Pilaf (page 219) (substitute water for the broth)

In a heavy skillet melt the butter over moderate heat. Add the fruits and nuts and sauté until lightly browned, stirring frequently. Combine the honey and water and add. Cook over low heat about 10 minutes or until the liquid is thickened, stirring occasionally. Arrange the hot pilaf on a serving dish and top with the fruit sauce.

Serves 4

ARARAT PILAF

Ararat Pilav

This dazzling pilaf, a jewel among jewels, will provide a dramatic spectacle for the most elegant of tables. Caucasian Armenians serve large amounts of it at banquets, surrounded by baked apples and quinces.

4 tablespoons butter
½ cup blanched almonds
1 cup dried apricots
1 cup dried prunes
1½ cups seedless raisins
¼ teaspoon ground cloves
2 tablespoons sugar or to taste
½ teaspoon cinnamon
2 apples
Warmed brandy
2 recipes Plain Rice Pilaf (page 219) (substitute water for the broth)

In a small skillet melt ½ tablespoon of the butter over low heat. Add the nuts and sauté until lightly browned, stirring frequently. Remove from the heat and set aside.

In a heavy skillet melt the remaining 3½ tablespoons butter. Add the dried fruits, cloves, and sugar. Cover and cook over low heat until the fruits are lightly browned, stirring frequently. Add the nuts, sprinkle with the cinnamon, and mix well. Remove from the heat and keep warm.

Scoop a hollow about 1½ inches deep out of the stem end of each apple. Line with aluminum foil and fill with the warmed brandy. On a large oval serving platter mound the hot pilaf in two separate peaks, one large, placed on the right, and one small, placed on the left, to resemble Mount Ararat.

Place the apples on the platter. Surround the pilaf with the fruit mixture to reach halfway up the "mountain." Ignite the brandy, turn off the lights, and serve.

Serves 8

RICE PILAF WITH DATES

Armavov Printz Pilav

4 tablespoons butter
½ cup slivered blanched almonds
1 cup coarsely chopped dates
½ cup seedless golden raisins
1 teaspoon orange flower water
1 recipe Plain Rice Pilaf (page 219) (substitute water for the broth)

In a heavy skillet melt 1 tablespoon of the butter. Add the almonds and sauté until golden, stirring frequently. Add the remaining 3 tablespoons butter, dates, and raisins to the skillet. Cook over low heat,

224

stirring, 5 to 6 minutes or until the nuts and fruits are lightly browned. Stir in the orange flower water and remove from the heat. Serve the hot pilaf on a heated platter, garnished with the date topping.

Serves 4

Variation: Simmer the pilaf 15 minutes, then stir in ¼ teaspoon powdered saffron or to taste, 2 tablespoons orange flower water, and 6 tablespoons sugar and mix well. Cover and simmer 10 minutes more or until the liquid is absorbed.

RICE PILAF WITH CHICKEN LIVERS AND SCALLIONS

Ich Pilav

6 tablespoons butter
2 tablespoons pine nuts
¼ pound chicken livers, coarsely chopped
12 scallions, chopped, including 2 inches of the green tops
3 tablespoons finely chopped fresh dill
Salt and freshly ground black pepper to taste
1 cup uncooked long-grain white rice
2 cups hot chicken broth
¼ cup dried currants

In a small skillet melt 1 tablespoon of the butter over moderate heat. Add the nuts and sauté until golden brown, stirring frequently. Remove the nuts to a plate.

Add 1 tablespoon of the butter, chicken livers, and scallions to the skillet and sauté until the livers and scallions are lightly browned. Stir in the dill and nuts and season with the salt and pepper. Remove from the heat and set aside.

In a heavy saucepan or casserole melt the remaining 4 tablespoons butter over moderate heat. Add the rice and cook 2 to 3 minutes or until the grains are thoroughly coated with butter but not browned, stirring constantly. Add the broth, currants, and additional salt and pepper. Bring to a boil, stirring. Cover, reduce the heat to low, and simmer about 20 minutes or until all the liquid has been absorbed and the rice is tender but still firm to the bite, not mushy.

Gently fold the chicken liver mixture into the rice with a fork, being careful not to mash the rice. Replace the lid of the saucepan or casserole and let stand 10 minutes in a warm place before serving. Serve with roast turkey or chicken or as a main course at lunch.

Serves 4

COLD MUSSEL PILAF

Midia Pilav

30 mussels in the shell
 4 medium onions, finely chopped
½ cup olive oil
¾ cup uncooked long-grain white rice
 2 tablespoons pine nuts
 2 medium tomatoes, peeled, seeded, and finely chopped
¼ cup dried currants
Salt and freshly ground black pepper to taste
 1 cup hot beef broth or water
Lettuce leaves (optional)

Scrub the mussels well and immerse in cold water. Pry open 20 of the mussels with the point of a knife. Trim off the beards, scoop out the flesh, and discard the shells. Set aside, along with the remaining 10 unopened mussels.

Sauté the onions in the olive oil in a heavy skillet over medium heat about 10 minutes or until soft and transparent, stirring constantly. Add the rice and nuts and sauté 5 minutes, stirring constantly. Add the tomatoes and sauté 5 minutes, stirring. Add the currants, salt and

226

pepper, and broth. Cook, uncovered, over high heat about 10 minutes. Scatter the opened and unopened mussels on top of the rice. Cover and cook on low heat 15 to 20 minutes or until all liquid is absorbed, the rice is done, and the shells have opened. Remove from the heat and cool. Serve cold, at a buffet or as an appetizer on a bed of lettuce if you wish.

Serves 6

NOTE: Canned mussels may be substituted when fresh mussels are not available. Place in a sieve and rinse thoroughly under running cold water. Remove any black spots.

SHRIMP PILAF

Garidos Pilav

2 tablespoons butter
2 tablespoons olive oil
¾ pound fresh shrimp, shelled and deveined (weighed after shelling), or uncooked frozen shrimp, thawed
Salt to taste
1 medium onion, thinly sliced lengthwise
2 medium cloves garlic, finely chopped
2 medium ripe tomatoes, peeled, seeded, and chopped
2 stalks celery, thinly sliced crosswise
1 teaspoon finely chopped parsley
¼ teaspoon powdered saffron or to taste
1 cup uncooked long-grain white rice
1⅓ cups broth made from shrimp trimmings, or clam juice (approximately)
Freshly ground black pepper to taste

In a heavy saucepan or casserole heat the butter and olive oil over moderate heat. Add the shrimp and salt and sauté 1 minute on each side. Remove and keep warm.

(continued)

Add the onion and garlic to the saucepan and sauté until golden brown, stirring frequently. Stir in the tomatoes, celery, and parsley and cook until they begin to soften. Add the saffron and rice and cook 2 minutes, stirring constantly. Add the broth, additional salt, and pepper and bring to a boil, stirring. Reduce the heat to low and place the shrimp on top of the rice. Cover and simmer 20 minutes or until all the liquid is absorbed and the rice is tender but still firm, not mushy. If necessary, more broth may be added. Serve as an entrée with Combination Salad (page 45).

Serves 3

NOTE: Scallops or clams, in the shell, that have been soaked in cold water 1 hour and drained may be substituted for the shrimp.

CHICKEN PILAF

Havov Pilav

1   3-pound chicken, cut into serving pieces
¼ cup butter
⅛ teaspoon cinnamon
⅛ teaspoon allspice
Salt and freshly ground black pepper to taste
2 large onions, finely chopped
1 six-ounce can tomato paste
1 cup cold water
2 cups boiling chicken broth
1 cup uncooked long-grain white rice or coarse bulghur

Dry the chicken with paper towels. In a large, heavy skillet melt the butter over moderate heat. Add the chicken, cinnamon, allspice, and salt and pepper and sauté, turning to brown evenly on all sides. Add the onions and cook until lightly browned. Add the tomato paste mixed with the water. Cover and simmer until chicken is tender. Add the broth and stir in the rice. Cover and simmer 20 minutes or until the rice is done. Serve as an entrée with a green salad.

Serves 4

LAMB AND RICE PILAF

Missov Pilav

1 recipe Rice Pilaf with Mushrooms (page 221) or Saffron Rice
    Pilaf with Toasted Almonds and Sesame Seeds (page 222)
1 tablespoon butter
½ pound boneless lean leg or shoulder of lamb, cut into thin
    1-inch-long strips
Salt and freshly ground black pepper to taste

Follow the recipe for either pilaf, making this addition:
In a small skillet melt the butter over moderate heat. Add the lamb and sauté until browned, stirring frequently. Drain off the liquid and season with the salt and pepper. Add to the rice along with the broth and proceed as directed.

Serves 4

LIVER PILAF

Gigerov Printz Pilav

    6 tablespoons butter
    ½ pound calf's, beef, or lamb's liver, trimmed and cut into
        ½-inch cubes
Salt and freshly ground black pepper to taste
    1 medium onion, finely chopped
    2 medium ripe tomatoes, peeled, seeded, and chopped
    ½ cup thinly sliced green pepper
    2 tablespoons pine nuts
    2 tablespoons dried currants
    1½ cups uncooked long-grain white rice
    2½ cups chicken broth (approximately)
    2 tablespoons finely chopped parsley

In a skillet melt 2 tablespoons of the butter over moderate heat. Add the liver and sauté a few minutes until no longer pink. Season with the salt and pepper, remove from the heat, and set aside.

Place the remaining 4 tablespoons butter in a heavy saucepan or casserole and melt over moderate heat. Add the onion and sauté until it begins to soften, stirring frequently. Add the tomatoes, green pepper, nuts, and currants and sauté a few minutes. Add the rice and cook a minute or so, stirring constantly. Add the broth and sprinkle with additional salt and pepper. Cook briskly, uncovered, a few minutes until the rice begins to absorb the liquid.

Place the sautéed liver on top of the rice, leaving the drippings in the skillet. Reduce the heat to low, cover, and simmer about 20 minutes or until all the liquid has been absorbed and the rice is tender but still firm to the bite, not mushy. If the liquid is absorbed before the rice is tender, add a little more broth. Garnish with parsley and serve as a luncheon or supper dish.

Serves 4

PLAIN CRACKED WHEAT PILAF

Bulghur Pilav

3 tablespoons olive oil or butter
1 small onion, finely chopped
1 cup medium or coarse bulghur
2 cups hot chicken or beef broth
Salt to taste

In a heavy saucepan or casserole heat the olive oil over moderate heat. Add the onion and sauté until soft but not browned, stirring frequently. Add the bulghur and sauté until the grains are thoroughly coated with the fat and are lightly browned, stirring constantly. Add the broth and salt and bring to a boil, stirring. Reduce the heat to low. Cover and simmer about 20 minutes or until all the liquid has been absorbed and the bulghur is tender. Serve with Tomato and Onion Salad (page 51) or as a side dish with roast lamb or chicken.

Serves 4

NOTE: You may also prepare this by simmering 15 minutes or until the bulghur is just tender. Then stir gently with a fork and set the saucepan, uncovered, in a preheated 325° oven 15 minutes. Stir again with a fork and bake 15 minutes or until the grains are dry and separate.

The pilaf may be flavored by adding ½ teaspoon curry powder, ground cumin, ground coriander, or dried basil with the broth, in which case ¼ cup minced green pepper may be sautéed with the onion.

CRACKED WHEAT PILAF WITH VERMICELLI

Telahaysov (Tel Shehrieyov) Bulghur Pilav

Follow the recipe (page 231) for Plain Cracked Wheat Pilaf, sautéing ½ cup vermicelli, broken into 1-inch pieces, in the olive oil until lightly browned. Add the bulghur and proceed as above.

Serves 4

CRACKED WHEAT PILAF WITH TOMATO

Loligov Bulghur Pilav

Follow the recipe (page 231) for Plain Cracked Wheat Pilaf, using butter and a medium onion. Before adding the bulghur, add 1 medium tomato, peeled, seeded, and minced, and ½ teaspoon dried basil (optional) and cook 3 minutes. Use 1½ cups broth or water. Simmer 15 minutes, then uncover and bake in a preheated 325° oven 30 minutes or until the grains are dry and separate.

Serves 4

Variation: Omit the basil. In a small skillet melt 3 tablespoons butter. Add 1 teaspoon curry powder or to taste and stir well. Pour over the cooked bulghur pilaf and fluff with a fork to distribute it evenly.

CRACKED WHEAT PILAF WITH LENTILS

Mujaddarah

4 cups chicken or beef broth (approximately)
1 cup lentils, washed and drained

1 cup coarse bulghur
Salt and freshly ground black pepper to taste
6 tablespoons butter
2 medium onions, sliced lengthwise

In a heavy saucepan combine the broth and lentils and bring to a boil over high heat. Lower the heat to moderate and cook, uncovered, 15 to 20 minutes or until the lentils are tender. Add the bulghur and salt and pepper. Bring to a boil, stirring. Reduce the heat to low, cover, and simmer 15 minutes or until the liquid is absorbed and the bulghur is tender. If the liquid is absorbed before the bulghur is done, add a little more hot broth.

Meanwhile, in a skillet melt the butter over moderate heat. Add the onions and sauté until golden brown, stirring frequently.

When the pilaf is done, add the onions with the butter and mix well. Cover and let stand in a warm place 5 to 10 minutes. Serve with Cucumber and Tomato Salad (page 50).

Serves 4

NOTE: You may substitute 1 cup long-grain white rice for the bulghur.

✤ CRACKED WHEAT PILAF WITH LIVER AND CHICK-PEAS

Gigerov Bulghur Pilav

  6 tablespoons butter
½ pound calf's or lamb's liver, coarsely chopped
Salt and freshly ground black pepper to taste
  1 medium onion, thinly sliced lengthwise
  2 medium ripe tomatoes, peeled, seeded, and finely chopped
½ cup thinly sliced green pepper or celery
1½ cups coarse bulghur
  2 tablespoons finely chopped fresh mint leaves or parsley
  1 cup drained canned chick-peas
2¼ cups chicken or beef broth (approximately)

In a skillet melt 2 tablespoons of the butter over moderate heat. Add the liver and sauté a few minutes until no longer pink, stirring frequently. Season with salt and pepper, remove from the heat, and set aside.

In a heavy saucepan or casserole melt the remaining 4 tablespoons butter. Add the onion and sauté until it begins to soften, stirring frequently. Add the tomatoes and green pepper and cook a few minutes. Add the bulghur and mint and cook a minute or so, stirring constantly. Add the chick-peas, broth, sautéed liver, and additional salt and pepper. Bring to a boil and reduce the heat to low. Cover and simmer 20 to 25 minutes or until the liquid in the pan is absorbed and the bulghur is tender. If the liquid is absorbed before the bulghur is done, add a little more hot broth. Serve as a luncheon or supper dish with a green salad.

Serves 4

NOTE: You may omit the chick-peas.

CRACKED WHEAT PILAF WITH MEAT SAUCE

1 recipe Plain Cracked Wheat Pilaf (page 231)
1 recipe Meat Sauce (page 293)

Spoon the hot pilaf onto heated individual serving plates and make an indentation in the center of each portion. Fill the indentation with the sauce. Serve with a green salad as a luncheon or supper dish.

Serves 4

11. Savory Pastries and Pastas

Left: Meat Tarts (page 238) and, right: Armenian Meat Pies (page 244)

This chapter includes appetizers, side dishes, and main dishes prepared with homemade, as well as commercially packaged, pastas. With the addition of a salad, they make quick, nutritious, and economical meals. It is not too well known that Armenians have delicious recipes using macaroni, such as Noodles with Rice and Macaroni with Lamb. For an Armenian version of spaghetti with meatballs see Meatballs Smyrna (page 163).

The various *boeregs* (filled pastries), *missahatz* (meat pies), and *manti* (meat-filled pastries baked in broth) are specialties of the Armenian kitchen, well worth the time they require to prepare.

Boeregs may be made with different doughs, such as paper-thin phyllo, flaky pastry, short dough, or yeast dough, and may be filled with meat, cheese, or vegetables. (For recipes using phyllo consult Chapter 1.) *Boeregs* may be baked, fried, or in the case of water *(sou)* *boereg*, dipped in water before baking. For a quickly prepared version of this last try Noodles and Cheese Bake. It is delicious hot or cold.

An excellent buffet or picnic dish, *missahatz*, better known by its Arabic name of *lahmajoon*, may be baked in advance, frozen, and reheated in a warm oven before serving. It is also good cold, accompanied by lemon wedges.

Manti, an ancient dish with variations throughout eastern Europe and Asia, makes a welcome meal on a cold winter day. For a soup version of *manti*, Dumpling Soup, see page 34.

MEAT TARTS

Missov Boereg

These superb little pastries are easily made with a simple dough. They make a splendid party dish and are certain to receive high praise.

1¼ cups sifted all-purpose flour
½ teaspoon salt
½ cup butter
3 tablespoons water (approximately)
Meat Filling (page 19)
1 egg, beaten

Sift the flour with the salt. Cut the butter in finely with a pastry blender or 2 knives. Add enough water to make a soft but not sticky dough. Roll out on a lightly floured board to 1/16-inch thickness or less. Cut into circles with a 3-inch cookie cutter. Place about 1½ teaspoons of the filling on the lower half of each circle. Dip a finger in cold water and moisten the edges. Fold over the other half to make a half moon and press the edges together. Brush with the egg. Place on a greased baking sheet and bake in a preheated 400° oven about 15 minutes or until golden brown and baked through. Serve warm, as an appetizer. *Boeregs* are also good served with light soups or salads.

Makes about 40

NOTE: You may substitute refrigerated buttermilk biscuit dough for the the dough in the recipe. Roll, fill, and bake in a preheated 350° oven until golden brown. For variety any of the fillings for *boeregs* (pages 18–20) may be used in this recipe.

238

CHEESE PASTRY

Banirov Boereg

1 egg
¼ cup milk
½ cup melted butter
¼ teaspon sugar
½ teaspoon salt
¼ cake compressed yeast
1½ teaspoons cold water
1½ cups plus 2 tablespoons all-purpose flour
2 recipes Cheese Filling (page 18)
Melted butter or beaten egg

In a large bowl beat the egg. Add the milk, ¼ cup of the butter, sugar, and salt and blend well. Dissolve the yeast in the water and add. Gradually add the flour. Place the dough on a lightly floured surface and knead until smooth. Divide into 15 portions and shape each into a small ball. Roll out each ball into a circle 6 inches in diameter. Brush with some of the remaining ¼ cup melted butter. Fold the lower third of each circle over the middle and brush with the butter. Bring the top third over this and brush it with the butter. Fold the left third over the center and brush with the butter. Finally, fold the right third over that, making a 2- to 2¼-inch square. Cover and place in the refrigerator. Repeat with the remaining dough and butter, refrigerating each *boereg* as it is filled.

After 1 hour remove each *boereg* one at a time as needed, and roll out into a 4½-inch square. Place a spoonful of the filling in the center. Dip a finger in cold water and moisten the edges. Fold the dough over into a triangle. Press the edges together to seal. Prick the top in three places with the point of a small sharp knife. Brush with the melted butter and place on a baking sheet. Leave in a warm place 3 to 3½ hours. Bake in a preheated 350° oven 20 minutes or until golden brown. Serve hot, as an appetizer.

Makes 15

NOODLES WITH RICE

The toasted almonds and sesame seeds are my personal suggestion and may be omitted, but they do provide an interesting flavor and unexpectedly crunchy texture.

½ cup uncooked long-grain white rice
2 cups ¼-inch-wide egg noodles
¼ cup melted butter
Salt to taste
2 tablespoons toasted sliced almonds (optional)
2 tablespoons toasted sesame seeds (optional)

Cook the rice in plenty of boiling salted water for 10 minutes. Add the noodles. Cook 8 minutes or until the rice and noodles are tender but still firm to the bite, not mushy, stirring frequently to prevent sticking. Drain quickly but thoroughly and return to the saucepan. Add the butter and salt, mix well, and turn into a heated ovenproof serving dish. Place in a preheated 350° oven 10 minutes or until heated through. Sprinkle the almonds and sesame seeds over the top just before serving.

Serves 4

To toast almonds and sesame seeds: Spread the nuts and seeds on separate baking sheets and place in a preheated 300° oven. Toast until golden brown, stirring occasionally and watching closely to prevent burning.

NOODLES AND CHEESE BAKE

8 ounces medium-wide egg noodles
4 tablespoons butter
2 eggs
½ pound Muenster cheese, freshly grated
6 ounces feta cheese, freshly grated
Salt to taste
¼ cup finely chopped parsley

Cook the noodles according to package directions. Drain well in a colander. Return to the hot pot in which they were cooked and toss gently but thoroughly with 2 tablespoons of the butter.

Place the eggs in a mixing bowl and beat slightly. Add the cheeses and salt, if needed, and blend well. Divide into 2 equal parts. Mix the parsley into one part.

Place half the noodles in a buttered 9-by-9-by-2-inch baking pan. Spread evenly with the cheese and parsley mixture. Cover with the remaining noodles and sprinkle the cheese mixture without parsley over the top. Dot with the remaining 2 tablespoons butter. Bake in a preheated 375° oven 45 minutes or until browned. Serve hot or chilled, cut into squares.

Serves 6

VARIATION

 Noodles and Spinach Bake

Sauté 1 medium onion, minced, in 3 tablespoons olive oil until soft but not browned. Add 1 pound spinach, washed, dried, stemmed, and chopped. Simmer about 10 minutes or until soft, stirring frequently. Mix in 2 tablespoons bread crumbs and remove from the heat. Beat the eggs as above. Omit the Muenster cheese. Add ½ pound feta, freshly grated, ¾ cup cottage cheese, 2 tablespoons freshly grated Parmesan or Romano cheese, and the spinach mixture and blend well. Add salt if needed, but omit the parsley. Cook the noodles, drain, and toss with 2 tablespoons of the butter. Divide the noodles in half. Layer them in the pan with the spinach and cheese mixture in between. Dot with the remaining 2 tablespoons butter. Cover and bake 30 minutes. Uncover and bake 15 minutes or until golden brown. Serve as above.

WATER PASTRY

Sou Boereg

3 eggs
1¾ cups sifted all-purpose flour (approximately)
3½ teaspoons salt
3 quarts water
5 tablespoons melted butter
1 pound brick cheese, shredded
½ cup finely chopped parsley
Salt to taste

In a large bowl beat the eggs. Gradually add the flour and ½ teaspoon of the salt and knead thoroughly until a firm dough is formed. Divide the dough into 8 equal parts. Shape each into a ball and place in a large pan, not touching one another. Cover with a damp cloth and let stand 1 hour.

On a lightly floured board roll out each ball of dough as thin as possible into a 9-by-9-inch square. Pile the rolled sheets one on top of each other, sprinkling each sheet lightly with flour and placing waxed paper between the layers. Cover with a cloth to prevent drying and set aside.

In a large pot bring the water and remaining 3 teaspoons salt to a boil. Have ready a large pot of cold water. Drop each sheet of pastry into the boiling water about 2 minutes. Remove, dip into the cold water, and lay out on a dry cloth.

Brush a 9-by-9-by-2-inch baking pan with some of the melted butter. Lay 4 of the sheets on top of each other in the pan, brushing each with

242

the butter. Mix the cheese, parsley, and salt together and spread evenly over the entire surface. Cover with the remaining pastry sheets, brushing each with the butter. Bake in a preheated 400° oven 35 minutes or until the surface is golden brown.

Cut into squares and serve warm, with Garlic Yogurt Sauce (page 288), if desired, as a side dish with roast chicken, ham, lamb, or veal. The *boereg* is good also as a luncheon dish, accompanied by a salad or one of the green vegetables cooked with olive oil (Chapter 12).

Serves 6

MACARONI WITH LAMB

Missov Titmaj

2 tablespoons butter
1 large onion, finely chopped
1 pound boneless lean lamb, trimmed of excess fat and cut into ½-inch cubes or ground
1 28-ounce can tomatoes, chopped
1 teaspoon dried basil or oregano or ½ teaspoon allspice
Salt and freshly ground black pepper to taste
12 ounces elbow macaroni or spaghetti

In a heavy skillet melt the butter over moderate heat. Add the onion and sauté until soft but not browned, stirring frequently. Add the lamb and cook until browned. Add the tomatoes, basil, and salt and pepper. Cover and simmer 35 minutes.

Meanwhile, cook the macaroni according to package directions until almost tender. Drain immediately and add to the meat sauce. Mix well, cook a few minutes, and serve hot or cold with a green salad, crusty bread, and plain yogurt or Garlic Yogurt Sauce (page 288) on the side if desired.

Serves 6 to 8

ARMENIAN MEAT PIES

Missahatz or Lahmajoon

This extremely popular and versatile pastry is to Armenians what pizza is to Italians.

DOUGH

> ¾ cup lukewarm water
> 1 cake compressed yeast
> 2¼ cups sifted all-purpose flour (approximately)
> ½ teaspoon salt
> ½ teaspoon sugar
> ¼ cup melted butter or margarine

MEAT TOPPING

> 1 pound lean ground lamb
> 2 medium onions, finely chopped
> ¼ cup finely chopped green pepper
> 1 medium ripe tomato, peeled, seeded, and finely chopped
> ¼ cup finely chopped parsley
> 1 teaspoon finely chopped fresh mint leaves
> 1 small clove garlic, finely chopped
> 2 tablespoons tomato paste
> 3 tablespoons freshly squeezed and strained lemon juice
> ⅛ teaspoon cayenne
> Salt and freshly ground black pepper to taste
> Paprika (optional)

To make the dough, pour ½ cup of the water into a small bowl and add the yeast. Let stand 3 minutes, then stir to dissolve yeast completely.

In a deep bowl combine the flour, salt, and sugar. Make a well in the

244

center and pour in the yeast mixture, melted butter, and remaining ¼ cup water. Using a large spoon, gradually blend the liquids into the flour mixture, working from the center out. Beat until the ingredients are well blended and form a soft dough.

Place the dough on a lightly floured surface and knead thoroughly, sprinkling occasionally with just enough flour to keep it from sticking. When it is smooth and elastic in texture, form into a lump and place in a lightly oiled bowl. Cover loosely with a kitchen towel and leave to rise in a warm place 2 to 3 hours or until doubled in size.

Meanwhile, combine all the topping ingredients except the paprika in a deep bowl and knead well until thoroughly blended. Taste for seasoning and set aside.

Punch down the dough and divide into 14 equal pieces. Form each into a ball and place on a lightly floured surface. Cover with a cloth and let rest 15 minutes.

On a lightly floured surface roll out each of the balls into a circle approximately 5 inches in diameter. Place ⅓ to ½ cup topping in the center of each circle, then spread it evenly to within about ¼ inch of the edge.

Arrange the pies on lightly oiled baking sheets. Bake in a preheated 450° oven about 12 minutes or until lightly browned. You may place the pies briefly under the broiler to brown the tops. Sprinkle with paprika and immediately wrap in aluminum foil, with meat sides against one another. Set aside 10 minutes. Serve hot or cold, with lemon wedges or with yogurt if desired, and with a green salad.

Makes 14

NOTE: Refrigerated buttermilk biscuit dough may be substituted for the homemade dough. Divide, roll, and spread with the topping as above. Bake in a preheated 400° oven about 10 minutes or until lightly browned.

ARMENIAN CHEESE PIES

Follow the recipe for Armenian Meat Pies (page 244), substituting this cheese topping for the meat topping.

        6 tablespoons olive oil
        2 medium onions, finely chopped
        2 cups tomato puree
        ½ cup tomato paste
        1½ tablespoons dried thyme
        2¾ teaspoons dried oregano
        ¾ teaspoon garlic powder
    Salt and cayenne to taste
        18 ounces Monterey Jack cheese, grated
    Olive oil

In a heavy saucepan heat the oil over moderate heat. Add the onions and sauté until lightly browned, stirring frequently. Add the tomato puree, tomato paste, thyme, oregano, garlic powder, and salt and cayenne. Cook over low heat 45 minutes. Remove from the heat and cool. Add the cheese and mix well. Spread about ⅓ cup of the topping on each circle of dough, drizzle ½ to 1 teaspoon of the olive oil over each, and bake as directed.

Makes enough topping for 14 pies

MEAT PASTRIES BAKED IN BROTH

Manti

DOUGH

3¼ cups all-purpose flour (approximately)
1 egg
2 tablespoons melted butter
1 cup water
Pinch salt

FILLING

1 pound lean ground lamb
2 medium onions, grated
⅓ cup finely chopped parsley
Salt and freshly ground black pepper to taste
¼ cup melted butter
6 cups chicken or beef broth, salted to taste

Combine all the dough ingredients in a large mixing bowl. Knead, sprinkling with flour when needed to prevent sticking, until smooth and elastic. Divide the dough into 2 equal parts, shaping each into a ball. Cover with a kitchen towel and let rest at room temperature 30 minutes.

Combine all the filling ingredients in a bowl. Mix together and knead with your hands until well blended and smooth. Taste for seasoning and set aside.

On a lightly floured surface roll out balls of dough one at a time to about 1/16-inch thickness. Cut into 2-inch squares. Place about 1 teaspoon of the filling on each square and form it into a canoe by moistening two opposite edges with water and pressing them together to seal.

Brush a large baking pan with the melted butter and arrange the filled canoes in the pan. Heat the broth and pour 2 cups evenly over the canoes. Bake in a preheated 350° oven 15 minutes. Pour an additional 2 cups of the broth over the canoes and bake 15 minutes. Pour in the remaining 2 cups and bake 15 minutes. Serve with Garlic Yogurt Sauce (page 288).

Serves 6

NOTE: You may flavor the broth with 2 tablespoons tomato paste. You may also bake the filled canoes 20 minutes or until slightly browned, pour the broth over them and bake 20 minutes longer, then serve with the broth and yogurt sauce.

12. Vegetables

Artichokes with Olive Oil (page 254)

Confirmed vegetable-haters usually change their minds after trying vegetables prepared in the Armenian style—and for good reason, since Armenian cuisine makes imaginative use of a wide variety of vegetables.

Seasoning plays an important role in cooking vegetables. Garlic, parsley, mint, dill, onions, and tomatoes (or tomato paste when fresh tomatoes are not in season) are essential in the preparation of many dishes.

Vegetables are prepared differently, depending upon their position on the menu. Cooked with olive oil (because it does not congeal) and served cold, they become wonderful appetizers, side dishes, or luncheon courses. Artichokes with Olive Oil, Armenian Green Beans, Stuffed Eggplant with Olive Oil and Garlic (*imam bayildi*), and the various rice *dolmas* in Chapter 9 belong to this category, which comprises a large number of dishes that should prove particularly attractive for entertaining, since they may be prepared in advance.

Vegetables cooked with butter make good hot side dishes. Green Beans with Tomatoes, Baked Pumpkin with Rice, and Vegetable Casserole are a few examples.

Stewed, grilled, baked, or stuffed with meat, vegetables constitute the main course. This group includes the numerous meat and vegetable stews, kebabs, and casseroles in Chapter 7 and the meat *dolmas* in Chapter 9.

Eggplant, a favorite vegetable, is prepared in all these different ways. Two kinds of eggplant are used: the larger, more common variety and the smaller type, sometimes known as Japanese eggplant, which is long and narrow and is used mainly for *dolmas*. If your supermarket does not carry the latter, it is available in Oriental and Middle Eastern grocery stores and sometimes in Italian ones.

252

Before frying eggplant, salt the slices generously and place a heavy weight on them for about 30 minutes. Then rinse and dry them with paper towels. Or you may soak the slices in salted water for 30 minutes and then rinse and dry them. This draws out the bitter juices and prevents the eggplant from absorbing too much oil in cooking.

It will be noticed that vegetables are almost never eaten boiled. Armenians prefer either to cook them in a sauce or to fry and serve them with a sauce. Among the fried vegetables, eggplant and zucchini are very popular side dishes, served with yogurt, lemon, *tarator*, or tomato sauce, depending on the rest of the meal.

Armenian cuisine also makes excellent use of some of the dried legumes, which are high in food value, including lentils, chick-peas, and beans. They are added to stews and pilafs or cooked in olive oil and served cold as *plaki*.

ARTICHOKES WITH OLIVE OIL

Tzitayoughov Gangar

A particularly excellent way of preparing artichokes.

 6 medium artichokes
Juice of 1 lemon
 2 cups hot water
 ½ cup olive oil
 12 small white boiling onions
Salt and white pepper to taste
 1 teaspoon sugar
 1½ tablespoons freshly squeezed and strained lemon juice
 3 tablespoons finely chopped fresh dill

Prepare each artichoke as follows: Peel the tough outer skin from the stem and trim off ⅛ inch of the stem end. Remove any coarse or discolored outer leaves and cut 1 inch off the top of the remaining leaves. Cut the artichoke in half lengthwise. Remove the fuzzy choke and thorny pinkish leaves from the center. Drop the artichoke into a large bowl of salted cold water mixed with the lemon juice (this prevents discoloration).

Place the hot water, olive oil, and onions in a heavy saucepan or casserole and cook over moderate heat about 10 minutes. Remove the artichokes from the salted water and arrange cut sides down in the saucepan. Sprinkle with the salt and pepper, sugar, lemon juice, and dill and baste thoroughly with the liquid in the pan. Lower the heat, cover, and simmer 20 minutes. Turn the artichokes cut sides up and place an onion in the center of each. Cover and simmer 30 minutes or until tender, basting occasionally. Remove from the heat and allow to cool in the saucepan. Serve chilled, as an appetizer or side dish.

Serves 6

JERUSALEM ARTICHOKES

Kednadantzi Adol

The following way of cooking this bland vegetable greatly enhances its flavor.

 1 pound Jerusalem artichokes
10 small white boiling onions
¼ cup olive oil
½ teaspoon sugar
Salt and freshly ground black pepper to taste
1½ cups water
Bibb lettuce leaves
 1 lemon, quartered

Pare the artichokes and cut in half (in thirds if large). Combine with the onions, olive oil, sugar, salt and pepper, and water in a heavy saucepan. Cover and cook over moderate heat until tender, about 30 minutes. Do not overcook. Remove from the heat and allow to cool in the saucepan. Serve cold over the lettuce leaves, as an appetizer or side dish, accompanied by the lemon wedges.

Serves 4

ARMENIAN GREEN BEANS

Tzitayoughov Ganach Lupia

This is one of the most popular and appetizing of Armenian vegetable dishes.

>   1 pound green beans, trimmed and halved lengthwise, or 2 ten-
>   ounce packages frozen French-cut green beans, thawed
>   1 medium onion, finely chopped
>   1 cup water
>   1 medium tomato, peeled, seeded, and finely chopped
>   ¼ cup olive oil
>   2 large cloves garlic, crushed (optional)
>   Salt and freshly ground black pepper to taste

Combine the beans, onion, and water in a heavy saucepan. Cover and cook over moderate heat 20 minutes. Add the tomato, olive oil, garlic, and salt and pepper. Cover and cook 20 minutes or until tender, adding more water if necessary. Remove from the heat and allow to cool. Serve cold, as an appetizer or side dish.

Serves 4

NOTE: You may add 1 tablespoon each finely chopped fresh mint leaves, parsley, and dill with the tomato if desired.

GREEN BEANS IN WALNUT SAUCE

This unusual way of preparing green beans is a specialty of Caucasian Armenians.

    1 cup walnut halves
    2 medium cloves garlic, finely chopped
    ⅓ cup finely chopped onion
    3 tablespoons finely chopped fresh coriander or 1 teaspoon ground coriander
1½ teaspoons paprika
Salt and cayenne to taste
    ¼ cup red wine vinegar
Chicken broth
    1 pound green beans, trimmed
    2 tablespoons finely chopped parsley (optional)

Pound the walnuts and garlic to a paste. Add the onion, coriander, paprika, salt and cayenne, and vinegar. Blend thoroughly, adding enough chicken broth to moisten to a paste consistency.

Drop the beans into boiling salted water. Boil, uncovered, about 10 minutes or until tender but still firm to the bite. Drain in a colander, then add to the walnut sauce. Being careful not to bruise the beans, toss thoroughly. Taste for seasoning. Serve chilled, sprinkled with the parsley.

Serves 6

FAVA BEANS

Tzitayoughov Paglah

1 pound fresh fava beans, shelled
1 bunch scallions, cut into 1½-inch pieces
⅓ cup chopped fresh dill
¾ teaspoon sugar
Salt to taste
¼ cup olive oil
1½ tablespoons freshly squeezed and strained lemon juice
1¼ cups water (approximately)

Combine all ingredients in a heavy saucepan. Place an inverted plate over the beans to keep them in place while cooking. Bring to a boil and reduce the heat to low. Cover and simmer 1 hour or until the beans are tender, adding more water if necessary. Remove from the heat and allow to cool in the saucepan. Serve chilled, as an appetizer or side dish.

Serves 4

VARIATION

Fava Beans with Tomatoes

In a heavy saucepan heat the olive oil over moderate heat. Add 1 large onion, finely chopped, and sauté until lightly browned, stirring frequently. Add 2 medium ripe tomatoes, finely chopped, and sauté a few minutes. Add the fava beans, 2 tablespoons finely chopped fresh dill or parsley, salt, pepper, and 1 cup water. Bring to a boil and continue as above.

WHITE BEAN PLAKI

Lupia Plaki

1 cup dried large white beans (Great Northern) (soak, if
  necessary)
6 cups boiling water (approximately)
Salt to taste
2 medium carrots, diced
½ cup diced green pepper
1 medium stalk celery, diced
2 medium cloves garlic, finely chopped
3 tablespoons finely chopped parsley
2 medium tomatoes, peeled, seeded, and finely chopped
Freshly ground black pepper or cayenne to taste
¼ cup olive oil
Bibb lettuce leaves
1 lemon, sliced

In a heavy saucepan combine the beans and 3 cups of the boiling
water. Cook over moderate heat 15 minutes. Drain and rinse under
running cold water. Wash the pot, return the beans to it, and add the
remaining 3 cups boiling water. Cook 1 hour. Add the salt, carrots,
green pepper, celery, garlic, parsley, tomatoes, and pepper. Cover and
cook 30 minutes. Add the olive oil and cook 20 minutes or until
vegetables are tender, adding more water if necessary. Serve cold on the
lettuce leaves, accompanied by the lemon slices, as an appetizer or side
dish.

Serves 4

NOTE: You may omit the green pepper and add 1 medium potato, peeled
and diced, and 1 medium onion, diced, along with the carrots.

Braised White Beans

Lupia Yahni

Bring the beans to a boil in 2½ cups water. Lower the heat and cook 1 hour and 15 minutes, adding more water if necessary. Sauté 2 medium onions, finely sliced, in the olive oil until golden brown. Stir into the beans with 1 tomato, peeled, seeded, and chopped, ½ teaspoon each sugar and paprika, and salt and black pepper to taste. Cook until tender, adding an additional 2 tablespoons oil 15 minutes before the end of cooking. Serve cold, with lemon wedges.

FRIED EGGPLANT

Simpoog Dabgodz

The recipe given below is one of the most basic ways of serving eggplant. The little-known variation with pomegranate sauce provides a brilliant and unexpected touch of fantasy and piquancy, and the oregano, which I must admit is my own addition, imparts a pleasantly pungent taste and aroma.

> 1 large eggplant
> Salt
> ½ cup olive oil (approximately)

Remove the stem and hull from the eggplant. Peel lengthwise in ½-inch strips, leaving ½-inch strips of skin between, making a striped design. Cut crosswise into ⅜-inch-thick slices and lay on paper towels. Sprinkle generously with the salt, weigh down with a heavy object, and let stand 30 minutes. Rinse and dry thoroughly with fresh paper towels.

In a large, heavy skillet heat the oil over high heat. Reduce the heat to moderate, add the eggplant slices, and fry until lightly and evenly browned on both sides. Drain on paper towels and arrange on a serving platter. Serve chilled, as an appetizer or side dish, with Garlic Yogurt Sauce (page 288), Lemon Sauce (page 288), or Garlic and Nut Sauce (page 290).

Serves 4

NOTE: The eggplant slices may be fried in olive oil as above or in Clarified Butter (page 355) and served hot as a side dish with fish, poultry, or meat.

VARIATION

Fried Eggplant with Pomegranate Sauce

Prepare, fry, and drain eggplant slices as above. Arrange on a serving dish. Sprinkle with ½ cup finely chopped green pepper. Dilute 2 tablespoons Pomegranate Sauce (page 291) with 1 or 2 tablespoons cold water, stirring with a small spoon to mix well. Crush 1 large clove garlic with a sprinkling of salt and add with ½ teaspoon dried oregano or to taste to the pomegranate mixture. Beat together until thoroughly blended. Spoon the mixture evenly over the eggplant slices. Serve chilled, as an appetizer or an accompaniment to meat, poultry, or fish.

STUFFED EGGPLANT WITH OLIVE OIL AND GARLIC

Sikhdoratz or Simpoog Imam Bayildi

Imam bayildi, the Turkish name of this classic dish, translates as "the priest fainted." This name's origin is explained by a tale that has several versions. Armenians say that one day an Armenian housewife was surprised by an unannounced visit from a priest, and not having been able to prepare anything in advance, created this dish impromptu. At the first mouthful the priest fainted from delight.

In other versions the imam, who was a gourmet, was so enamored of this dish when his wife prepared it that he fainted for one of the following reasons: upon sniffing it, as it has a strong garlic aroma; from ecstasy at its magnificent flavor; from gorging himself on it, because it was so rich; in desolation at being denied it.

Still another story exists, which draws attention to the large amount of olive oil used in this recipe. The imam, who was tight with his money, was so impressed by the excellence of an eggplant dish prepared by his fiancée that he specified that her dowry, which was considerable, consist of enough oil in which to cook it, he thought, for many years to come. Huge jars of oil were stored in the couple's new home. For the first two nights the imam was in a gastronome's heaven, but on the third night the dish failed to materialize. When queried anxiously by the imam, his wife burst into tears, saying, "Alas, we have no more oil," whereupon the imam fainted.

The following recipe uses a more modest amount of oil than is usually specified. If desired, you may increase the amount (short of to the fainting point).

1 eggplant (about 1¼ pounds)
Salt
½ cup olive oil
2 medium onions, halved lengthwise and sliced
3 medium ripe tomatoes, peeled, seeded, and finely chopped
4 medium cloves garlic, finely chopped
¼ cup finely chopped parsley
1 tablespoon finely chopped fresh mint leaves (optional)
Salt and freshly ground black pepper to taste
⅓ cup water (approximately)

Remove the stem and hull from the eggplant. Peel lengthwise in 1-inch strips, leaving 1-inch strips of skin in between, making a striped design. Make lengthwise slashes through the peeled parts, sprinkle with the salt, and let stand 30 minutes. Rinse under running cold water and pat dry with paper towels.

In a heavy casserole heat ¼ cup of the olive oil. Add the eggplant and fry until lightly and evenly browned on all sides.

Combine the remaining ¼ cup olive oil with the onions, tomatoes, garlic, parsley, mint, and salt and pepper. Mix well. Stuff the eggplant pockets with this mixture. Replace the eggplant in the casserole, add the water, and spread any leftover stuffing mixture over the top. Bring to a boil and cover. Reduce the heat to low and simmer 50 minutes or until tender, adding more water if necessary. Remove from the heat and allow to cool. Place on a platter and serve cold, as an appetizer.

Serves 4

NOTE: 8 small (6 by 2 inches each) cylindrical eggplants may be substituted for the 1 large eggplant. Slit each lengthwise on one side down the middle, without quite cutting through, leaving 1 inch at each end uncut.

Variation: Here is the Caucasian Armenian version of this dish. Stem and slit small cylindrical eggplants lengthwise on one side. Scoop out the insides and chop. Add minced garlic; chopped celery; minced fresh coriander, dill, and parsley; salt; and pepper. Mix well and fry in olive oil. Stuff the eggplants with this mixture. Melt butter in a skillet and arrange the eggplants, cut sides up, in a single layer. Cover with peeled, seeded, and chopped tomatoes and finely chopped fresh dill and coriander. Sprinkle with salt and pepper and pour in a little water. Cover and cook over low heat until the eggplants are tender. Serve hot or cold.

BRAISED LEEKS

Bras Yahni

1½ pounds leeks
½ cup olive oil
1 large onion, halved lengthwise and thinly sliced
1 large tomato, peeled, seeded, and chopped
Salt and freshly ground black pepper to taste
1 cup beef broth
¼ cup finely chopped fresh dill (optional)
1 lemon, cut into wedges

Cut off the roots from the leeks and remove any tough or discolored outer leaves. Cut into 2-inch-long pieces and wash thoroughly under running cold water. Drain and dry with paper towels.

In a heavy saucepan heat the olive oil over moderate heat. Add the onion and sauté until soft but not browned, stirring frequently. Add the leeks and sauté a few minutes. Add the tomato, salt and pepper, and broth. Cover and cook over low heat about 35 minutes or until tender. Serve cold, sprinkled with the dill and accompanied by the lemon wedges. The leeks may also be served hot.

Serves 6

BRAISED MUSHROOMS

Soung Yahni

This is a particularly delicious and unusual way of preparing mushrooms.

    ½ cup olive oil
    2 large onions, halved lengthwise and sliced
    2 medium cloves garlic, finely chopped
    1 pound mushrooms, halved lengthwise if small or quartered if large
    1 cup chopped parsley
Salt and freshly ground black pepper to taste
    1 cup water
    2 tablespoons finely chopped fresh dill or mint leaves
Lemon slices

In a heavy saucepan heat the olive oil over moderate heat. Add the onions and garlic and sauté until soft, stirring frequently. Add the mushrooms and sauté, turning to brown evenly on all sides. Add the parsley, salt and pepper, and water. Cover and cook about 35 minutes or until the mushrooms are tender.

To serve hot: Transfer to a heated serving platter, sprinkle with

264

the dill, and serve, accompanied by the lemon slices, as a side dish with poultry, game, or veal.

To serve cold: Remove from the heat and allow to cool. Transfer to a serving platter lined with lettuce leaves, cover with clear plastic film, and chill. Just before serving, sprinkle with the dill, and garnish with the lemon slices. Serve as an appetizer or as a side dish with cold meats.

Serves 4

ARMENIAN PEAS AND CARROTS

Here is a novel and appetizing way of preparing a familiar combination.

    6 tablespoons olive oil
    1 medium onion, finely chopped
    3 medium carrots, sliced crosswise ¼ inch thick
    1 small tomato, peeled, seeded, and chopped
    ½ teaspoon sugar
    Salt to taste
    1 cup water (approximately)
    1 18-ounce can peas, drained
    1 tablespoon finely chopped fresh dill or basil or to taste
    1 lemon, cut into wedges

In a heavy saucepan heat 4 tablespoons of the olive oil over moderate heat. Add the onion and sauté until golden brown, stirring frequently. Add the carrots and tomato and cook 3 to 4 minutes. Add the sugar, salt, and water. Cover and cook over moderate heat 30 minutes or until the carrots are almost tender, adding more water if necessary. Stir in the peas and the remaining 2 tablespoons olive oil. Cover and simmer 15 minutes. Remove from the heat and cool to room temperature. Transfer to a serving dish, cover with clear plastic film, and chill. Sprinkle with the dill and garnish with the lemon wedges. Serve as an appetizer or a side dish with meat and poultry.

Serves 4

POTATO PLAKI

Kednakhintzor Plaki

This is one way of transforming simple ingredients into an exciting taste experience.

6 medium potatoes, peeled and sliced
2 medium carrots, diced
1 medium stalk celery, diced
1 large tomato, peeled, seeded, and diced
4 medium cloves garlic, finely chopped
3 tablespoons finely chopped parsley
1 tablespoon finely chopped fresh dill (optional)
Salt and freshly ground black pepper to taste
2 cups water (approximately)
¼ cup olive oil
Bibb or romaine lettuce leaves
1 lemon, sliced

In a heavy saucepan or casserole combine the potatoes, carrots, celery, tomato, garlic, parsley, and dill. Add the salt and pepper and water. Cover and cook over low heat 40 minutes or until the vegetables are almost tender, adding more water if necessary. Pour in the olive oil and cook 20 minutes or until the vegetables are done. Serve cold on the lettuce leaves, as an appetizer or side dish, accompanied by the lemon slices.

Serves 6

NOTE: Cleaned and shelled mussels, clams, oysters, or shrimp may be added toward the end of cooking.

266

TURNIPS WITH OLIVE OIL

Tzitayoughov Shoghkam

If, like many people, you are convinced that you do not like turnips, you are in for a discovery and a pleasant surprise.

    1 pound small turnips
    10 small white boiling onions
    ¼ cup olive oil
    Salt and freshly ground black pepper to taste
    1 teaspoon sugar
    1½ cups water
      3 tablespoons each finely chopped parsley and fresh dill or 4
        tablespoons finely chopped fresh mint leaves
    Lemon slices (optional)

Pare and quarter the turnips. Combine with the onions, olive oil, salt and pepper, sugar, and water in a heavy saucepan. Cover and cook over moderate heat about 45 minutes or until tender.

To serve hot: Transfer to a heated serving platter, sprinkle with the parsley and dill, and serve, accompanied by the lemon slices, as a side dish with lamb, poultry, or game.

To serve cold: Remove from the heat and allow to cool. Transfer to a serving platter lined with lettuce leaves, cover with clear plastic film, and chill. Just before serving, sprinkle with the parsley and dill. Garnish with the lemon slices. Serve as an appetizer.

Serves 4

FRIED ZUCCHINI

Titoum Dabgodz

4 medium zucchini, scraped and sliced crosswise ⅜ inch thick
½ cup sifted all-purpose flour, seasoned with salt and freshly
    ground black pepper to taste
½ cup olive oil

Coat the zucchini with the seasoned flour. In a skillet heat the olive oil
and fry the zucchini slices, a few at a time, until golden brown on both
sides. Drain on paper towels and arrange on a serving platter. Serve cold,
as an appetizer or side dish, with Garlic Yogurt Sauce (page 288), or
with Lemon Sauce (page 288) flavored with chopped fresh dill if desired.

Serves 6

NOTE: The zucchini slices may be fried in olive oil as above or in
Clarified Butter (page 355) and served hot as a side dish with fish,
poultry, or meat. If desired, you may serve them with tomato sauce.

STUFFED ZUCCHINI WITH OLIVE OIL AND GARLIC

Sikhdoratz or Titoum Imam Bayildi

This delightful preparation is the zucchini counterpart to the renowned eggplant dish on page 261.

4 medium zucchini, scraped
1 bunch scallions, chopped

3 medium cloves garlic, finely chopped
½ cup finely chopped parsley
2 tablespoons finely chopped fresh mint leaves
2 tablespoons finely chopped fresh dill
Salt to taste
1 medium tomato, peeled, seeded, and chopped
¼ cup olive oil
1½ tablespoons freshly squeezed and strained lemon juice
⅓ cup water (approximately)
Romaine or Bibb lettuce leaves
1 lemon, cut into wedges

Slit the zucchini lengthwise on one side, down the middle without quite cutting through, leaving 1 inch at each end uncut. Combine the scallions, garlic, parsley, mint, dill, and salt and mix well. Stuff the zucchini pockets with the mixture. Arrange the zucchini side by side, cut sides up, in a heavy saucepan or casserole. Spread any leftover stuffing mixture over the top. Add the tomato, olive oil, lemon juice, and water. Bring to a boil and cover. Reduce the heat to low and simmer 50 minutes or until tender, adding more water if necessary. Remove from the heat and let cool. Serve chilled on the lettuce leaves as an appetizer, garnished with the lemon wedges.

Serves 4

ASPARAGUS FRITTERS

Dznepeg Khmorapatik

Armenians, particularly those living in the Caucasus, prize asparagus and prepare it in many interesting ways.

1 cup asparagus tips
1 cup flour
1 teaspoon baking powder

½ teaspoon salt
 1 egg
½ cup milk (approximately)
 1 teaspoon vegetable oil or melted butter
Vegetable oil for deep frying
Salt to taste
 1 lemon, cut into wedges (optional)

Peel the asparagus tips and parboil in boiling salted water. Drain and cut crosswise into 1½-inch pieces.

Sift together the flour, baking powder, and salt. Beat the egg, then add the milk and oil. Add to the flour mixture and beat until smooth. Dip the asparagus pieces one at a time in the batter to coat thoroughly. Drop into the hot vegetable oil (365 to 370°). Fry until golden brown and drain on absorbent paper. Sprinkle with the salt and serve as an hors d'oeuvre or vegetable with the lemon wedges.

Serves 4

NOTE: Other parboiled vegetables such as mushrooms, carrots, zucchini or eggplant slices, broccoli or cauliflower flowerets, and young tender okra may be prepared in the same way.

GREEN BEANS WITH TOMATOES

Loligov Ganach Lupia

2 tablespoons butter
1 medium onion, finely chopped
2 medium ripe tomatoes, peeled, seeded, and chopped
1 pound green beans, trimmed and halved lengthwise, or 2 ten-
  ounce packages frozen French-cut green beans, thawed
Salt and freshly ground black pepper to taste
1 cup water

In a heavy casserole melt the butter over moderate heat. Add the onion and sauté until lightly browned, stirring frequently. Add the tomatoes and sauté a few minutes. Add the beans, salt and pepper, and water. Lower the heat, cover, and simmer 40 minutes or until tender. Serve as a side dish with fowl or meat.

Serves 4

CABBAGE WITH TOMATOES

Loligov Gaghamp

Follow the recipe (above) for Green Beans with Tomatoes, substituting for the beans a 1½- to 2-pound head of white cabbage, washed and halved. Place cut sides down on a board and slice very thinly. Sauté 2 medium onions, minced, in ¼ cup butter. Add 4 medium tomatoes, peeled, seeded, and chopped, and sauté as above. Stir in the cabbage, salt, pepper, and 2 tablespoons water. Cover and simmer 30 minutes or until tender. Stir in ¼ cup finely chopped fresh dill.

Serves 4

OKRA WITH TOMATOES

Loligov Bami

Follow the recipe (page 270) for Green Beans with Tomatoes, substituting for the beans 1 pound okra, washed and trimmed of stem ends, or 2 ten-ounce packages frozen okra, defrosted. Use 1½ cups broth or water and simmer 30 minutues or until the okra is tender, adding 1½ tablespoons freshly squeezed and strained lemon juice during the last 5 minutes of cooking. Serve as a side dish with meat.

Serves 6

ZUCCHINI WITH TOMATOES

Loligov Titoum

Follow the recipe (page 270) for Green Beans with Tomatoes, substituting for the beans 2 medium zucchini, sliced crosswise ½ inch thick. Use ½ cut hot water or broth and simmer 30 minutes or until the zucchini is tender. Serve as a side dish with broiled or roasted meats or poultry.

Serves 3

EGGPLANT WITH TOMATOES

Loligov Simpoog

  1 medium eggplant
Salt
⅓ cup olive oil or Clarified Butter (page 355)
  2 tablespoons butter
  1 medium onion, finely chopped
  2 medium tomatoes, peeled, seeded, and finely chopped
Freshly ground black pepper to taste
½ cup water

Remove the stem and hull from the eggplant. Peel and cut in 2-inch cubes. Lay side by side on paper towels. Sprinkle generously with the salt and let stand 30 minutes. Rinse and dry thoroughly with fresh paper towels.

In a large, heavy skillet heat the olive oil over moderate heat. Add the eggplant and fry until golden brown on all sides. Remove from the heat and set aside.

In a heavy saucepan heat the butter over moderate heat. Add the onion and sauté until golden brown, stirring frequently. Add the tomatoes and cook 5 minutes. Add the eggplant, additional salt, pepper, and water. Cover and cook over low heat 25 minutes or until the eggplant is tender and the sauce is slightly thickened. Serve as a side dish with broiled or roasted meats or poultry.

Serves 4

Variation: Peel and slice the eggplant. Salt and fry as above. Place in a buttered shallow baking pan. Cover with fried minced onion and top with lightly sautéed tomato halves. Bake in a 350° oven 10 minutes. Serve with Garlic Yogurt Sauce (page 288), on the side.

EGGPLANT PUREE

Hunkar Beyendi

This delicate puree traditionally accompanies Potted Lamb (page 141). It also makes an excellent side dish with roast or braised chicken or lamb.

    3 medium eggplants (about 1 pound each)
    1 tablespoon freshly squeezed and strained lemon juice
    3 tablespoons butter
    3 tablespoons flour
    ½ cup hot milk
    ¼ cup freshly grated Parmesan or Romano cheese
    Salt and freshly ground black pepper to taste

Cut the stems and hulls from the eggplants and discard. Broil each eggplant as follows: Using a long-handled fork, prick the skin of the eggplant in several places. Insert the fork in it. Broil over charcoal or a gas flame, turning the eggplant frequently, until the flesh is very soft and the skin is charred. The eggplants may also be broiled in an electric oven. Place them in a baking pan and broil 4 inches from the heat 20 to 30 minutes, turning to char evenly on all sides.

(continued)

When the eggplants are cool enough to handle, peel off the skins, remove any badly charred spots, and slit them open. Scoop out the seeds and discard. Place the eggplant pulp in a heavy saucepan and beat in the lemon juice. Simmer over low heat about 10 minutes, stirring frequently.

Meanwhile, in a small saucepan heat the butter over moderate heat. Add the flour and cook until it turns golden brown, stirring constantly. Stir this into the eggplant. Gradually beat in the milk until the mixture is smooth and creamy. Add the cheese and salt and pepper. Cook a few minutes more until the mixture turns into a thick puree, stirring constantly.

Serves 6

BAKED EGGPLANT WITH CHEESE

Yepvadz Banirov Simpoog

Decorative and delicious, this is an elegant yet simple way of preparing eggplant.

1 eggplant (about 1¼ pounds)
1¼ cups freshly grated Gruyère or Parmesan cheese
1 large egg, beaten
2 tablespoons finely chopped parsley
Dried oregano or basil to taste (optional)
Salt and freshly ground black pepper to taste
2 large tomatoes, sliced and seeded
3 tablespoons butter

Remove the stem and hull from the eggplant. Peel lengthwise in ½-inch strips, leaving ½-inch strips of skin in between, making a striped design. Cut crosswise into ¼-inch-thick slices and arrange in one layer in a buttered shallow baking pan.

Mix together the cheese, egg, parsley, oregano, and salt and pepper.

Cover the eggplant slices evenly with the mixture. Place the tomato slices over each eggplant slice and dot the entire surface with the butter. Bake in a preheated 325° oven 30 to 40 minutes or until the eggplant is tender. Serve as a side dish with meat or poultry or as a first course.

Serves 4

Variation: Mix together 2 hard-cooked eggs, finely chopped, ¼ pound Swiss cheese, grated, and ¼ cup melted butter. Cover the eggplant slices evenly with the mixture. Arrange in a buttered shallow baking pan and sprinkle the eggplant slices with melted butter. Bake as above. Serve with Garlic Yogurt Sauce (page 288).

EGGPLANT FRIED IN EGGS

This is an exquisite eggplant delicacy.

    1 medium eggplant
    Salt
    ½ cup olive oil or Clarified Butter (page 355) (approximately)
    ½ cup fine cracker crumbs made from Nabisco Waverly Wafers
    2 small eggs, beaten until frothy

Remove the stem and hull from the eggplant. Peel lengthwise in ½-inch strips, leaving ½-inch strips of skin in between, making a striped design. Cut crosswise into ¼-inch-thick slices and place on paper towels. Sprinkle generously with the salt, weigh down with a heavy object, and let stand about 30 minutes. Rinse and dry thoroughly with fresh paper towels.

In a heavy skillet heat the oil over moderate heat. Coat the eggplant slices lightly with the cracker crumbs, then dip in the eggs. Fry until golden brown on both sides. Drain on absorbent paper and serve hot or cold, as an accompaniment to roast lamb, roast chicken, or broiled fish. Or serve as an appetizer with Pomegranate Sauce (page 291).

Serves 4

ZUCCHINI FRIED IN EGGS

Follow the recipe for Eggplant Fried in Eggs (page 275), substituting for the eggplant unpeeled sliced zucchini. (Do not salt and weigh down the zucchini.)

Serves 4

MUSHROOMS FRIED IN EGGS

Follow the recipe for Eggplant Fried in Eggs (page 275), substituting for the eggplant 1 pound mushrooms, cooked in boiling salted water and drained. (Do not salt and weigh down the mushrooms.)

Serves 4

BAKED PUMPKIN WITH RICE

In America we seem to associate pumpkin mainly with Halloween and pie. Armenians, however, especially those living in the Caucasus, have created a fascinating repertoire of pumpkin dishes, ranging from soups to delectable desserts and jams.

4 cups water
1 teaspoon salt
1 cup uncooked long-grain white rice
½ cup raisins
2 tablespoons butter
2 pounds pumpkin, peeled and sliced lengthwise ½ inch thick
8 tablespoons sugar
6 tablespoons melted butter
¼ cup toasted chopped almonds (see page 342)
½ teaspoon cinnamon

276

In a heavy saucepan bring the water and salt to a boil over high heat. Gradually stir in the rice, being careful not to disturb the boiling, and cook 15 minutes. Add the raisins and cook a few minutes. Remove from the heat and drain thoroughly in a sieve.

In a heavy skillet melt the butter over moderate heat. Add the pumpkin slices and sauté lightly on both sides. Arrange half of the sautéed slices in a buttered shallow baking pan and sprinkle evenly with 2 tablespoons of the sugar and 2 tablespoons of the melted butter. Sprinkle the rice and raisin mixture with 2 tablespoons of the sugar, 2 table-spoons of the melted butter, and the toasted nuts. Mix well and spread evenly over the pumpkin slices. Cover with the remaining sautéed pumpkin slices and sprinkle the entire surface evenly with the remaining 2 tablespoons melted butter, remaining 4 tablespoons sugar, and cinnamon. Cover with aluminum foil and bake in a preheated 350° oven 45 minutes or until the pumpkin is tender and well glazed. Serve as an accompaniment to poultry or pork.

Serves 4

Variation: Caucasian Armenians use a whole pumpkin for this dish. To prepare, cut about 1 inch off the top of a small unpeeled pumpkin and reserve. This will later serve as a lid. Clean out the inside of the pumpkin. (Do not discard the seeds. Save them to prepare Toasted Pumpkin Seeds, page 4.) Scoop out 1 cup of the pulp and chop finely. Combine with 1 cup half-cooked rice, ¼ cup raisins, ½ cup chopped prunes, 1 apple, minced, and sugar and cinnamon to taste and mix well. Stuff the pumpkin with the mixture, cover with the reserved lid, and place in a buttered shallow baking dish just large enough to hold the pumpkin comfortably. Bake in a 350° oven until tender, about 1½ hours. Serve cut in wedges, with a portion of the rice stuffing on top of each piece. If desired, spoon melted butter over each serving.

GLAZED PUMPKIN

Shakar Titoum

1 4-pound pumpkin
½ cup water (approximately)
1 cup sugar
1 small piece gingerroot (about 1 inch), peeled and halved
¼ teaspoon salt
2 tablespoons freshly squeezed and strained lemon juice
¼ cup toasted chopped almonds or hazelnuts (see page 342)

Peel the pumpkin. (Do not discard the seeds. Save them to prepare Toasted Pumpkin Seeds, page 4.) Cut into 1-inch cubes. In a heavy saucepan or casserole bring the water to a boil. Add the sugar and gingerroot and stir until the sugar dissolves. Add the pumpkin and salt and cook over moderate heat until tender and well glazed, adding more water if necessary. Remove the gingerroot and discard. Add the lemon juice and transfer to a heated serving platter. Garnish with the nuts. Serve as an accompaniment to turkey or pork.

Serves 4

SPINACH WITH CHICK-PEAS

Siserov Sbanakh

¼ cup butter
½ cup finely chopped onion
1 pound spinach, washed, drained, stemmed, and coarsely
   chopped

¼ cup tomato paste
¼ cup water (approximately)
Salt and freshly ground black pepper to taste
1 cup drained cooked or canned chick-peas

In a heavy saucepan melt the butter over moderate heat. Add the onion and sauté until golden, stirring frequently. Add the spinach, tomato paste, water, and salt and pepper and bring to a boil. Reduce the heat to low. Cover and simmer 20 minutes, adding a little more water if necessary. Stir in the chick-peas. Cover and simmer 5 to 10 minutes or until the spinach is tender and the chick-peas are heated through.

Serves 3

NOTE: You may substitute Swiss chard for the spinach.

VEGETABLE CASSEROLE

Ailazan

1 small eggplant, sliced crosswise ½ inch thick
2 medium zucchini, halved lengthwise and then sliced crosswise
   2 inches thick
1 medium green pepper, seeded, deribbed, and cut into 8 pieces
1 cup green beans, trimmed and halved crosswise
2 carrots, scraped and sliced crosswise
2 medium potatoes, peeled and sliced ½ inch thick (optional)
2 large onions, thinly sliced lengthwise
4 large ripe tomatoes, peeled, seeded, and chopped
2 tablespoons finely chopped parsley
2 tablespoons finely chopped fresh dill or mint leaves
2 medium cloves garlic, finely chopped (optional)
Salt and freshly ground black pepper to taste
¼ cup butter

Combine the eggplant, zucchini, green pepper, green beans, carrots, potatoes, and onions in a baking dish. Cover with the tomatoes and sprinkle with the parsley, dill, garlic, and salt and pepper. Dot with the butter. Bake, covered, in a preheated 350° oven 1 hour or until the vegetables are tender, adding a little water if the mixture seems too dry. Serve as a side dish with roast chicken or lamb.

Serves 4

NOTE: You may substitute olive or vegetable oil for the butter and serve cold.

Variation: Omit the carrots and potatoes. Sauté each vegetable separately in Clarified Butter (page 355) or olive oil, then arrange in layers in a baking dish and proceed as above, reducing the amount of butter to 2 tablespoons.

ZUCCHINI AND CHEESE BAKE

4 medium zucchini, scraped
4 eggs
1 cup freshly grated Gruyère cheese
½ cup freshly grated feta cheese
2 tablespoons finely chopped parsley
2 tablespoons finely chopped fresh mint leaves
6 scallions, chopped, including 2 inches of the green tops (optional)
½ cup all-purpose flour
Salt and freshly ground black pepper to taste
¼ cup butter

Grate the zucchini into a large mixing bowl. Add the eggs, cheeses, parsley, mint, scallions, flour, and salt and pepper and mix thoroughly. Pour into a buttered 9-by-9-by-2-inch baking dish and dot with the butter. Bake in a preheated 350° oven 45 minutes or until the zucchini is tender and the surface is golden brown. Drain off the excess butter, if any, by tilting the pan. Serve hot or cold, as a side dish with poultry or meat.

Serves 6

VARIATION

Zucchini Cheese Balls

The above mixture may also be fried. Add enough flour to make the mixture the consistency of a thick pancake batter. Drop by tablespoonfuls into hot vegetable oil and fry until golden brown on all sides. Serve as a side dish or as an hors d'oeuvre.

13. Sauces

Ingredients for Garlic and Nut Sauce (page 290)

SERVED COLD

Yogurt   286

Cinnamon Yogurt Sauce   287

Garlic Yogurt Sauce   288

Lemon Sauce   288

Egg Sauce   289

Garlic and Nut Sauce   290

Onion and Parsley Sauce   291

Pomegranate Sauce   291

SERVED HOT

Egg and Lemon Sauce   292

Lemon Curry Sauce   292

Tomato Sauce   293

Meat Sauce   293

DESSERT SAUCES

Sweet Yogurt Sauce   294

Heavy Cream Topping   294

Armenian cuisine does not as a rule rely on separate sauces to give it variety, interest, or flavor. Instead, the characteristic taste of each dish is achieved by skillful seasoning and by the addition of a little water or broth to the liquid the particular vegetable, fish, bird, or meat has yielded in cooking. Many of the dishes owe their appearance, flavor, and fragrance to the use of fresh herbs, onions, and tomatoes.

Among the few sauces that are prepared and served separately, the most basic is *madzoon*, or yogurt. Plain *madzoon* or *madzoon* flavored with cinnamon or garlic is a usual accompaniment to various meat *dolmas*, kebabs, and fried vegetables. It is never served with fish. For desserts *madzoon* is sweetened with sugar and may be laced with cinnamon or another flavoring.

A favorite Armenian sauce is *terbiyeh*, an egg-lemon mixture that is added at the end of cooking to thicken and flavor many soups and meat dishes, giving them a wonderful tart taste. A few dishes are finished with the simple addition of melted butter with paprika for a subtle taste and color.

Tarator, an unusual and interesting garlic and nut sauce, is served over fish and fried vegetables. For an exotic appetizer try Fried Mussels (page 12) with *tarator* sauce.

Two other sauces are a sweet syrup prepared from grapes known as *roub* (Turkish *bekmez*); and *narsharab* (pomegranate syrup), which lends a rich color and superb taste to fried eggplant, grilled fish, lamb, and pork.

Some Armenian pastries and desserts are served with a rich cream topping called *kaymak*, which has a thick yet pliable consistency, making it possible for one to slice or roll it. *Kaymak* has a distinctive taste of its own which is especially compatible with *tel kadayif* (Shredded Pastry with Walnut Filling, page 321).

285

YOGURT

Madzoon

Yogurt is a healthful food that has been used in Middle Eastern cookery since biblical times. It is a very nourishing food and one that helps digestion. It appears under different names in different communities. Armenians call it *madzoon,* and in Arabic-speaking countries it is called *laban.* In the United States it is known as yogurt, which is derived from the Turkish word *yoghourt.*

Yogurt is an essential food in Armenian cuisine and is served in many different ways. It may be eaten as a snack, either alone or with honey or preserves, diluted with water to make a cool summer drink, mixed with diced cucumbers and mint leaves to make a refreshing salad, made into a cheese spread, used to make wonderful hot or cold soups, and served as a sauce for meat dishes, stews, vegetables, pilafs, cakes, and desserts. Homemade yogurt is economical, flavorful, and simple to make. It is important, however, to maintain a proper temperature during its preparation because one is working with living bacteria that will die if the temperature is over 120° and will not grow if it is under 90°. This can easily be done by checking the temperature of the milk used to make the yogurt with a candy thermometer. In order for the yogurt to form, the milk must remain warm for about eight hours or overnight. Putting it in a thermos bottle will accomplish this very well.

Fresh live yogurt, available in health-food stores and in some supermarkets, is used as a starter. (Armenians call this *magart.*) If the bacteria in the starter have been killed by sterilization, you will of course be unsuccessful, as you will if the milk has been treated with antibiotics.

Here is the recipe for making yogurt. In an enameled or flameproof glass saucepan bring 2 cups milk to a boil over moderate heat. As the milk begins to rise, reduce the heat to low and simmer about 2 minutes. Remove from the heat, pour into a glass bowl, and cool to a temperature of about 110°. (The Middle Eastern cook will test the temperature by waiting until he can put his finger in the milk and count to ten without any pain, or he will put a little on his wrist to see if it feels more than lukewarm.) Working quickly, put 1 tablespoon live yogurt into a small glass bowl and mix it thoroughly with a few tablespoons of the warm milk until smooth. Then stir it into the remaining milk in the bowl and mix well. Pour into a thermos bottle, preferably a wide-mouthed one, and close the bottle at once. Leave it undisturbed about 8 hours or overnight. When ready, the yogurt should have a thick custardlike consistency. Well-made yogurt is rich and creamy, with a mild flavor, not watery and sour, as is so often the case.

Using a rubber scraper, empty the yogurt into a glass container or jar and store in the refrigerator. (Reserve a few tablespoons in a small glass jar and refrigerate to use as a starter for your next batch of yogurt.) It will improve in flavor and thicken slightly as it cools.

Makes 2 cups

NOTE: For yogurt with a thicker consistency and richer flavor, ¼ to ½ cup heavy cream may be added to the milk before boiling. A firmer yogurt with a texture similar to that of cream cheese may be made by pouring the yogurt into a bag made from a double thickness of cheesecloth or muslin. Suspend the bag several hours or overnight to allow the excess liquid to drip out (place a bowl underneath to catch the drippings). Prepared this way, yogurt may be salted to taste, covered with a thin layer of olive oil, and served as a spread or hors d'oeuvre with Armenian Thin Bread (page 301), or crackers. Black olives, tomatoes, and cucumbers make a good accompaniment.

CINNAMON YOGURT SAUCE

Ginamonov (Tarchinov) Madzoon

1 cup chilled unflavored yogurt
1½ teaspoons cinnamon

Pour the yogurt into a chilled serving bowl and sprinkle the top evenly with the cinnamon. This sauce is good served with meat *dolmas*, especially Grapevine Leaves Stuffed with Meat (page 200).

Makes 1 cup

GARLIC YOGURT SAUCE

Sikhdorov Madzoon

1 cup unflavored yogurt
1 medium clove garlic or to taste
¼ teaspoon salt
½ teaspoon crushed dried mint leaves (optional)

Pour the yogurt into a bowl. Pound the garlic with the salt and mint. Add to the yogurt and mix well. Cover and chill several hours before serving. This is excellent on fried eggplant or zucchini, some meat *dolmas*, and some lamb dishes.

Makes 1 cup

NOTE: 2 tablespoons finely chopped fresh mint leaves and/or dill may be used instead of the dried mint.

LEMON SAUCE

½ cup olive oil
½ cup freshly squeezed and strained lemon juice
Salt and freshly ground black pepper to taste
½ cup finely chopped parsley
½ cup finely chopped scallions, including 2 inches of the green tops

Combine the olive oil, lemon juice, and salt and pepper in a small bowl. Beat together with a fork or whisk until well blended. Add the parsley and scallions and mix well. This sauce is used in salads, on boiled or fried vegetables, and on broiled or fried fish.

Makes about 1 cup

EGG SAUCE

1 egg yolk
1¼ tablespoons freshly squeezed and strained lemon juice
Salt and freshly ground black pepper to taste
6 tablespoons olive oil (approximately)
1 or 2 hard-cooked eggs
3 sprigs parsley

Combine the egg yolk, lemon juice, and salt and pepper in the container of an electric blender. Cover and blend just a few seconds, then uncover, and with the motor still running, slowly add the olive oil in a thin, steady stream until the mixture thickens (you may not need all of the olive oil). Add the egg and parsley and blend until smooth. Cover and chill thoroughly. Serve with broiled or fried fish.

Makes about ¾ cup

GARLIC AND NUT SAUCE

Tarator

½ cup walnut halves, hazelnuts, blanched almonds, or pine nuts
1 medium clove garlic or to taste, pounded
2 slices white bread, trimmed of crusts, soaked in water, and squeezed dry
½ cup olive oil
1 tablespoon wine vinegar
Salt, cayenne, and paprika to taste

Place the nuts in the container of an electric blender and pulverize. Add the garlic and blend well. Add the bread and blend several seconds. Add the olive oil, vinegar, and salt, cayenne, and paprika. Blend slowly until a smooth sauce is obtained. Taste for seasoning, cover, and refrigerate. Serve with baked, boiled, or fried seafood or boiled or fried vegetables such as cauliflower, beans, and eggplant.

Makes 1 cup

NOTE: If you have no blender, *tarator* may be prepared by hand: Mash the garlic in a mortar with a little salt until thoroughly crushed. Add the nuts and pound until well blended. Crumble the bread into the mixture and pound. Gradually add the olive oil and vinegar, beating thoroughly after each addition, until a smooth sauce is obtained. Season to taste and blend well. Cover and refrigerate.

ONION AND PARSLEY SAUCE

Piaz

3 small onions, halved lengthwise and very thinly sliced
1 tablespoon salt
½ cup chopped parsley

Place the onion slices in a bowl, sprinkle with the salt, and mix well. Let stand a few minutes, then knead with your hands to release the juices. Rinse the onion thoroughly with cold water to remove the salt and place in a small serving bowl. Add the parsley and mix well. Mixed with fresh lemon juice, *piaz* makes a good topping for broiled or fried fish.

Makes about 1 cup

POMEGRANATE SAUCE

Narsharab

The homemade version of this sauce is preferable to the bottled one.

Juice from seeds of 8 fresh pomegranates
1 cup sugar

Heat the pomegranate juice in a small enameled saucepan over moderate heat. Add the sugar and cook until it dissolves, stirring constantly. Lower the heat and cook 15 minutes or until the mixture thickens to a syrup. Remove from the heat. Serve hot or cold, with barbecued meat or fish or with fried eggplant.

Makes about ¾ cup

EGG AND LEMON SAUCE

Terbiyeh

2 eggs
3 tablespoons freshly squeezed and strained lemon juice
1 cup hot chicken or meat broth

In a small saucepan beat the eggs with a whisk until frothy, then beat in the lemon juice. Gradually add the hot broth. Heat over low heat, stirring constantly, until the sauce is thickened. Do not allow it to boil or the eggs will curdle. Taste for seasoning. This is a very common sauce in Armenian cooking. It is added to many soups, meat stews, meat *dolmas*, and boiled fish dishes before serving.

Makes 1 cup

❀ LEMON CURRY SAUCE

¼ cup butter
1 teaspoon mild curry powder or to taste
¼ cup freshly squeezed and strained lemon juice
Salt to taste
⅛ teaspoon garlic powder
2 tablespoons chopped chives or toasted almonds (page 342)

In a small skillet melt the butter. Stir in the curry powder. Add the remaining ingredients, mix well, and heat through. This is a good sauce

292

for broiled seafood, chicken, or lamb; rice or bulghur pilafs; or boiled potatoes.

Makes about ½ cup

TOMATO SAUCE

¼ cup butter
1 small onion, finely chopped
4 large ripe tomatoes, peeled, seeded, and finely chopped
2 medium cloves garlic, crushed
2 tablespoons finely chopped parsley
1 bay leaf
Salt and freshly ground black pepper to taste

In a heavy saucepan melt the butter over moderate heat. Add the onion and sauté until golden and soft, stirring frequently. Add the tomatoes, garlic, parsley, bay leaf, and salt and pepper. Cook over low heat about 15 minutes or until the sauce is thickened, stirring often. Put through a food mill or sieve and keep warm.

Makes about 2 cups

MEAT SAUCE

¼ cup butter
2 medium onions, halved lengthwise and thinly sliced
¼ cup pine nuts
1 pound lean ground lamb
4 large ripe tomatoes, peeled, seeded, and chopped
2 large green peppers, seeded, deribbed, and sliced lengthwise
⅜ inch thick
1 teaspoon dried basil leaves, crushed
Salt and freshly ground black pepper to taste

In a skillet melt the butter over moderate heat. Add the onions and sauté until soft but not browned, stirring frequently. Stir in the pine nuts and sauté until the onions and nuts turn golden brown. Add the lamb and cook 5 minutes, breaking it up with a fork. Stir in the tomatoes, green peppers, basil, and salt and pepper. Cook, covered, over low heat about 25 minutes, stirring occasionally. This is a good sauce for Plain Cracked Wheat Pilaf (page 231). It may also be served over Raw Lamb and Wheat Patties (page 174) or Baked Lamb and Wheat without Stuffing (page 176), Plain Rice Pilaf (page 219), or macaroni.

Serves 4

SWEET YOGURT SAUCE

1 cup chilled unflavored yogurt
3 tablespoons confectioners' sugar or to taste
1 teaspoon cinnamon

Pour the yogurt into a small bowl, add the sugar, and beat thoroughly. Sprinkle with the cinnamon. Serve over fruit desserts and pancakes.

Makes 1 cup

NOTE: Yogurt may also be flavored with orange flower water, vanilla, or raspberry syrup.

HEAVY CREAM TOPPING

Kaymak

Pour 1 quart heavy cream into a shallow enameled saucepan and bring to a boil over very low heat. Using a ladle, remove some cream and pour it back into the pan from as high up as possible. This will cause bubbles to form. Do this for 1 hour, then turn off the heat. Leave the saucepan in a warm place 2 or 3 hours to set. Place the saucepan in the refrigerator at least 10 hours or overnight. With a sharp knife, loosen the edges of the *kaymak*, then cut it into strips. Using a spatula, carefully remove the strips to a plate. Cut into squares or roll the strips up and then slice. Serve as a topping for pastries. *Kaymak* may also be spread on toast with honey.

Serves 20

NOTE: You can make an imitation *kaymak* that takes much less time to prepare. Pour 1 quart heavy cream into a shallow enameled saucepan, reserving a little bit. In a small bowl dissolve 4 tablespoons cornstarch in the reserved cream to make a thin paste. Bring the cream in the saucepan almost to boiling and gradually add the cornstarch mixture and 1 teaspoon vanilla. Cook about 10 minutes or until thickened, stirring constantly. Remove from the heat and cool. Cover and chill thoroughly before using.

Serves 20

14. Breads and Coffee Cakes

A selection of Armenian breads

Through the ages bread has occupied an essential place in the diet of Armenians, who serve it at every meal. Eaten with *banir* (cheese), bread constitutes the most popular snack and has been the traditional breakfast of Armenian peasants for centuries.

Lavash is a very thin, crisp, cracker-type bread that keeps well in a dry place. It has been baked the same way, in a large outdoor oven called a *tonir*, since antiquity. It can be made into small rounds or rolled out to a diameter of sixteen inches or more. It is eaten crisp as is, or it may be sprinkled with water thirty minutes or so before serving, then wrapped in a kitchen towel and set aside to absorb the water and soften until serving time. *Lavash* goes particularly well with Armenian appetizers, and it is fun to wrap a piece of it around a stuffed grapevine leaf or a slice of cheese before eating. It is uniquely adaptable for sandwiches.

Another bread that Armenians favor is *pideh,* a crusted yeasty white bread baked in either large round loaves or smaller individual ones. *Pideh* is brushed with milk and sprinkled generously with sesame seeds before baking. It is especially good for dipping into meat, vegetable, or salad juices.

Simit is a breakfast roll with good keeping qualities. A delicious roll known as *choereg* or *keghkeh* is served at breakfast or with afternoon tea or coffee. There are many variations of *choereg* which are shaped into breads or rolls and flavored with *mahlab,* an unusual spice with a wonderful aroma and taste. Other flavorings for *choereg* include grated lemon or orange rind and ground aniseed. *Choeregs* are traditionally baked during holidays, especially at Easter.

Two unusual coffee cakes are *tahinov gatah* and *koritzov gatah.* The first has a filling of *tahini,* sugar, and cinnamon. It is very good served with jam. The second has a stuffing of butter, flour, nuts, sugar, and cinnamon. It may be shaped either in the form of a small pie or into small egg-size balls.

ARMENIAN THIN BREAD

Lavash

½ package active dry yeast
1½ teaspoons sugar
 1 cup plus 2 tablespoons warm water (110 to 115°)
3½ cups sifted all-purpose flour (approximately)
 ¼ cup melted butter, cooled to lukewarm
1½ teaspoons salt

In a small bowl sprinkle the yeast and ½ teaspoon of the sugar over 2 tablespoons of the water. Let stand a couple of minutes, then stir to dissolve the yeast completely.

Pour the flour into a large bowl and make a well in the middle. Pour in the yeast mixture, remaining 1 cup water, melted butter, salt, and remaining 1 teaspoon sugar. With a large spoon, stir the center ingredients together, then gradually blend into the flour. Knead in the bowl or on a floured surface until a soft and elastic dough is formed, adding more flour if necessary. Shape into a ball. Place in a clean oiled bowl and turn dough to coat with the oil. Cover loosely with a kitchen towel and leave in a warm place (85°) that is free from drafts (such as an unlit oven with a pan of hot water on the bottom rack) until the dough doubles in bulk, about 3 hours.

Punch down the dough and divide into 14 equal parts. On a lightly floured board roll out one part as thin as possible, forming a circle approximately 9 to 10 inches in diameter. Occasionally sprinkle the dough lightly with flour to keep it from sticking. Place on a baking sheet and prick the entire surface of the dough with a fork. Bake in a preheated 450° oven about 5 to 6 minutes or until golden brown and crisp, watching closely to prevent burning. Repeat the rolling, pricking, and baking procedure with the remaining dough. Cool the *lavash* on a rack and store in a covered container in a dry place.

Serve the crisp *lavash* as it is. If you want softer *lavash*, about 30 minutes before serving, sprinkle it lightly with water (too much will make it soggy) or hold it briefly under running water on both sides and then shake off the excess water. Wrap the dampened *lavash* in a kitchen towel and set aside to absorb the water and soften. *Lavash*, either crisp or soft, is excellent with appetizers, cheese, and kebabs.

Makes 14

NOTE: *Lavash* can also be rolled into small circles or circles with a diameter of 16 inches or more. The small rounds may be brushed with water beaten with a little egg and then sprinkled with sesame seeds before baking. These are delicious eaten crisp, with appetizers and cocktails. The very large rounds should be softened, folded into triangles, and served at dinner.

Lavash can be made without butter; use 1¼ cups water and proceed as above.

ARMENIAN BREAD

Pideh

> 2 cups warm water (110 to 115°)
> 2 packages active dry yeast
> 5½ cups sifted all-purpose flour (approximately)
> 2 teaspoons salt
> 2 tablespoons sugar
> 2 tablespoons butter, softened
> **Milk**
> **Sesame seeds**

Pour the water into a large mixing bowl and sprinkle with the yeast. Let the mixture rest 5 minutes, then stir to dissolve the yeast. Add 3 cups of the flour, salt, and sugar and beat with a large spoon until smooth. Add the butter and the remaining 2½ cups flour, a little at a time, mixing first with the spoon and then with your hands until thoroughly blended.

Turn out the dough onto a lightly floured surface and knead until smooth and spongy, sprinkling with a little flour if necessary to keep it from sticking. Form into a ball and place in a lightly oiled bowl, turning to grease the top. Cover loosely with a kitchen towel and let rise in a warm place (85°) free from drafts (such as an unlit oven with a pan of hot water on the bottom rack) about 45 minutes.

Punch down the dough, turn over, and let rise 15 minutes. Punch down again, divide into 4 equal pieces, and shape each into a ball. Place on an oiled baking sheet and gently press down with your knuckles, flattening the balls so that they are about 8 inches in diameter and ¾ inch thick. With a small sharp knife, score the top of each loaf to form a design of diamonds. Brush with the milk and sprinkle evenly with the sesame seeds. Let rise in a warm place 30 minutes or until doubled in volume. Bake in a preheated 425° oven 15 to 20 minutes or until golden brown. Remove loaves from baking sheets and let cool slightly on racks. Serve warm.

Makes 4

Armenian Rolls

For smaller-sized *pideh* divide the dough into 10 equal pieces, shaping each into a ball. Place on the baking sheet and flatten each so that it is about 5 inches in diameter and ¾ inch thick. Bake these for about 12 minutes or until golden brown.

SESAME ROLLS

Shoushmayov Gatah

These rolls may be eaten at any time and are particularly delicious with cheese.

    1 cake compressed yeast
    ½ cup lukewarm water (95°)
    5 cups sifted all-purpose flour (approximately)
    2 eggs
    ½ cup melted butter, cooled to lukewarm
    ½ cup condensed milk
    ½ cup sugar
    1 egg, beaten
    Sesame seeds

In a small bowl dissolve the yeast in the water. Place the flour in a large bowl. Make a well in the center and add the eggs, melted butter, milk, and sugar. With a large spoon stir the center ingredients together, then gradually blend into the flour. Knead in the bowl or on a floured surface until a soft dough is formed. Shape into a ball and place in a clean bowl. Cover loosely with a kitchen towel and let rise in a warm place (85°) free from drafts (such as an unlit oven with a pan of hot water on the bottom rack) 3 hours or until doubled in bulk.

Punch down the dough. With lightly floured hands, break off small portions of dough one at a time and roll into ropes about 12 inches long and ½ inch thick. Beginning at one end, wind up each rope around itself into a snail-shaped circle.

Carefully arrange the rolls 2 inches apart on a baking sheet. Brush the tops with the beaten egg and sprinkle generously with the sesame seeds. Cover and let rise in a warm place 2 hours. Bake in a preheated 375° oven 15 to 20 minutes or until golden brown.

Makes about 18

NOTE: You may omit the sesame seeds.

BREAKFAST ROLLS

Simit

3½ cups sifted all-purpose flour
¾ teaspoon salt
2 eggs, beaten
½ cup melted butter, cooled to lukewarm
2 tablespoons olive oil
2 tablespoons milk
2 tablespoons water
Milk or beaten egg
Sesame seeds

Combine the flour and salt in a large bowl. Make a well in the center and pour in the eggs, melted butter, olive oil, milk, and water. With a large spoon stir the center ingredients together, then gradually blend into the flour mixture until a medium-light and somewhat oily dough is formed.

With lightly floured hands, break off small portions of the dough one at a time and roll into ropes 8 inches long and ½ inch thick. Press the ends of each rope together to form a ring.

Place the rings on baking sheets. Brush the tops with the milk and sprinkle with the sesame seeds. Bake in a preheated 400° oven 25 minutes or until golden brown.

Makes about 16

NOTE: You may shape the dough into snail-like rolls or sticks. To form snails, roll small portions of dough into ropes about 12 inches long and ½ inch thick. Beginning at one end, wind up each rope around itself into a snail-shaped circle. To form sticks, cut the ½-inch-thick rolled dough into 4-inch-long pieces. Dip in beaten egg, roll in sesame seeds, and bake as above.

COFFEE ROLLS

Choereg or Keghkeh

¼ cup warm water (110 to 115°)
1 package active dry yeast
1¼ cups lukewarm milk
2 eggs, beaten
1 cup melted butter, cooled to lukewarm
¼ cup sugar
1 teaspoon salt
1½ teaspoons ground *mahlab* or ground aniseed
1½ teaspoons baking powder
6 cups sifted all-purpose flour (approximately)
1 egg, beaten
Sesame seeds (optional)

Pour the warm water into a large bowl and sprinkle it with the yeast. Let the mixture stand a few minutes, then stir to dissolve the yeast. Add the milk, eggs, melted butter, sugar, salt, *mahlab*, and baking powder and blend well. Stir in the flour, a little at a time, until a soft dough is formed. Turn out onto a lightly floured surface and knead 3 to 4 minutes or until smooth. Place the dough in a lightly oiled bowl, turning it over to grease the top. Cover with a kitchen towel and let rise in a warm place (85°) free from drafts (such as an unlit oven with a pan of hot water on the bottom rack) about 2 hours or until doubled in bulk.

Punch down the dough and transfer it to a lightly floured surface. Divide it into 32 equal pieces. Form into snail-shaped rolls (or other shapes, as you wish). To form into snails, roll each piece of dough into a rope about 12 inches long. Beginning at one end, wind up the rope around itself into a snail-shaped circle.

Carefully arrange the rolls 2 inches apart on a greased baking sheet. Cover and let rise in a warm place 50 to 60 minutes or until almost doubled in volume. Brush the tops of the rolls with the beaten egg and sprinkle with the sesame seeds. Bake in a preheated 350° oven 20 minutes or until a rich golden brown. Serve warm, or cool on a rack and serve at room temperature.

Makes 32

NOTE: Some Armenians like to sprinkle *mahlab* with a little sugar while grinding in order to help bring out its flavor.

ARMENIAN PANCAKES

Dabagaplit

 1 egg, beaten
1½ tablespoons melted butter, cooled to lukewarm
 ½ cup water
 2 cups sifted all-purpose flour (approximately)
 ½ teaspoon salt
1½ teaspoons double-acting baking powder
Clarified Butter (page 355)
Sugar

In a mixing bowl combine the egg, melted butter, and water and blend well. Gradually stir in the flour, salt, and baking powder until a soft, smooth dough is formed. With the hands lightly floured, shape into 1¼-inch balls. Using a rolling pin on a floured surface, roll each ball into a circle about 5 inches in diameter.

In a small, heavy skillet melt a little of the clarified butter. Add the circles of dough and fry one at a time until golden brown on each side. Keep the cakes warm while the others are cooking. Add more butter to the pan as needed. Sprinkle with the sugar and serve hot. These pancakes are good at breakfast or brunch, with sautéed bacon slices and Fruit Paste Dipped in Egg (page 75).

Serves 6

COFFEE CAKE WITH SESAME SEED PASTE

Tahinov Gatah

1 package active dry yeast
¼ cup warm water (110 to 115°)
½ cup lukewarm milk
¼ cup melted butter, cooled to lukewarm
2 eggs, beaten
4 tablespoons sugar
1 teaspoon salt
3¼ to 3½ cups sifted all-purpose flour (approximately)
¾ teaspoon cinnamon
2 tablespoons finely chopped walnuts (optional)
4 tablespoons *tahini*
1 egg, beaten

Sprinkle the yeast over the water in a large bowl. Let stand a few minutes and then stir to dissolve the yeast. Add the milk, melted butter, eggs, 1 tablespoon of the sugar, and salt and mix together. Gradually stir in the flour and blend until a soft dough is formed. Shape into a ball and place in a clean bowl. Cover loosely with a kitchen towel and leave in a warm place (85°) free from drafts (such as an unlit oven with a pan of hot water on the bottom rack) until doubled in volume, about 1 hour. Meanwhile, mix together the remaining 3 tablespoons sugar, cinnamon, and nuts.

Punch down dough. Transfer it to a lightly floured surface and knead 1 minute or until smooth. Divide into 4 equal pieces. Roll each piece into a rectangle 5 by 8 inches. Brush the surface of each rectangle with 1 tablespoon of the *tahini* and sprinkle evenly with ¼ of the sugar mixture. Fold each rectangle in half to make a rectangle 4 by 5 inches. Place on a lightly oiled baking sheet, cover with clear plastic film, and place in the refrigerator for 30 minutes.

Transfer the chilled rectangles to a lightly floured surface and again roll each into a 5-by-8-inch rectangle. Fold in half and arrange

1 inch apart on the baking sheet. Cover and leave to rise in a warm place 1 hour or until doubled. Brush with the beaten egg. Bake in a preheated 350° oven about 25 minutes or until golden brown. Cool about 10 minutes, then slice and serve warm, with jam.

Makes 4

COFFEE CAKE WITH FILLING

Koritzov Gatah

DOUGH

    1 cake compressed yeast
    2 cups lukewarm milk (95°)
    ¾ cup sugar
    1 cup melted butter, cooled to lukewarm
    6½ cups sifted all-purpose flour (approximately)
    ½ teaspoon salt

FILLING (KORITZ)

    ½ cup butter
    1 cup sifted all-purpose flour
    ⅓ cup chopped walnuts or almonds
    6 tablespoons sugar
    ½ teaspoon cinnamon

Melted butter
    1 egg, beaten
Sesame seeds

Make the dough: In a large bowl soften the yeast in 1 cup of the milk. Combine the sugar with the remaining 1 cup milk and stir to dissolve completely. Add to the yeast mixture with the melted butter and mix together. Combine the flour and salt and gradually add to the liquid ingredients, blending well. Knead thoroughly on a floured surface until a soft dough is formed. Shape into a ball and place in a clean oiled bowl, turning until the dough is coated with oil. Cover with a kitchen towel and leave to rise in a warm place (85°) free from drafts (such as an unlit oven with a pan of hot water on the bottom rack) until doubled, about 2 to 3 hours.

Meanwhile, prepare the filling: In a heavy skillet melt the butter over low heat. Add the flour, nuts, sugar, and cinnamon and stir until thoroughly blended. Continue cooking over low heat until a thick paste is formed and the mixture turns pink, stirring frequently. Remove from the heat and set aside.

Punch down the dough and divide into six equal pieces. With a rolling pin, roll out each piece on a floured surface ⅛ inch thick. Brush the surface of each piece with some of the melted butter. Fold up the dough like a package into a 5-inch square, brushing the top surface with butter each time you make a fold. Place 1 tablespoon of the filling on the lower half of each square. Fold the square over in half, covering the filling. Press the edges together to seal. With a rolling pin, flatten the square to about ¼-inch thickness.

Carefully arrange the *gatahs* 1 inch apart on a lightly greased baking sheet. Brush the tops with the beaten egg and sprinkle with the sesame seeds. Cover and leave in a warm place to rise about 1 hour, or until doubled in bulk. Bake in a preheated 350° oven about 20 minutes or until golden brown. Cool on racks.

Makes 6

NOTE: The *gatahs* may also be shaped into small rolls. To prepare, divide the dough into 40 equal pieces. Form each into a little ball and indent with your thumb, pressing gently to make a round opening. Place a little of the filling in the hollow, bring the edges together, and seal. With a rolling pin, flatten each ball into a circle ¼ inch thick. Arrange on a baking sheet, brush with the beaten egg, and sprinkle with the sesame seeds. Prick with a fork and bake as above.

15. Desserts

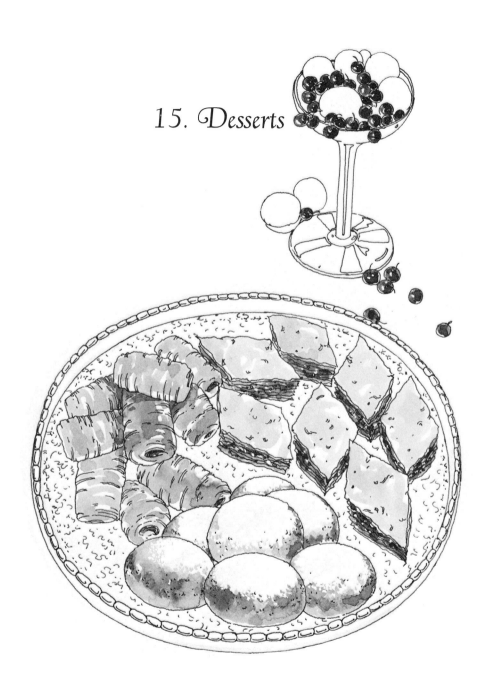

*Armenian pastries, clockwise from bottom: Kurabia (page 323),
Bourma (page 319) and Baklava (page 316),*

FRUIT DESSERTS

This chapter includes recipes for some of the most fabulous and mouth-watering pastries in the world, for which Armenians have long been famous. Many of these sweets are prepared with paper-thin phyllo dough. Making this exquisite dough is time-consuming and involves a great deal of patience. Fortunately it can be bought ready-made by the pound from Middle Eastern bakeries or the stores listed in the Shoppers' Guide (page 385–95). Before using phyllo, you should read the entry for it in the Glossary.

Baklava, the best known of these pastries, has many variations, depending on the shape and filling used. It may be made with many layers of buttered phyllo, assembled in a pan with a filling of nuts, cheese, or cream, and scored into small diamonds. Or the phyllo is wrapped around the filling to form triangles, rolls, or other shapes. After baking, a honey or simple syrup of sugar and water which has been flavored with lemon juice is poured over the *baklava*. Apple, custard, and nut pastries are rolled versions of *baklava*, differing mainly in their fillings.

Another great Armenian favorite is *tel kadayif*, made with long threads of partially cooked and dried pastry that resembles shredded wheat and is obtainable from Middle Eastern groceries or bakeries. The pastry is stuffed with nuts, drenched with syrup, and served with *kaymak*, a special cream topping (see Heavy Cream Topping, page 294). Cheese *kadayif* is a variation of *tel kadayif* which substitutes a filling of cheese for the nuts.

Kurabia is a rich butter cookie similar to shortbread, coated generously with confectioners' sugar and often topped with a blanched almond or pistachio nut. Large trays of *kurabia* are traditionally served at weddings and at Christmas or Easter. Armenians also make a version

314

of *kurabia* stuffed with chopped nuts. Sometimes the nuts are mixed with the dough before baking.

As a rule, cakes and pastries do not form part of an everyday meal in the Middle East but are served with afternoon or late evening tea or coffee, on special occasions, and during holidays. Dessert usually consists of a bowl of cold fresh fruit, accompanied by cheese.

Fruits have been abundantly cultivated in Armenia from ancient to modern times. Soviet Armenia produces an enormous variety of grapes. Armenian peaches are especially prized, and apples are found everywhere. Many varieties of apricots, pears, and plums, including damsons and the local yellow sour plums, are grown. There are cherries (sweet, sour, and the native cornelian, or *kizil*), lemons, melons, oranges, pomegranates, and quinces, as well as berries, including barberries and mulberries. Nuts are also cultivated, and green almonds and walnuts are considered a delicacy. Compotes made of fresh or dried fruits, often including nuts, are also popular, as are puddings.

MANY-LAYERED PASTRY WITH FILLING

Baklava

This celebrated pastry of rare perfection is perhaps one of the world's most exquisite sweets. It is enjoyed by all the peoples of the Middle East, who call it by its above name. The specific Armenian word for it is *hazaratertik*, meaning *mille-feuille* or "sweet of a thousand leaves."

A little more syrup or a slightly sweeter one may be used, but be careful not to overdo it. Well-made *baklava* is light, crisp, and subtle and bears no relation to what usually passes for it: a heavy, soggy mess drowning in syrup and so sweet that it hurts one's teeth!

Before making *baklava*, please read the entry for phyllo in the Glossary.

FILLING

    ¾ cup finely chopped or ground walnuts
    ¾ cup finely chopped or ground blanched almonds
    2 tablespoons sugar
    1 teaspoon cinnamon

PASTRY

    ½ cup melted Clarified Butter (page 355) (approximately)
    30 sheets phyllo pastry, each 9 by 9 inches

SYRUP

    1 cup sugar
    ¾ cup water
    1 teaspoon freshly squeezed and strained lemon juice

Combine all the filling ingredients in a small bowl. Set aside.

To assemble the pastry, brush a 9-by-9-by-2-inch baking pan with some of the melted clarified butter. Line it with 10 sheets phyllo, brushing each with the butter. Sprinkle half the nut mixture evenly over the entire surface. Top with another 10 sheets phyllo, brushing each with the butter. Sprinkle with the remaining nut mixture. Cover with the last 10 sheets phyllo, brushing each with the butter. With a sharp knife, cut the pastry in vertical lines 2¼ inches apart, then cut diagonally into diamond shapes. Bake in a preheated 325° oven 30 minutes. Reduce the heat to 250° and bake 1 hour and 15 minutes or until golden, crisp, and baked through.

While the *baklava* bakes, prepare the syrup: Combine the sugar, water, and lemon juice in a small saucepan. Bring to a boil over high heat, stirring constantly to dissolve the sugar. Reduce the heat and simmer, uncovered, about 20 minutes or until the syrup reaches a temperature of 225° on a candy thermometer. Remove from the heat and keep warm.

When the *baklava* is done, remove it from the oven and allow to cool slightly. Spoon the syrup evenly over the pastry. Cool to room temperature before serving.

Serves about 20

ROLLED PASTRY WITH NUT FILLING

Before making this recipe, please read the entry for phyllo in the Glossary.

FILLING

¾ cup ground walnuts
½ cup ground blanched almonds
2 teaspoons sugar
¼ teaspoon cinnamon
⅛ teaspoon nutmeg

    20 sheets phyllo pastry, each 12 by 16 inches

    1 cup melted butter, preferably Clarified Butter (page 355) (approximately)

    1 cup sugar

    ⅔ cup water

    1 teaspoon freshly squeezed and strained lemon juice

    1 stick cinnamon, 2 inches long

    ¼ cup honey

Combine all the filling ingredients in a small bowl. Mix well and set aside.

Prepare each pastry as follows: Place one sheet phyllo on a flat surface and brush with some of the melted butter. Fold in half crosswise to make a rectangle about 12 inches long and 8 inches wide. Brush the top with the butter and sprinkle with 1 tablespoon of the filling. Beginning at the lower edge of the sheet, roll up tightly like a jelly roll into a cylinder. Cut in half to make two rolls, each about 4 inches long. Place seam sides down on a lightly buttered baking sheet. Repeat the procedure with the remaining phyllo sheets and filling. Brush the tops of the rolls with the butter. Bake in a preheated 350° oven about 20 minutes or until crisp and golden.

While the rolls bake, prepare the syrup: In a small, heavy saucepan bring the sugar, water, lemon juice, and cinnamon stick to a boil over moderate heat. Cook until the sugar dissolves, stirring constantly. Stir in the honey. Remove from the heat and keep warm.

When the pastry rolls are done, dip them while still hot one at a time in the syrup and place on racks to drain. Serve warm or cold.

Makes 40

ROLLED SHIRRED PASTRY
WITH NUT FILLING

Bourma

Use the ingredients in the recipe (page 317) for Rolled Pastry with
Nut Filling, omitting the almonds and nutmeg and using 1 cup ground
walnuts, 16 sheets phyllo, and about ¾ cup melted butter. Mix the
nuts, sugar, and cinnamon and set aside.

Prepare each *bourma* as follows: Place 1 sheet phyllo on a flat
surface, shorter end nearest you, and brush with some of the butter.
Sprinkle 1 tablespoon of the nut mixture evenly over the sheet. Place
a dowel or an old curtain rod, about 15 inches long and ⅜ inch in
diameter, along the bottom edge of the sheet. Fold the lower edge of
the sheet over the dowel and roll the length of the sheet, like a jelly
roll. Gently squeeze both ends of the rolled sheet as far as possible
toward the center like an accordion, forming creases. Carefully pull
out the dowel. Place the *bourma*, seam side down, on a lightly buttered baking sheet. Brush the rolls and bake as directed on page 318.

Meanwhile, prepare the syrup. When the pastry is done, remove
from the oven and cut each *bourma* in half. Dip each piece in the
syrup and place on racks to drain and cool.

Makes 32

NOTE: The rolled-up unbaked *bourma* may also be shaped into snails
and baked as above. After dipping in syrup, sprinkle the centers with
finely chopped pistachios.

ROLLED PASTRY WITH CUSTARD FILLING

FILLING (ABOUT 3½ CUPS)

    2 eggs, separated
    ¾ cup sugar
    ½ cup rice flour
    3 cups scalded milk
    1 teaspoon vanilla

SYRUP

    1⅓ cups sugar
    1 cup water
    1 tablespoon lemon juice

    About 28 phyllo pastry sheets as needed
    Melted butter, preferably Clarified Butter (page 355)

Prepare the filling: In a mixing bowl beat the egg yolks. Add the sugar and rice flour and blend. Beat the eggs whites until stiff, add to the rice flour mixture, and blend thoroughly until smooth. Combine the mixture with the milk in a double boiler and cook 10 to 15 minutes or until thickened, stirring constantly. Remove from the heat, stir in the vanilla, and cool.

While the filling cools, prepare the syrup: Combine the sugar, water, and lemon juice in a small saucepan. Bring to a boil over moderate heat, stirring constantly until the sugar is dissolved. Reduce the heat to low and simmer 10 minutes. Remove from the heat and cool to lukewarm.

Form the phyllo into Boereg Rolls (page 17) or Boereg Triangles (page 18), using the cooled custard as a filling. After pastries are baked, dip one at a time in the syrup and place on racks to drain and cool. Serve cold, allowing two pastries per person.

ROLLED PASTRY WITH APPLE FILLING

    2 tart apples, peeled and finely chopped
    3 tablespoons sugar
    1 tablespoon finely chopped walnuts
    1 tablespoon finely chopped blanched almonds
    ¼ teaspoon cinnamon
    1 teaspoon freshly squeezed and strained lemon juice
    About 24 phyllo pastry sheets as needed
    Melted butter, preferably Clarified Butter (page 355)
    1 recipe syrup from Rolled Pastry with Nut Filling (page 317)

In a small bowl combine the apples, sugar, nuts, cinnamon, and lemon juice and mix well. Form the phyllo into Boereg Rolls (page 17) or Boereg Triangles (page 18), using the apple mixture as a filling. After the pastries are baked, dip one at a time in the syrup and place on racks to drain. Serve warm, allowing two pastries per person.

SHREDDED PASTRY WITH WALNUT FILLING

Tel Kadayif or Knafe

This splendid pastry is almost as famous as *baklava* and equally delectable. Like *baklava*, well-made *kadayif* is light and crisp and, despite appearances to the contrary, not difficult to prepare. A company dessert par excellence, it will do honor to any occasion.

FILLING

    1½ cups finely chopped walnuts
    3 tablespoons sugar
    1½ teaspoons cinnamon

1 pound *tel kadayif*, defrosted if frozen
1 cup melted butter

1½ cups sugar
¾ cup water
1 teaspoon freshly squeezed and strained lemon juice
1 tablespoon honey

Heavy Cream Topping (page 294) or 1 cup heavy cream, whipped (optional)
3 cups fresh strawberries, sweetened to taste (optional)

To make the filling, combine the nuts, sugar, and cinnamon in a small bowl and mix well. Set aside.

Loosen and separate the *tel kadayif*, discarding any coarse particles of dough. Sprinkle ¾ cup of the melted butter over the *kadayif* and blend with your hands (or with one hand and a fork in the other) until the shreds are evenly and thoroughly coated with the butter.

Divide the *kadayif* into two equal parts. Arrange one part in a buttered 9-by-13-by-2-inch baking pan. Spread the filling evenly over the *kadayif*. Cover with the remaining *kadayif* and press lightly with your hands to smooth the top. Brush the entire surface with the remaining ¼ cup melted butter. Bake in a preheated 350° oven about 45 minutes or until golden brown and cooked through.

Meanwhile, prepare the syrup: Combine the sugar, water, lemon juice, and honey in a small saucepan. Cook over medium heat until the sugar dissolves, stirring constantly. Bring to a boil, then reduce the heat and simmer, uncovered, about 15 minutes, or until the syrup reaches a temperature of 220° on a candy thermometer. Remove from the heat and keep warm.

When the pastry is done, remove it from the oven and cool 10 minutes. Spoon the syrup evenly over the warm pastry. Cover and let stand 15 minutes. Cut into squares and serve warm or cold, with the cream topping and strawberries.

Serves 12

SHREDDED PASTRY WITH CHEESE FILLING

Banirov Tel Kadayif

Follow the recipe (above) for Shredded Pastry with Walnut Filling, substituting for the nut filling this cheese filling: In a small bowl combine ¾ pound mild Muenster cheese, grated, 1½ cups small-curd cottage cheese, 3 tablespoons sugar, and ½ teaspoon cinnamon and blend well.

After spooning the syrup over the pastry, sprinkle the top evenly with chopped unsalted pistachio nuts. Omit the Heavy Cream Topping and strawberries. Serve the cheese *kadayif* warm.

Serves 12

NOTE: You may use the imitation *kaymak* described in the note on page 295 in place of the cheese filling in this recipe.

BUTTER COOKIES

Kurabia

This is another of the outstanding Armenian pastries which are popular throughout the Middle East. These cookies are simple to prepare, and so light and delicate that they melt in the mouth.

    1 cup melted butter, cooled
    ¼ cup sugar
    ½ teaspoon vanilla or almond extract
    1 teaspoon double-acting baking powder
    2⅓ cups all-purpose flour, sifted (approximately)
    ¼ cup finely chopped walnuts or blanched almonds (optional)
    ¼ cup confectioners' sugar

Place the butter, sugar, vanilla, and baking powder in a large bowl and mix together with a spoon. Gradually beat in the flour, a little at a time, until it is well blended and forms a soft dough. Stir in the nuts.

With lightly floured hands shape the dough into round cookies about 1½ inches in diameter and ½ inch thick. Or form into small crescents, S-shapes, balls, or other shapes. Place the cookies 1 inch apart on an ungreased baking sheet. Bake in a preheated 350° oven about 15 to 20 minutes or until golden and set. Remove from the oven and cool slightly. Sift the confectioners' sugar over the cookies to cover them completely. Allow to cool thoroughly before storing.

Makes about 24

NOTE: Instead of using the nuts, you may gently press a blanched almond or unsalted pistachio nut on each cookie before baking.

VARIATION

Stuffed Butter Cookies

In a small bowl combine 1 cup ground walnuts, 2 tablespoons sugar, ½ teaspoon cinnamon, and 1 egg white, stiffly beaten. Mix well. Stuff each *kurabia* as follows: Take a small portion of the dough and form into a ball about 1 inch in diameter. Indent with your forefinger, pressing gently to make a hollow. Place about 1 teaspoon of the nut mixture in the hollow, bring the edges together, and seal. Gently flatten the ball with the palms of your hands. Or form into small egg shapes and place on a baking sheet. Bake and sugar as above.

WALNUT PASTRY

Unguyzov Khmoreghen

Although this Armenian favorite can be served at dessert, it usually shows up at afternoon tea.

PASTRY

½ cup butter
2¾ cups sifted all-purpose flour
½ teaspoon salt
2 teaspoons double-acting baking powder
½ cup milk
2 eggs, beaten

FILLING

6 tablespoons ground walnuts
¼ cup chopped seedless golden raisins
¾ cup sugar
1 teaspoon cinnamon
⅛ teaspoon nutmeg (optional)

2 tablespoons melted butter
1 egg
1 tablespoon water

Make the pastry: In a large bowl, using a pastry blender or two knives, cut the butter into the flour, salt, and baking powder until the mixture attains the consistency of cornmeal. Make a well in the center and pour in the milk and eggs. With a large spoon stir the center ingredients together, then blend thoroughly with the flour mixture and gather into a ball. Divide the dough into 3 equal pieces and shape each into a ball. Cover with clear plastic film and refrigerate 1 hour.

Meanwhile, combine the filling ingredients in a bowl and mix well. Set aside.

Remove one ball of dough at a time from the refrigerator and roll out on a lightly floured surface into a circle about 10 or 11 inches in diameter. Cut into 8 wedge-shaped pieces. Brush each lightly with the melted butter. Sprinkle generously and evenly with the filling, leaving 1 inch of dough uncovered at the tip. Beginning at the wide end, roll up each wedge toward the point. Curve into a crescent shape and place point side up on an ungreased baking sheet. Repeat the entire procedure with the remaining two balls of dough. Beat the egg with the water and brush the tops of the crescents with the mixture. Bake in a preheated 375° oven 25 minutes or until golden brown.

Makes 24

NOTE: Caucasian Armenians use a filling of ground walnuts or blanched almonds, sugar, cardamom, cinnamon, and honey.

COFFEE COOKIES WITH SESAME SEEDS

Shoushmayov Khmoreghen

These extremely popular cookies are usually prepared in large quantities to be served at informal parties or at teatime.

   1 cup butter
¾ cup sugar
½ cup milk
   1 teaspoon double-acting baking powder
½ teaspoon cinnamon
   3 cups sifted all-purpose flour (approximately)
   1 egg
   1 tablespoon water
Sesame seeds

In a large bowl cream the butter until fluffy, then gradually beat in the sugar. Add the milk, baking powder, and cinnamon and mix well. Stir in the flour, a little at a time, to make a soft dough. Form into small rings, fingers, or other shapes, as desired. To form rings, with lightly floured hands break off small portions of the dough one at a time and roll out into ropes about 5 inches long and ⅜ inch thick. Press the ends of each rope together to form a ring. Or form dough into 2-inch-long finger shapes. Beat the egg and water together. Dip each cookie into the mixture, then roll in the sesame seeds to coat evenly on all sides. Arrange the cookies on two baking sheets. Bake in a pre-heated 350° oven until golden brown, about 20 minutes.

Makes about 3 dozen

Variation: Cream the butter with 1 cup sugar. Add 4 eggs, one at a time, beating well after each addition. Stir in ½ cup freshly squeezed orange juice and ½ teaspoon vanilla. Sift together about 4 cups all-purpose flour and 1½ teaspoons baking soda and gradually stir into the egg mixture. Shape as above or into braids (braid 3 ropes together, pressing the ends firmly to fasten). Arrange on baking sheets, brush with the egg beaten with the water, and bake as above. This will make about 4 dozen cookies.

DATE COOKIES

Armavov Khmoreghen

Rich and cakelike, these irresistible pastries keep well, if you can keep them! They are excellent served with afternoon coffee or tea.

FILLING

> 1 8-ounce package pitted dates, ground
> 1 cup ground walnuts
> 2 tablespoons sugar
> 1 teaspoon cinnamon
> ⅛ teaspoon ground cloves
> ⅛ teaspoon nutmeg

      1 cup melted butter
    ¼ cup sugar
      2 eggs, beaten
    ½ cup milk
    ½ teaspoon vanilla
      3 cups sifted all-purpose flour (approximately)
      2 teaspoons baking powder

      1 egg, beaten

Combine all the filling ingredients and mix well. Roll the mixture 1½ teaspoonfuls at a time into tiny finger shapes. Set aside.

To make the pastry, combine the butter and sugar in a mixing bowl and stir well. Add the eggs, then gradually stir in the milk and vanilla. Sift the flour with the baking powder and beat in a little at a time until well blended and a soft dough is formed. Roll out the dough ⅛ inch thick on a floured surface and cut into circles with a 3-inch cookie cutter.

Place one "finger" of the date filling on each circle near one edge and roll up, forming cylinder-shaped cookies. Press the edges together, smoothing with your fingers. Brush with the beaten egg. Place on a buttered cookie sheet. Bake in a preheated 350° oven about 20 minutes or until golden brown. Remove from the oven and allow to cool thoroughly before storing in a tightly closed container.

Makes about 3 dozen

NUT-FILLED COOKIES

Mamoul

FILLING

      1 cup ground walnuts
      1 tablespoon sugar
      1 teaspoon cinnamon
      1 egg white, stiffly beaten

¼ cup milk
¾ cup sugar
¾ cup melted butter, cooled
1 egg, well beaten
3½ to 3¾ cups sifted all-purpose flour (approximately)
¼ teaspoon baking soda

Confectioners' sugar

Combine all the ingredients for the filling in a small bowl and mix well. Set aside.

Prepare the dough by combining the milk and sugar in a small saucepan. Cook over low heat until sugar is completely dissolved, stirring frequently. Remove from the heat and cool. Place the melted butter and egg in a large bowl and blend together. Add the milk mixture and mix well. Gradually blend in the flour and soda to make a soft dough.

Prepare each cookie as follows: Take a small portion of dough and form into a ball about 1 inch in diameter. Indent with your forefinger, pressing gently to make a hollow. Place about 1 teaspoon of the filling in the hollow, bring the edges together, and seal. Gently flatten the ball with the palms of your hands or form into small egg shape. Place on a baking sheet. Bake the cookies in a preheated 325° oven about 20 minutes or until very lightly browned. Remove from the oven and cool slightly on racks. Sift the confectioners' sugar generously over the tops and cool.

Makes about 4 dozen

COOKIES DIPPED IN SYRUP (LADYFINGERS)

FILLING

1 cup coarsely ground walnuts
2 tablespoons sugar
1 teaspoon cinnamon

    1 cup melted butter, cooled to lukewarm
    ¼ cup freshly squeezed and strained orange juice
    ¼ teaspoon finely grated orange peel
    1 tablespoon brandy
    3 tablespoons sugar
    3 teaspoons double-acting baking powder
    ¼ teaspoon salt
    2½ to 2¾ cups sifted all-purpose flour
    1 small egg
    2 tablespoons water

SYRUP

    1½ cups sugar
    1 cup water
    2 tablespoons honey
    2 teaspoons freshly squeezed and strained lemon juice
    ½ orange slice, including the rind

GARNISH

Finely chopped walnuts or unsalted pistachio nuts
Flaked coconut

To make the filling, combine the nuts, sugar, and cinnamon in a small bowl and mix well. Set aside.

Make the pastry: In a large bowl combine the melted butter, orange juice, orange peel, brandy, sugar, baking powder, and salt and mix well. Gradually add the flour, stirring after each addition, until a soft dough is formed.

Prepare each cookie as follows: Take a walnut-size piece of dough and form into a ball. Indent with your forefinger, pressing gently to make a hollow. Place 1 to 1½ teaspoons of the filling in the hollow, bring the edges together, and seal. Gently roll between the palms of your hands into an oval shape. Place the cookies 1 inch apart on an ungreased baking sheet. Beat together the egg and water. Brush the tops of the cookies with this mixture. Bake in a preheated 350° oven about 25 minutes or until golden brown.

While the cookies bake, prepare the syrup: Combine the sugar, water, honey, lemon juice, and orange slice in a small saucepan. Bring to a boil over high heat, stirring constantly until the sugar dissolves. Reduce the heat and simmer 5 minutes. Remove from the heat and keep warm.

When the cookies are baked, remove them from the oven and cool. Dip, a few at a time, in the syrup placed over very low heat. Allow the cookies to remain in the syrup about 1 minute, then remove and place on racks to drain. Sprinkle at once with the garnish of chopped nuts and coconut. Cool thoroughly before storing.

Makes about 30

DEEP-FRIED FRITTERS WITH SYRUP

Lokma

FRITTERS

> 1 package active dry yeast
> ⅛ teaspoon sugar
> 1¼ cups plus 2 tablespoons warm water (110 to 115°)
> ½ cup warm milk (110 to 115°)
> ½ teaspoon salt
> 1 egg, beaten
> 3 cups all-purpose flour

SYRUP

> 1 cup sugar
> ¼ cup honey
> ½ cup water
> 1 teaspoon freshly squeezed and strained lemon juice
> 1 stick cinnamon, 2 inches long

Vegetable oil for deep frying

GARNISH

> 1 teaspoon cinnamon
> ½ cup finely chopped walnuts or unsalted pistachio nuts
> 1 cup heavy cream, whipped (optional)

To make the fritters, dissolve the yeast and sugar in ¼ cup of the water. Combine the remaining water, milk, yeast mixture, salt, and beaten egg in a large bowl and stir together. Gradually add the flour and beat thoroughly until a smooth and thick but not stiff batter is formed. Cover with a kitchen towel and allow to rise in a warm place (85°) free from drafts (such as an unlit oven with a pan of hot water on the bottom rack) about 45 minutes or until doubled.

Meanwhile, prepare the syrup: Place the sugar, honey, water, lemon juice, and cinnamon stick in a small saucepan. Cook over moderate heat until the sugar dissolves, stirring constantly. Bring to a boil and cook, uncovered, about 10 minutes, or until the syrup reaches a temperature of 220° on a candy thermometer. Remove from the heat and cool.

In a deep-fryer or heavy saucepan heat 4 inches of the oil to a temperature of 375°. Drop 1 tablespoon of the batter at a time into the hot oil, being careful not to crowd the pan. Fry the fritters about 2 minutes or until golden brown on all sides. Remove from the oil with a perforated spoon and drain on absorbent paper.

Dip the fritters in the syrup and heap on a serving platter. Sprinkle with the cinnamon and nuts and garnish with the whipped cream. Pour the remaining syrup into a pitcher and serve on the side.

Serves 8

FARINA CAKE WITH SYRUP

BATTER

> 6 eggs, separated
> ¾ cup sugar
> ¾ cup regular-grain farina
> ½ cup finely chopped blanched almonds
> 1½ teaspoons double-acting baking powder
> 1½ tablespoons brandy
> Pinch salt

    1 cup sugar

1¼ cups water

    2 teaspoons freshly squeezed and strained lemon juice

    1 stick cinnamon, 2 inches long

    1 cup heavy cream, whipped

    3 cups strawberries

To make the batter, place the egg yolks and sugar in a mixing bowl and beat until light. Combine the farina, nuts, and baking powder and gradually stir into the mixture. Add the brandy and blend well. Beat the egg whites with the salt until very stiff and fold into the egg yolk mixture. Turn into a greased 9-by-9-by-2-inch pan. Bake in a preheated 350° oven about 30 minutes or until a cake tester comes out clean.

Meanwhile, prepare the syrup: Combine the sugar, water, lemon juice, and cinnamon stick in a small saucepan. Bring to a boil, stirring constantly to dissolve the sugar. Reduce the heat and simmer 15 minutes. Remove from the heat and cool to lukewarm.

When the cake is done, remove from the oven. Spoon the syrup evenly over it, using only as much as the cake will absorb readily without becoming soggy. Cool to room temperature, then cover and refrigerate several hours or overnight. Just before serving, cut into diamonds or squares and serve with the whipped cream and strawberries.

Serves 12

YOGURT CAKE

Madzoonov Gargantag

½ cup butter
2 cups sugar
1 cup unflavored yogurt
3 eggs, beaten
1 tablespoon freshly squeezed and strained lemon juice
1 teaspoon grated lemon rind
2½ cups all-purpose flour, sifted
½ teaspoon baking soda
Confectioners' sugar

In a large mixing bowl cream the butter and sugar until smooth. Add the yogurt and mix well. Beat in the eggs, lemon juice, and lemon rind. Gradually add the flour and baking soda, a little at a time, and blend well. Pour the mixture into a greased and floured 9-by-9-by-2-inch cake pan. Bake in a preheated 350° oven 45 minutes or until a cake tester comes out clean. Remove from the oven and cool. Just before serving, sift the confectioners' sugar evenly over the cake.

Serves 12

NOTE: Instead of using the confectioners' sugar, you may serve the cake with sweetened strawberries and whipped cream.

RICE FLOUR DESSERT

Muhallebi

An exquisite and delicate dessert fragrant with the incomparable scent of cinnamon. The date garnish is my idea and may be omitted.

½ cup rice flour or cornstarch
4 cups cold milk
½ cup sugar
1 teaspoon vanilla
1 teaspoon cinnamon
2 tablespoons finely chopped dates
2 tablespoons unsalted pistachio nuts, finely chopped

Dissolve the rice flour in 1 cup of the milk. Place the remaining 3 cups milk and the sugar in a heavy saucepan. Bring to a boil over high heat, stirring constantly until the sugar is completely dissolved. Lower the heat and add the rice flour mixture. Simmer until the mixture thickens, about 10 minutes, stirring continuously. Stir in the vanilla. Spoon the custard into heatproof individual dessert bowls. Sprinkle the tops evenly with the cinnamon and garnish with the chopped dates and pistachios. Cool to room temperature, cover with clear plastic film, and refrigerate several hours or overnight until thoroughly chilled. Serve with coconut or vanilla cookies if desired.

Serves 6

ARMENIAN RICE PUDDING

Gatnabour

The addition of orange flower water or rose water transforms a simple pudding into a memorable delicacy.

  1 cup water
Pinch salt
⅔ cup uncooked long-grain white rice, washed and drained
  4 cups milk
½ cup sugar
  1 teaspoon orange flower water or rose water
  1 teaspoon cinnamon
Toasted blanched almonds (page 342) or shelled unsalted pistachio nuts

In a heavy saucepan bring the water and salt to a boil over high heat, stirring constantly to dissolve the salt. Add the rice and reduce the heat to low. Cover and simmer about 5 minutes or until all of the water is absorbed. Add the milk and bring to a boil. Cover and simmer 35 to 40 minutes, stirring frequently. Add the sugar and cook 10 minutes, stirring often. Remove from the heat and add the orange flower water. Spoon the pudding into individual heatproof dessert bowls. Sprinkle the tops with the cinnamon and decorate with the almonds. Cool to room temperature, cover with clear plastic film, and refrigerate several hours or overnight until thoroughly chilled.

Serves 6

ARMENIAN CHRISTMAS PUDDING

Anoush Gorgodabour

This traditional pudding has been made for centuries.

½ cup skinless whole-grain wheat, washed and drained
6 cups water (approximately)
¾ cup dried apricots, halved
¾ cup seedless golden raisins
1 cup sugar
1 teaspoon vanilla
¼ cup walnuts, coarsely chopped
¼ cup whole blanched almonds

Combine the wheat and water in a heavy saucepan and bring to a boil over high heat. Remove from the heat and set aside to soak overnight.

The next day cook the mixture over low heat 1½ hours. Add the apricots, raisins, sugar, and a little more water if necessary and stir to dissolve the sugar. Simmer 30 minutes, stirring occasionally. Remove from the heat and stir in the vanilla. Ladle the pudding into a large heatproof serving bowl or individual heatproof dessert bowls. Garnish with the nuts. Refrigerate several hours or overnight until thoroughly chilled.

Serves 8

NOTE: If desired, you may toast the walnuts and almonds in a 300° oven, turning frequently, until golden brown, about 15 minutes. Watch closely so they will not burn. This pudding is sometimes flavored with cinnamon. Other good flavorings are almond extract and apricot liqueur.

PUMPKIN DESSERT

Titoum Anoush

An unusual dessert with exquisite color, smooth texture, and delicate flavor.

    1 4-pound pumpkin
    2 cups sugar
    ½ cup water
    ¾ cup finely chopped toasted almonds or walnuts (page 342)
    Cinnamon
    ½ cup heavy cream, whipped (optional)

Peel the pumpkin, remove the seeds, and cut into 1-inch-thick slices. Place in a heavy saucepan in layers, sprinkling each layer with the sugar. Pour in the water. Cover and cook over moderate heat until all the water has been absorbed and the pumpkin is tender, stirring occasionally. Remove from the heat, mash the pumpkin, and transfer it to a serving dish. This may now be served hot, as a vegetable, or cold, as a dessert.

To serve hot, cover the top with the chopped nuts, sprinkle with the cinnamon, and serve at once as an accompaniment to roast turkey, chicken, or ham.

To serve cold, cool to room temperature, cover with clear plastic film, and refrigerate until thoroughly chilled. Just before serving, cover with the nuts, sprinkle with the cinnamon, and garnish with the whipped cream.

Serves 4

NOTE: You may also sprinkle the top with shredded coconut if desired.

338

FLOUR HELVA

Aliurov Helva or Oun Helva

1 cup sugar
½ cup water
1½ tablespoons honey
¼ teaspoon freshly squeezed and strained lemon juice
⅛ teaspoon rose water or vanilla
½ cup butter, preferably Clarified Butter (page 355)
2½ cups sifted all-purpose flour
Toasted almond or walnut halves (page 342)

In a small saucepan combine the sugar, water, honey, and lemon juice. Bring to a boil, stirring constantly to dissolve the sugar. Add the rose water. Remove from the heat and cool to lukewarm.

In a heavy skillet melt the butter. Add the flour and cook over low heat about 20 minutes or until very lightly browned, stirring constantly. Remove from the heat and stir in the syrup until thoroughly blended. Pour onto a serving plate and press into a thick rectangle. Cut into 1½-inch squares and top each with a toasted nut half.

Serves 4

VARIATION

Flour Helva with Cream

Khavitz

Dissolve 1 cup sugar in 1 cup heavy cream. Melt ½ cup butter, add 2 cups flour, and cook as above until the mixture is lightly browned. Add the cream mixture and cook over very low heat until thoroughly blended, stirring constantly. Serve as above.

FARINA HELVA

Imrig Helva

1 cup sugar
1 cup water
1 cup milk
½ cup butter
1 cup regular-grain farina
¼ cup pine nuts or slivered blanched almonds
1 teaspoon cinnamon
½ cup heavy cream, whipped (optional)

Combine the sugar, water, and milk in a heavy saucepan. Bring to a boil, stirring constantly until the sugar is completely dissolved. Lower the heat and simmer 10 minutes. Remove from the heat and set aside.

In a heavy skillet melt the butter over low heat. Add the farina and nuts and sauté 10 minutes or until the mixture is lightly browned, stirring continuously. Gradually stir the milk syrup into the farina mixture and mix well. Cover and simmer over very low heat until all the syrup is absorbed and the mixture is thickened. Remove from the heat, place a kitchen towel over the skillet to absorb the steam, and replace the lid. Leave in a warm place, covered, 30 minutes.

To serve, stir the *helva* well and pour onto a serving platter. Smooth the top and sprinkle with the cinnamon. Serve warm, with the whipped cream.

Serves 8

VARIATION

Cheese Helva

Five minutes before the *helva* is cooked, add 1 cup shredded domestic Muenster, Monterey Jack, or other mild cheese. Cook until cheese is melted, stirring frequently. Serve at once, omitting the whipped cream.

340

POACHED STUFFED APPLES IN HONEY

This is a rich and delicately spiced dessert, a perfect ending to a light meal.

FILLING

¼ cup chopped walnuts
2 tablespoons chopped seedless golden raisins
¼ teaspoon cinnamon
⅛ teaspoon nutmeg
1 teaspoon sugar

4 medium firm cooking apples, peeled and cored

SYRUP

½ cup sugar
½ cup honey
1 cup water
1 teaspoon freshly squeezed and strained lemon juice
1 small stick cinnamon

Whipped cream

Combine the filling ingredients in a small bowl and mix well. Fill the cavities of the apples with the mixture and set aside.

In a heavy saucepan bring the syrup ingredients to a boil over high heat, stirring constantly to dissolve the sugar. Arrange the apples side by side in the saucepan and baste with the syrup. Lower the heat and cover. Simmer about 15 minutes or until the apples are tender, basting occasionally with the syrup. Serve warm or chilled, with the whipped cream.

Serves 4

APRICOT AND ALMOND DELICACY

Noushov Dziran

The apricot (*Prunus armeniaca*) is native to Armenia; it was brought from there into Italy by the Romans. Armenians treasure it and use it generously throughout their cuisine.

As many blanched almonds as dried apricot halves
1 pound best-quality dried apricots
1¾ to 2 cups sugar
1 cup heavy cream, whipped

Place the almonds in a baking pan. Toast in a preheated 300° oven until golden brown, turning frequently. Watch closely; do not let them burn. Remove to a plate and set aside.

In a saucepan combine the apricots with just enough water to cover and cook over moderate heat 3 minutes. With a perforated spoon, remove the fruit from the liquid onto a plate and set aside.

Add the sugar to the liquid in the saucepan and stir until completely dissolved. Cook over moderate heat until a heavy syrup is obtained. Return the apricots to the syrup and simmer 5 minutes. Remove from the syrup and arrange cut sides up on a serving platter. Press a toasted almond in the center of each apricot and spoon the syrup evenly over all. Cool to room temperature, then cover with clear plastic film and refrigerate until thoroughly chilled. Serve with the whipped cream, allowing 4 or 5 apricots per person.

✿ APRICOTS IN WHIPPED CREAM

This lavish temptation can provide a brilliant finale to a superb meal.

¾ cup sugar
1¼ cups water
1½ cups dried apricots
3 tablespoons apricot liqueur or to taste
1 cup heavy cream
½ teaspoon vanilla
2 tablespoons sifted confectioners' sugar
½ cup toasted blanched almonds, chopped (to toast, see page 342)

In a heavy saucepan combine the sugar and water. Bring to a boil over high heat, stirring constantly to dissolve the sugar. Add the apricots and return to a boil. Cover, reduce the heat to low, and simmer 15 minutes or until tender but not mushy. Remove from the heat and stir in the apricot liqueur. Cool to room temperature, then transfer to a deep dish. Refrigerate, covered, until thoroughly chilled.

Just before serving, whip the cream with the vanilla and confectioners' sugar. Dice the apricots. Reserve 2 tablespoons for a garnish; mix the rest with the whipped cream and half the nuts. Transfer to a glass compote or individual compotes. Decorate with the reserved apricots and nuts. Serve cold, with vanilla wafers.

Serves 6

CHILLED FRUIT SOUP

Anoushabour

¾ pound mixed dried fruits
1 stick cinnamon, 1 inch long
5½ cups water
½ to ¾ cup sugar
1 tablespoon freshly squeezed and strained lemon juice
Whipped cream
Toasted sliced almonds (page 342)

In a heavy saucepan combine the dried fruits, cinnamon stick, and water. Bring to a boil over high heat. Reduce the heat to low and simmer about 25 minutes or until the fruit is very tender. Remove the fruit, purée, and set aside. Add the sugar to the liquid in the saucepan. Bring to a boil, stirring constantly to dissolve the sugar. Add the lemon juice and remove from the heat. Mix with the puréed fruit. Cool to lukewarm, then pour into individual dessert dishes. Cover with clear plastic film and refrigerate until thoroughly chilled. Serve topped with the whipped cream and garnished with the nuts.

Serves 6

DRIED FRUIT COMPOTE

Mirkatan or Khoshab

The hauntingly delicate taste and fragrance of this ancient dessert evoke the nostalgic memory of summer on a cold winter night.

5 cups water
¾ cup sugar

344

½ cup dried pitted prunes
½ cup dried peaches or pears
½ cup dried apricots
¼ cup seedless golden raisins
1 stick cinnamon, 2 inches long
2 tablespoons pine nuts

In a heavy saucepan boil the water and sugar 10 minutes, stirring to dissolve the sugar. Add the prunes and boil 5 minutes. Add the peaches, apricots, raisins, and cinnamon stick. Lower the heat and simmer about 15 minutes or until the fruits are tender. Remove from the heat and stir in the pine nuts. Cool to room temperature. Transfer to a deep serving bowl, cover, and refrigerate until thoroughly chilled.

Serves 4 or 5

NOTE: Dried cherries, not available commercially in America, are a delicious addition to this compote. (They are also good eaten by themselves.)

VARIATION

Apricot Soup

Armenians also make a soup with whole dried apricots. To prepare, cover 2 cups dried apricots with 4 cups hot water and cook 15 minutes. Stir in 1 cup sugar until dissolved and simmer 5 minutes. Serve warm or chilled. This will serve 4.

16. Candies and Preserves

Pedestal dish: Strawberry Preserves (page 354); table: soudjuk (page 350); plate: candied nuts (page 353)

Some of the recipes in this chapter have been specialties of Armenian cuisine for centuries. Preserved grapevine leaves in brine, home-cured olives, clarified butter, and other staples that were formerly made at home can now be bought in prepackaged form in this country, in the Middle East, and in the Caucasus.

Factories in Soviet Armenia manufacture many different kinds of preserved foods, a large number of which are made from fruits. They include appetizers, compotes, jams, juices, marinades, and purees. Some of the more unusual jams are cornelian cherry, white cherry, eggplant, mulberry, melon, yellow plum, pumpkin, quince, rose petal, tomato, and walnut. In spite of the wide and excellent selection, some Armenians still prefer to make their own preserves.

My memories of childhood summers at our country house include a seemingly unending preparation of food, not only for daily needs but also for the entire year ahead. An especially busy time occurred at the end of summer, when we would make trips every day at dawn and at sunset to our vineyard in order to gather large basketfuls of grapes for use in the preparation of two Armenian confections, *bastegh* and *soudjuk* (also called *sharots* or *chuchkhella*).

To make *bastegh* the grapes were pressed and the juice boiled with sugar and thickened with flour. This was poured over heavy muslin sheets to an even ⅛-inch thickness and left to dry overnight. The following day the fruit-paste-covered sheets were hung outdoors to finish drying. When the fruit paste was completely dry, the reverse sides of the sheets were sprayed with water. The *bastegh* was then peeled off, cut into the desired shapes, and kept in covered jars. *Bastegh* was served with walnuts on the side, or it was stuffed with a filling of nuts, sugar, and cinnamon and rolled into triangles.

349

Soudjuk was made by stringing walnut halves on heavy thread and dipping them into grape juice thickened as for *bastegh* several times until the nuts were evenly covered with ⅛ inch of the paste. They were then hung to dry thoroughly for several days. Then the thread was pulled out and the *soudjuk* cut into the desired lengths, rolled in powdered sugar, and stored in covered jars. *Bastegh* and *soudjuk* can also be made from the juice of other fruits besides grapes, such as apples, apricots, cherries, peaches, plums, quinces, raspberries, and strawberries.

Very popular with Armenians and other Middle Eastern peoples is *lokhoum* ("peace candy"), better known as Turkish delight, which is offered with Armenian coffee to visitors. It is available at Middle Eastern groceries.

For an after-dinner treat Candied Almonds or Walnuts or Almond, Fig, and Date Confection may be enjoyed with a glass of brandy or port.

ALMOND, FIG, AND DATE CONFECTION

1 cup toasted blanched almonds (see page 342)
1 cup dried figs
1 cup pitted dates
¼ cup sugar
½ teaspoon cinnamon

Put the nuts and fruits through the coarsest blade of a meat grinder. Combine the sugar and cinnamon. Form the mixture into small balls and roll in the sugar-cinnamon mixture. Store in a tightly covered container. These are good with brandy or port.

Makes about 2 dozen

Variation: Grind ½ cup toasted blanched almonds or hazelnuts and 1 cup each dried apricots and pitted dates as above, form into small balls, and roll in confectioners' sugar. This makes about 16 balls.

QUINCE PASTE

Sergevil Bastegh

2 pounds fresh quinces, peeled
Sugar

In a saucepan combine the quinces with just enough water to cover and bring to a boil over moderate heat. Cook about 30 minutes or until soft. Remove the cores, mash, and purée.

Weigh the puree. Combine with an equal weight of the sugar in a heavy saucepan. Cook, stirring, over moderate heat about 20 to 30 minutes or until the mixture is reduced to a thick, stiff consistency and

351

it comes away from the bottom and sides of the pan. Watch the heat, regulating to prevent scorching. Spread the mixture ½ to 1 inch thick on a wet shallow pan and leave to set overnight. Cut into squares, dip in additional sugar, and dry on racks. When thoroughly dry, wrap in waxed paper and store in a cool, dry place.

Apricot Paste

Dziran Bastegh

Substitute 1 pound dried apricots for the quinces. Cook as above until very soft. Purée and return to the saucepan. Add 2¼ cups sugar. Cook until the mixture is reduced to a thick, stiff consistency, stirring frequently. After spreading the mixture, sprinkle with finely chopped unsalted pistachio nuts or toasted almonds if desired. Continue as above.

STRAWBERRY FRUIT ROLL

Yelag Bastegh

Commercial varieties of this age-old confection are becoming increasing popular in the United States, so much so that even some supermarkets are now featuring them. *Bastegh* should be made in dry, sunny weather, preferably in the morning.

Line a shallow roasting pan with clear plastic film and fasten with tape. Bring 2 cups hulled washed ripe strawberries and 3 tablespoons sugar to a full rolling boil, stirring to dissolve the sugar. Remove from the heat and put through a food mill or wire strainer to remove the seeds. Cool to lukewarm, then pour into the film-lined pan, spreading it about $\frac{1}{16}$ inch thick. Cover the pan tightly with cheesecloth to keep the fruit clean while drying and fasten with tape to prevent the cloth from touching the puree. Place outdoors in full sun a whole day, bringing it indoors in the evening. Return to the sun the next morning and leave until firm to the touch. Do not leave in the sun longer than necessary.

The fruit should be dry enough that it can be peeled off the plastic in one piece but not so dry that it cracks. The amount of time needed for drying depends on the type of fruit used and the sun's heat. To store, roll up the sheet, plastic and all. Cover with additional plastic and seal.

Makes 1

Variation: Other ripe fruit, including raspberries, apricots, Mariposa or Nubiana plums, nectarines, peeled peaches, or a combination of bananas and apricots (for each peeled banana use 2 sliced pitted apricots) may be used. For raspberries, combine 2 cups fruit with ¼ cup sugar and boil until the liquid seems syrupy, stirring; proceed as above. For other fruits, remove the pits and slice. Combine 2 cups fruit with ¼ cup sugar. Boil until the liquid seems syrupy, crushing the fruit and stirring. Whirl in an electric blender or put through a food mill, then proceed as above.

CANDIED ALMONDS OR WALNUTS

Gozinakh

½ cup honey
½ cup sugar
1¼ cups chopped blanched almonds or walnuts
Pinch cinnamon

In a heavy saucepan combine the honey and sugar and bring to a boil, stirring constantly to dissolve the sugar. Cook without stirring until the syrup reaches 220° on a candy thermometer. Lower the heat. Add the nuts and cinnamon and cook 10 to 15 minutes or until the nuts turn golden brown, stirring frequently. Remove from the heat and pour into a wet shallow pan. Cool. When firm, place the pan briefly over low heat and loosen the edges of the candy with a knife. Cut into squares or diamonds.

Makes about ¾ pound

STRAWBERRY PRESERVES

Yelag Anoush

2 pounds ripe perfect strawberries
Cognac
2 pounds sugar
¼ cup freshly squeezed and strained lemon juice

Hull, wash, and dry the strawberries. Dip each in the Cognac and place in layers in a glass container, crushing some of the berries to release the juices and sprinkling each layer with the sugar. Cover and refrigerate 8 hours.

Pour the strawberry juice that has formed into a heavy stainless steel or enameled saucepan. Cook over high heat about 5 minutes. Add the strawberries and boil slowly 6 to 8 minutes or until thickened, stirring occasionally and skimming off foam as it rises to the surface. Add the lemon juice 1 minute before the end of cooking. Ladle into 4 sterilized ½-pint jars, filling to the top. Seal at once.

Makes 2 pints

QUINCE CONFITURE

Sergevil Anoush

2 medium quinces
3 cups sugar
1 cup water
1 stick cinnamon, 2 inches long
1 teaspoon freshly squeezed and strained lemon juice

Remove the core and seeds from the quinces, peel, and cut into thin slices. In a heavy saucepan combine the sugar and water. Bring to a boil, stirring constantly to dissolve the sugar. Boil until the mixture

354

attains a medium-thick syrupy consistency. Add the quinces and cinnamon stick. Reduce the heat to low and simmer until the fruit is tender and the liquid is thickened. Stir in the lemon juice and cook 1 or 2 minutes longer. Remove from the heat and cool. Pour into 3 sterilized ½-pint jars and seal.

Makes 1½ pints

PRESERVED GRAPEVINE LEAVES

Choose leaves that are young, tender, and as uniform in size as possible. Wash thoroughly, remove the stems, and arrange dull sides up in piles of 15. Beginning with the stem ends, roll up each pile like a jelly roll and tie with string.

In a saucepan combine 2 quarts water and ½ cup salt. Bring to a boil. Drop the bundles of leaves, a few at a time, into the boiling brine. Cook for a minute or so—just until the leaves change color. Remove the rolls one at a time. Cool slightly, then pack tightly into sterilized pint jars. Return the brine in the saucepan to a boil. Cover the leaves with the boiling brine and seal immediately.

CLARIFIED BUTTER

Armenians use clarified butter extensively, particularly for frying and for making pastries. It is superior to ordinary butter in that it does not burn at high temperatures.

Place 2 pounds butter in a heavy saucepan. Melt over low heat, being careful not to let it brown. Skim off the foam with a spoon as it rises to the surface. Remove from the heat and let rest several minutes, then skim off any foam that still appears on the surface. Carefully spoon the clear butter into a container, discarding the milky residue in the bottom of the pan. Cover and refrigerate.

Makes about 1½ pounds

NOTE: A type of clarified butter, known as *ghee*, may be purchased in specialty shops.

17. Beverages

Armenian Coffee (page 361) and tea (pages 362–363) with Turkish delight

A pitcher of cold water is a must at every Armenian meal, no matter what other beverages are served. Armenians are very sensitive about their drinking water. As children, during the summer holidays we would make daily excursions, carrying our water jugs to a particular spring that was close to half an hour's walk away. There were several other springs much closer to home, and the temptation to shorten our long trip was a great one, but we knew that our secret would easily be revealed with the first sip of water taken by the older members of the family. It was not long before we too became aware of different tastes in water, and an appreciation of good water has stayed with me ever since.

Armenians are also very particular about the wine they drink. The art of wine-making has been known in Armenia since earliest recorded history, and many ornaments with grape designs have been found at the site of excavations. Vineyards flourish today on the plain of Ararat, below the celebrated glacier-crowned mountain of ancient Armenia, which lies mostly in what is now Turkey, close to the border of Soviet Armenia, and which can be seen from the Armenian capital of Yerevan.

Red, white, and rosé wines, champagne, brandy, and vodka are produced in Soviet Armenia. Forty different kinds of wines and ten brandies are bottled. Armenian madeira and sherry are famous for their flavor and color, and Armenian malaga and muscat rank along with those of the Crimea as the most outstanding in all the Soviet Union, winning many gold medals. The average brandy is fourteen years old, although some brandy is kept forty or fifty years before it is ready to drink! Armenian brandy is considered among the finest in the world.

With such a long tradition of viticulture, it is not surprising, however, that in spite of the high standard of Soviet Armenian wines and brandies, many Armenians make their own wine and brandy at home. This is also true of Armenians living in other lands.

With *meza,* or appetizers, Armenians serve *oghi* (Turkish *raki,* Arabic *arak*), a strong, very dry spirit distilled from grapes, which becomes a cloudy white with the addition of water. Beer also goes well with Armenian food and may be served with *meza.*

In summer Armenians drink lemonade and *tahn,* which is yogurt diluted with cold water and salted to taste. Refreshing beverages made with strawberries, grapes, cherries, apricots, and other fruits are also popular.

An Armenian meal always ends with Armenian coffee or tea, both of which are also served in the afternoon with cakes, pastry, or some kind of sweet.

ARMENIAN COFFEE

Soorj

Coffee originated in Ethiopia. Introduced into Arabia, it soon became one of the most important necessities of life in the Middle East. It was brought to Europe during the first half of the seventeenth century but did not become popular until 1669, when the Turkish ambassador to France created a sensation in high society by offering it to all his guests. Three years later an Armenian named Pascal capitalized on the vogue by opening a coffee shop at the Saint-Germain Fair with outstanding success. It was not long before coffee, despite its high price, was in great demand throughout Europe. Many cafés sprang up in the cities, there being some six hundred in Paris alone by the end of the eighteenth century.

Soorj, coffee, is the most popular Armenian hot beverage, served after dinner and offered on social and business occasions. Variations of this pulverized coffee are enjoyed throughout the Middle East under the names of Arabic, Greek, Turkish, or Armenian coffee. In this country it can be purchased (often under the names of Greek or Turkish coffee) from the Middle Eastern food stores in the Shoppers' Guide (pages 385–95).

Armenian coffee is made and served from a narrow-necked, long-handled brass or enamel pot called a *soorjaman* (Turkish *jezve*), also available from stores specializing in Middle Eastern foods. The *soorjaman* comes in several sizes, the largest holding only about six servings, since this kind of coffee is at its best when made in small quantities.

Armenian coffee is always made to order. For maximum flavor and aroma many people roast and pulverize the beans in a coffee mill (*soorjaghatz*) just before brewing. It can be made with or without sugar, which is stirred into it while it is being heated. Since this coffee is strong, it is traditionally served in small demitasse cups. It is sipped slowly while still very hot but after a suitable pause of a minute or two, which gives the grounds a chance to settle to the bottom of the cup.

Often after the last sip the cups are turned upside down and left on their saucers so that the black sediment can run down the sides of the cups, forming various patterns that are "read" to reveal one's future. If one's cup sticks to the saucer, it is believed that his wish will be fulfilled, making it unnecessary to read his cup. Those whose cups do not stick have to endure the bad predictions along with the good!

1 demitasse cup fresh cold water
1 teaspoon sugar
1 heaping teaspoon pulverized coffee

Combine the water and sugar in a small *soorjaman* and bring to a boil, stirring constantly, until the sugar is dissolved.

Add the coffee, stir well, and bring slowly to a boil. As soon as coffee reaches the rim of the *soorjaman*, remove from the heat immediately to avoid overflowing. Carefully skim off the foam that has formed on top and spoon into a demitasse cup. Return the *soorjaman* to the heat and allow the coffee to boil to the rim one or two more times. Remove from the heat and gently pour into the cup, being careful not to disturb the foam, which will rise to the top as you pour the coffee. Do not stir.

Makes 1 medium-strength demitasse cup

NOTE: The measurements given above may be increased, according to the number of cups you wish to make. More or less sugar may be used, according to taste. A little more coffee may be used if a stronger brew is desired.

CINNAMON CLOVE TEA

Haigagan Tey

4 cups fresh cold water
1 stick cinnamon, 1 inch long
2 whole cloves

1 tablespoon tea leaves or 2 tea bags
Sugar to taste
Coarsely chopped almonds or walnuts (optional)

In a flameproof glass or enameled teapot combine the water, cinnamon, and cloves. Bring to a rolling boil over high heat, then lower the heat and simmer 5 minutes. Turn off the heat, add the tea leaves or bags, and steep 3 minutes. If using tea leaves, stir and then strain the tea; if using tea bags, remove. Serve at once, with the sugar. Garnish each serving with the almonds.

Makes 4 cups

MINT TEA

Ananoukhov Tey

Mint tea is considered to be good for upset stomachs or colds.

1 tablespoon crushed dried mint leaves
2 cups boiling water
2 cups freshly made hot tea
Sugar to taste
Lemon slices (optional)

Add the mint to the boiling water and steep 5 minutes. Strain and mix with the hot tea. Serve at once, with the sugar and lemon slices.

Makes 4 cups

CHILLED YOGURT DRINK

Tahn or Ayran

An Armenian version of buttermilk, *tahn* is the most popular beverage for serving with meals. It is especially refreshing in hot weather, when one can consume many glassfuls throughout the day. An Armenian will offer his guest a tall glass of ice-cold *tahn* just as one would offer a soft drink here.

1 cup unflavored yogurt
½ to 1½ cups ice-cold water
Salt to taste
Ice cubes

Place the yogurt in a deep bowl and stir until smooth. Gradually beat in the water until well blended. (The amount of water depends on whether thin or thick *tahn* is desired.) Add salt and mix well. Serve well chilled, over ice cubes.

Serves 2

NOTE: You may combine the yogurt, water, and salt in the container of an electric blender, cover, and blend until well mixed and smooth.

❀ STRAWBERRY LEMONADE

Yelagov Limonachour

½ cup water
½ cup sugar

½ cup plus 1 tablespoon freshly squeezed and strained
   lemon juice
1¾ cups cold water
½ cup crushed strawberries
Crushed ice

In a small saucepan combine the water and sugar. Bring to a boil
over high heat, stirring to dissolve the sugar. Lower the heat and cook
5 minutes. Remove from the heat and cool. Combine with the lemon
juice and water. Put 2 tablespoons of the crushed berries into the
bottom of each of 4 glasses. Fill with the crushed ice and lemonade.

Serves 4

ARMENIAN CHERRY BRANDY

Haigagan Gerasoghi

Sour cherries
Sugar
Brandy
Whole cloves
Cinnamon sticks
Whole nutmegs

Wash, stem, and pit the sour cherries. Place equal amounts of the
cherries and sugar in alternate layers in a heavy enamel saucepan, ending with a layer of sugar on top. Let stand 12 hours or overnight. The
following day bring the mixture slowly to a boil, stirring constantly
until the sugar is dissolved. Drain off the cherry juice and measure.
(Reserve the cherries.) To each cup of cherry juice add ½ cup brandy.
To 8 cups of the cherry-brandy mixture add 1½ teaspoons whole
cloves, 1 small cinnamon stick, 1 whole nutmeg, and ½ cup of the
cherries. Pour into sterilized bottles and seal. Store in a cool place. The
brandy will be ready in one month. Serve chilled.

Menus

Grapes or Melon
Coffee Rolls (page 306) or Coffee Cake with Sesame Seed Paste (page 308)
Apricot, Strawberry, and Raspberry Jam
Butter
Coffee or Tea

Fresh Sweetened Pomegranate Juice
Fruit Paste Dipped in Egg (page 75)
Armenian Pancakes (page 307)
Sautéed Bacon
Coffee or Tea

Fresh Orange and Grapefruit Sections
Sausage with Eggs (page 74)
Cheese and Olives
Armenian Thin Bread (page 301), Sesame Rolls (page 304), or Breakfast Rolls (page 305)
Coffee or Tea

LUNCHEON

Chicken Soup with Egg and Lemon Sauce (page 30)
Artichokes Stuffed with Meat (page 196)
Plain Saffron Rice Pilaf (page 222)
Tomato and Onion Salad (page 51)
Lemon Sherbet with Raspberries
Nut-Filled Cookies (page 328)
Coffee or Tea

Chilled Tomato Juice or Mixed Pickles (page 8)
Curried Broiled Chicken (105)
Plain Cracked Wheat Pilaf (page 231)
Cucumber and Tomato Salad (page 50)
Beer or Iced Tea
Chilled Fruit Soup (page 344)
Coffee

Clear Chicken Broth
Armenian Broiled Fish (page 93) with Lemon Sauce (page 288)
Fried Eggplant (page 260) or Fried Zucchini (page 268)
Spinach Salad made with Lemon Juice (page 48)
Chilled Light Dry White Wine
Poached Stuffed Apples in Honey (page 341)
Coffee or Tea

Jerusalem Artichokes (page 255)
Meatballs Smyrna (page 163)
Spaghetti with Grated Cheese
Endive or Escarole Salad
Light Red Wine
Melon or Grapes with Cheese
Coffee or Tea

Lamb and Mixed Vegetable Casserole (page 144)
Plain Rice Pilaf (page 219)
Romaine Salad (page 47)
Chilled Yogurt Drink (page 364) or Iced Tea
Rice Flour Dessert (page 335)
Coconut or Vanilla Cookies
Coffee

Hard-Cooked Egg and Tomato Slices, Dressed with Carp Roe Dip
    (page 6)
Lamb and Rice Pilaf (page 229)
Belgian Endive or Bibb Lettuce Salad
Chilled Rosé
Dried Fruit Compote (page 344)
Coffee or Tea

368

Fried Almonds (page 4)
Eggplant Caviar (page 5) or Carp Roe Dip (page 6)
Black and Green Olives and Feta Cheese
Fried Mussels (page 12) with Garlic and Nut Sauce (page 290) or
      Stuffed Mussels (page 12)
Meat and Egg Rolls (page 14)
Small Boereg Rolls or Triangles with Cheese or Spinach-Cheese
      Filling (page 17)
Grapevine Leaves Stuffed with Rice and Olive Oil (page 9)
Sliced Cucumbers and Tomatoes
Oghi or Cocktails or Beer

DINNER

Boereg Rolls or Triangles with Spinach-Cheese Filling (page 17)
Fried Fish with Garnish (page 88)
French-Fried Potatoes or Homemade Potato Chips
Chilled Light Dry White Wine
Yogurt Cake (page 334) with Strawberries and Whipped Cream
Coffee or Tea

Boereg Rolls or Triangles with Cheese Filling (page 17)
Chicken with White Sauce (page 111)
Buttered Noodles
Buttered Green Peas or Asparagus Tips
Bibb Lettuce Salad
Chilled Full-Bodied Dry White Wine
Apricots in Whipped Cream (page 343)
Gaufrettes
Coffee or Tea

Boereg Rolls or Triangles with Meat Filling (page 17)
Clear Chicken Broth
Roast Goose with Apricots in Wine (page 114)
Plain Rice Pilaf (page 219)
Buttered Green Peas and Sautéed Small White Onions
Belgian Endive Salad
Full-Bodied Red Wine or Brut Champagne
Shredded Pastry with Cheese Filling (page 323)
Coffee or Tea

Targhana Soup (winter) (page 24) or Chilled Yogurt and Cucumber
   Soup (summer) (page 27)
Broiled Skewered Lamb (page 124)
Rice Pilaf with Vermicelli (page 220), Cracked Wheat Pilaf with
   Vermicelli (page 232), or Plain Saffron Rice Pilaf (page 222)
Combination Salad (page 45)
Medium-Bodied Red Wine
Many-Layered Pastry with Filling (page 316)
Coffee or Tea

Chicken Soup with Egg and Lemon Sauce (page 30)
Artichokes with Olive Oil (page 254)
Roast Leg of Lamb (page 131)
Saffron Rice Pilaf with Toasted Almonds and Sesame Seeds (page 222)
Romaine Salad (page 47)
Medium-Bodied Red Wine
Pistachio Ice Cream
Butter Cookies (page 323)
Coffee or Tea

BUFFET SUPPERS

Carp Roe Dip (page 6)
Black Olives, Tomato Wedges, and Scallions
Boereg Rolls or Triangles with Cheese Filling (page 17)
Baked Eggplant, Ground Meat, and Tomato Casserole (page 164)
Rice Pilaf with Tomatoes (page 221)
Tossed Green Salad
Armenian Bread (page 302) or French Bread
Chilled Rosé
Rolled Shirred Pastry with Nut Filling (page 319)
Coffee or Tea

Boereg Rolls or Triangles with Spinach-Cheese Filling (page 17)
Green Peppers and Tomatoes Stuffed with Meat (page 201)
Fried Stuffed Lamb and Wheat Balls (page 178) or Baked Lamb
   and Wheat with Stuffing (page 175)
Cabbage Salad (page 47)
Chilled Rosé
Shredded Pastry with Walnut Filling (page 321) with Whipped
   Cream and Strawberries
Coffee or Tea

370

Grapevine or Swiss Chard Leaves Stuffed with Rice and Olive Oil
  (pages 9 and 209)
Broiled Skewered Lamb (page 124) or Ground Lamb on Skewers
  (page 160)
Roasted Corn
Combination Salad (page 45)
Armenian Thin Bread (page 301) or French Bread
Iced Tea or Lemonade or Beer
Watermelon and Cheese
Walnut Pastry (page 325)
Coffee

Mixed Pickles (page 8)
Grapevine, Cabbage, or Swiss Chard Leaves Stuffed with Rice and
  Olive Oil (pages 9, 208, and 209)
Fried Stuffed Lamb and Wheat Balls (page 178)
Armenian Meat Pies (page 244) with Lemon Slices
Combination Salad (page 45) or Green Bean Salad (page 52)
Sesame Rolls (page 304)
Fresh Fruit and Cheese
Date Cookies (page 327)
Chilled Yogurt Drink (page 364) or Lemonade or Iced Tea or Beer

Glossary

ABOUR (Turkish CHORBA). Soup.

AGHTSAN (Turkish SALATA). Salad.

ALIUR. Flour.

ANANOUKH. See MINT.

ANOUSH. Sweet, jam.

ANOUSH GORGODABOUR. A traditional pudding made with skinless whole-grain wheat, dried fruits, and nuts.

ANOUSHABOUR. Literally, "sweet soup": a chilled fruit soup made with dried apricots or other fruits.

ARISHTAH. Noodle.

ARMAV. Date.

AZADKEGH. See PARSLEY.

BAKLAVA (PAKLAVA, PAHKLAVA; Armenian HAZARATERTIK). The most famous Middle Eastern dessert, made with many paper-thin layers of buttered homemade dough or phyllo. The pastry is stuffed with a mixture of nuts, baked, and then drenched with syrup.

BAMI (BAMYA). Okra.

BANIR (PANIR). Cheese. The term often refers to firm white cheese made from goat's milk.

BASIL (Armenian RAHAN, SHAHASBRAM). A fragrant herb with a subtle flavor; used fresh or dried in salads, pickled vegetables, stuffings, and vegetable and meat dishes.

BASTEGH (PASTEGH). A paste prepared with fruit and sugar. A very popular sweet.

BASTERMA. (BASTURMA, PASTERMA). 1) Salted beef, wind-dried, cured with a hot fenugreek paste (see CHAIMEN) prepared with a mixture of various spices and seasonings, and dried again. It is available in specialty stores. 2) Caucasian grilled marinated meat.

BDOUGH. Fruit.

BIGHBEGH (Turkish BIBER). Pepper.

BOEREG. 1) Dough with filling. 2) A stuffed and baked or fried dish made with many layers of paper-thin pastry, either in the form of a pie or folded into rolls or triangles. Served as an hors d'oeuvre, main course, or dessert, depending on the stuffing used. 3) A stuffed vegetable.

BOURMA. A rich dessert made with paper-thin pastry that is stuffed with a nut filling, rolled, shirred, baked, and then dipped in syrup. *Bourma* has a taste similar to that of *baklava*.

BOZBASH. A substantial soup, popular in the Caucasus, with many variations. It is prepared with lamb, vegetables, and fresh herbs and may also include fruits.

BRAS (PRAS; Turkish PRASA). Leek.

BULGHUR (Armenian TZAVAR). Cooked, dried, cracked wheat that comes three ways: fine (No. 1), medium (No. 2), and coarse (No. 3). The first two are used mainly for making *keufteh*, while coarse bulghur is used to make pilaf and stuffed vegetables (*dolma*). Bulghur is available in bulk at Middle Eastern groceries.

CHAMAN. See CUMIN SEED.

CHAIMEN (CHAIMAN, HOROM CHAMAN). Fenugreek, an unusual Asiatic herb with tiny reddish brown seeds, aromatic and slightly bitter. It is ground and employed in the preparation of a spicy hot paste used in making *basterma*, the famous Armenian cold cut.

CHEE KEUFTEH. Uncooked *keufteh*. This is Armenian-style steak *tartare* and is based on ground lamb and bulghur.

CHICK-PEA (Armenian SISER; Turkish NOHUT). Also known as *ceci* beans in Italian and garbanzo beans in Spanish, chick-peas are available canned in supermarkets. Dried chick-peas may be obtained from Middle Eastern and Mediterranean specialty stores and occasionally from supermarkets. In the Middle East chick-peas are used extensively. They appear in dips, salads, vegetable dishes, stews, and *keuftehs*. They are also roasted and salted and eaten like peanuts as *meza* (hors d'oeuvres) or roasted and coated with sugar and served as candy. These last two items may also be purchased at the specialty stores mentioned.

CHIKHIRTMA. A popular soup in the Caucasus, usually made with chicken, although it can also be made with lamb. It is thickened with egg yolk, flavored with lemon juice or vinegar for a tart taste, sometimes colored with saffron, and served sprinkled with minced fresh herbs.

CHOEREG (KEGHKEH). A slightly sweetened coffee roll.

CINNAMON (Armenian GINAMON; Turkish TARCHIN). One of the most important spices in Armenian cookery. It is used in stuffings, soups, and meat, poultry, and vegetable dishes, as well as in pilafs, desserts, confections, and beverages.

374

CORIANDER (Armenian GINTZ, KINTZ; Turkish KISHNISH). An aromatic herb resembling flat-leaf parsley but having a much stronger flavor. Fresh coriander is widely used, particularly in Caucasian Armenian cookery, both in food preparation and as a garnish. In the United States it can be found in Latin America, Puerto Rican, or Chinese markets and is also known as *cilantro* or Chinese parsley. Dried coriander or crushed coriander seeds may be substituted if fresh coriander is not available. If you dislike the distinctive odor and taste of this herb, you can omit it entirely or substitute flat-leaf parsley (often called Italian parsley).

CUMIN SEED (Armenian CHAMAN, KIMON; Turkish KIMION). Ground and used to flavor meat dishes.

DABAGAPLIT (DABAGI GATAH). Pancake.

DABGVADZ. Fried.

DEREVAPATAT (DEREVI SARMA, DEREVI DOLMA; Turkish YA-PRAKH DOLMASI). A dish made with grapevine leaves, which are stuffed and steamed. If the leaves are stuffed with rice and cooked with olive oil, they are served cold and are better known by their Turkish name of *yalanchi dolma*. If meat stuffing is used, they are served hot, often accompanied by a yogurt sauce. Cabbage or chard leaves are sometimes substituted for the grapevine leaves.

DILL (Armenian SAMIT). Used extensively in Armenian cooking: in salads, soups, stuffings, pickles, and egg, meat, and vegetable dishes.

DOLMA. Literally, any stuffed food, most often a vegetable stuffed with meat and rice or bulghur, simmered or baked, and served hot. Alternately, the vegetable may be stuffed with rice and cooked with olive oil, in which case it is served cold.

DZIRAN. Apricot.

DZNEPEG (ASBOURAG). Asparagus.

FAVA BEANS (Armenian PAGLAH). Broad beans, also known as horse beans.

FETA CHEESE. A firm white cheese with a slightly sharp taste, sold in the United States. Similar to the white cheeses prevalent in the Balkans, Middle East, and Caucasus, it is usually made from the milk of sheep or goats. Covered with brine, it keeps well in the refrigerator.

FRUIT ROLL. See BASTEGH.

GAGHAMP (Turkish LAHANA). Cabbage.

GAKAV. Partridge.

GANGAR (Turkish ENGINAR). Artichoke.

GARAK. Butter.

GARGANTAG. Coffee roll, cake, or pie.

GARIDOS. Shrimp.

GATAH (KATAH). A roll, bread, or coffee cake with many variations.

GATNABOUR. Literally, "milk soup": rice pudding.

GIGER (Turkish; Armenian LEART). Liver.

GOZINAKH. An Armenian candy prepared with walnuts or almonds, honey, and sugar and cut into diamond shapes.

GRAPEVINE LEAVES. Used fresh or preserved in the preparation of stuffed grapevine leaves, the famous Armenian specialty. In the Middle East and the Caucasus the fresh, tender leaves of grapevines are preferred whenever available. In America preserved grapevine leaves are sold in jars or cans in many specialty shops and groceries.

GUEVECH (Turkish; Armenian KCHUCH). A very basic dish that can be made with meat or poultry and various vegetables and served as a main course, or just with vegetables and served as a side dish. Traditionally it is baked in small individual earthenware casseroles and served piping hot. One eats directly out of the casserole. Plain yogurt or a yogurt sauce often accompany *guevech*.

HAIGAGAN. Armenian.

HARPUT KEUFTEH (POROV KEUFTEH; Turkish ICHLI KEUFTEH). *Keufteh* made with ground lamb and bulghur, stuffed with nuts, boiled, and served in tomato broth.

HATZ. Bread.

HAV. Chicken.

HAVGIT. Egg.

HAZAR (Turkish MAROUL). Romaine lettuce.

HELVA (HALVA, KHALVA, HALWA). 1) A popular candy bar throughout the Middle East, the Caucasus, and Central Asia, usually made commercially, though homemade versions of it also exist. There are many varieties of *helva*, prepared with different types of flour, nuts, and flavors. They are usually formed into a stiff paste that is pressed into blocks and cut into pieces. 2) A version of *helva* made with sesame seeds which is sold in the United States in many supermarkets and groceries under the name of halvah. 3) Desserts prepared with farina or flour and flavored with nuts, cinnamon, rose water, vanilla, cream, or soft white unsalted cheese.

HINTGAHAV. Turkey.

HUNKAR BEYENDI. Turkish for "the sultan liked it"; a dish of puréed eggplant served with *tas kebab*.

376

IMAM BAYILDI (Armenian SIKHDORATZ). Turkish for "the priest fainted"; a famous dish of eggplant, tomatoes, onions, garlic, parsley, and olive oil which is served cold. For an explanation of this title, consult the recipe on page 261. A zucchini version of *imam bayildi* may be found on page 268.

IMRIG (Turkish IRMIK). Farina (Cream of Wheat).

IMRIG BAKLAVA. Farina cake with syrup.

INTAGAGHAMP (DZAGHGAGAGHAMP; Arabic KARNABIT). Cauliflower.

IZMIR KEUFTEH. Meatballs as made in Izmir (ancient Smyrna), a city on the Aegean.

JAGINTEGH. Beet.

JAJIK. A cold Armenian soup or salad made with yogurt and cucumbers, ideal for summer menus.

KABOURGA. Roast rack of lamb with stuffing.

KARNI YARIK. Baked eggplant stuffed with ground lamb.

KAYMAK. A rich, concentrated cream, served as a topping for *kadayif* and other Armenian desserts.

KEBAB. 1) Cooked meat. There are various ways of preparing *kebab*. The method by which the particular dish is prepared is described by the word preceding it: i.e., shish kebab (meat on a skewer), *tas kebab* (meat cooked in a pot). 2) Barbecued.

KEDNAKHINTZOR. Potato.

KESHKEG (HERISSAH). A traditional dish of lamb or chicken and whole wheat, cooked for many hours until the mixture attains the consistency of a puree.

KEUFTEH. A meat, fish, wheat, or vegetable mixture, usually shaped into balls, patties, or small sausages with or without stuffing, and eaten raw or cooked. Occasionally, as in *sini keufteh*, the mixture is turned into a shallow pan before cooking.

KEYMA. 1) Ground meat (AGHATZADZ MISS). 2) The ground meat or vegetable mixture that forms the exterior of stuffed *keuftehs*.

KHASH (Turkish PACHA). Boiled or stewed lamb shanks. Lambs' tongues and stomach and calves' feet may also be used.

KHINTZOR. Apple.

KHMOREGHEN. Pastry.

KHOROVADZ. 1) Broiled, roasted, barbecued. 2) Armenian term for SHISH KEBAB.

KHOZI MISS (KHOZENI). Pork.

KINI. Wine.

KIRKOUM. See SAFFRON.

KIZIL. The cornelian cherry, native to the Caucasus. Used extensively in Armenian cookery there.

KORITZOV GATAH. A coffee cake stuffed with toasted flour, butter, nuts, sugar, and cinnamon.

KOUZOU KZARTMA. Lamb baked with potatoes.

KURABIA (GURABIA, KHOURABIA). A rich butter cookie similar to shortbread, coated generously with powdered sugar and stuffed or topped with chopped nuts. An Armenian favorite, traditionally served at weddings and other festive occasions.

KYURDYUK. Fat procured from under the tail (*tmag*) of a certain species of sheep bred in the Middle East, Caucasus, and Central Asia. *Kyurdyuk* is alternated with lean meat on shashlik skewers, used in stuffings, and melted and used for cooking.

LAHMAJOON (Arabic; Armenian MISSAHATZ). Armenian meat pies.

LAVASH. Thin white Armenian bread.

LEHZOU. Tongue.

LIMONACHOUR. Lemonade.

LOKHOUM (Turkish RAHAT LOKUM). Although the Turkish translates as "peace candy," this is known in the United States as Turkish delight. It is a soft, chewy confection, often stuffed with bits of toasted almonds or pistachios and coated with powdered sugar. In the Middle East *lokhoum* is frequently served with Turkish coffee.

LOKMA. Deep-fried fritters, served warm as dessert with honey syrup and sprinkled with cinnamon and chopped nuts.

LOLIG (Turkish DOMATES). Tomato.

LULEH (LYULYA) KEBAB or KEYMA KEBAB. Ground meat on skewers, broiled over charcoal or wood embers.

LUPIA (Turkish FASSOULIA). Bean. *Ganach lupia* are string beans, *garmir lupia* (LOVIAS) are red beans, *germag lupia* are white beans.

MADZOON. Yogurt.

MAHLAB (MAHLEB). An unusual spice derived from black cherry kernels which is used to flavor breads, rolls, and desserts. It should be finely ground before using. The addition of a little sugar while grinding helps to release its full fragrance.

MANTABOUR (Arabic SHISH BARAK). A soup made with dumplings stuffed with ground lamb and cooked in either a yogurt or a tomato broth.

MANTI. Small, canoe-shaped pastry boats stuffed with ground meat, baked in broth, and served hot with a yogurt sauce.

MEZA (MEZE, MAZZA). Assorted hors d'oeuvres, usually accompanied by *oghi*, a potent anise-flavored aperitif, or beer.

378

MIDIA (Armenian TSIGNAGANCH). Mussels. *Midia dolma* are stuffed mussels.

MINT (Armenian ANANOUKH; Turkish NANÉ). A popular herb in Armenian cooking which is used fresh or dried in salads, soups, stuffings, and egg, vegetable, fish, and meat dishes. Dried mint is sold in Middle Eastern groceries. When it is in season, fresh mint is sometimes found in a few markets in the United States. It can easily be grown at home.

MIRKATAN. Fruit compote.

MISS. Meat.

MISSOV. A dish made with meat; often, a meat and vegetable stew.

MOUSSAKA. Ground meat and eggplant casserole, a renowned Middle Eastern dish with many variations. Armenians also make *moussaka* with potatoes, pumpkin, and zucchini.

MUHALLEBI. A milk pudding made with rice flour or cornstarch and served cold.

MUJADDARAH (Arabic). A dish of lentils and rice or bulghur.

NABASDAG. Rabbit.

NARINCH. Orange.

NARSHARAB. A tart syrup made from the juice of pomegranate seeds. Available in Middle Eastern specialty shops.

NOUSH. Almond.

OGHI (Turkish RAKI; Arabic ARAK; Greek OUZO). A potent anise-flavored aperitif, popular throughout the Middle East. In Armenia it is distilled from grapes; in Turkey from grapes, plums, grains, potatoes, or molasses; in Greece from grains; and in Iraq and Egypt from dates. *Oghi* looks like water but turns a cloudy white when water or ice is added to it.

ORANGE FLOWER WATER. A concentrated liquid flavoring with an exotic fragrance, distilled from the blossoms of the bitter orange tree. Used to flavor ice cream, puddings, and other desserts. Sold at Middle Eastern groceries and some gourmet shops.

PAGLAH. See FAVA BEANS.

PANJAR (PANCHAR). Swiss chard.

PANJAREGHEN (PANCHAREGHEN). Vegetables.

PARSLEY (Armenian AZADKEGH; Turkish MAYDANOS). One of the most common herbs used in Armenian cookery. Armenians prefer the flat-leaf variety known in the United States as Italian parsley. Parsley keeps well in the refrigerator, stored with the stems in a jar of water.

PASEAN. Pheasant.

PAT. Duck.

PHYLLO (FILO; Turkish YUFKA). Paper-thin sheets of dough, used in making the many-layered Armenian, Middle Eastern, and Greek pastries and the strudels of Eastern Europe (phyllo and strudel dough are the same thing). Available fresh or frozen in Armenian, Greek, and Middle Eastern groceries and bakeries, some Eastern European, German, and Austrian groceries and bakeries, and in certain specialty shops. This ready-made dough comes by the pound, wrapped in clear plastic, in long, narrow packages containing anywhere from twenty-five to fifty sheets, depending on how thin each manufacturer makes his phyllo sheets. The size of the sheets also varies from brand to brand; therefore filling ingredients should be adjusted accordingly. *Note on handling phyllo*: It is best to use phyllo immediately after purchasing; however, it may be kept in the refrigerator for about a week. Since the paper-thin sheets are very fragile, dry up easily, and break, handle each sheet gently and work quickly to prevent drying. Cover the pile of sheets to be used with a barely dampened kitchen towel. Take from the pile only the sheet you need at a particular moment; keep the rest of the sheets covered. Any portion of the dough which will not be used for the recipe at hand should be kept in the refrigerator, well sealed in its plastic cover.

PIAZ. 1) Bean salad. 2) An onion and parsley mixture that, with the addition of lemon juice, makes a pleasant dressing for broiled or fried fish.

PIDEH. Crusty Armenian yeast bread, shaped in a round loaf.

PILAV (PLAV). Long-grain rice or bulghur (medium or coarse) cooked in the Armenian style, usually in chicken or meat broth with butter and flavorings.

PINE NUTS (Armenian GONAHUND, SNOBAR). The kernels of pine cones, also known as pignoli, pignolia, or pignola. They are used in stuffings, pilafs, desserts, employed as a garnish, or just eaten by themselves. Available in Middle Eastern groceries, nut shops, and health-food stores.

PLAKI. A method of cooking vegetables or fish with olive oil, tomatoes, parsley, and onion or garlic. The dish is served cold.

POMEGRANATE (Armenian NOUR). A fruit much appreciated by Armenians, particularly those living in the Caucasus, who eat it raw, make a syrup from it, and use it in soups, stuffings, pilafs, and fish and meat dishes.

POROV. With stuffing.

PRINTZ. Rice.

QUINCE (Armenian SERGEVIL). A fruit with a tart and astringent flavor, a sweet fragrance, and a high pectin content. It is usually cooked before eating. Not too well known in the United States, where it is used mainly for making jams, jellies, and marmalades, this delicate fruit is

380

much favored by Armenians, who, in addition to using it for preserves and compotes, feature it in soups and lamb and beef dishes. They also stuff it with ground lamb and rice and serve it alone or in combination with other different fruits and vegetables as a main course.

ROSE WATER (Armenian VARTACHOUR). A fragrant concentrated liquid flavoring, distilled from the petals of the pink damask rose, used to flavor desserts. It may be found at Middle Eastern groceries and some gourmet shops.

ROUB (ROUP; Turkish BEKMEZ). A thick sweet syrup or sauce prepared with undiluted grape juice and used on meats and in making candy.

SAFFRON (Armenian KIRKOUM). The dried stigmas of a variety of crocus. Armenians use it to flavor and color rice pilafs a delicate yellow. They also use it in pastries and in meat, chicken, and vegetable dishes.

SALOR. Plum. CHORTZADZ SALOR. Dried plum (prune).

SAQ. Goose.

SBANAKH (SHOMIN). Spinach.

SEKH. Melon, cantaloupe.

SERGEVIL. See QUINCE.

SESAME SEED (Armenian SHOUSHMA). Armenians use the seeds whole in candies and sweets and to flavor and decorate breads, rolls, cakes, cookies, and pastries. The ground seeds are used to make sesame seed paste (*tahini*).

SHAKANAG. Chestnut.

SHISH KEBAB (Armenian KHOROVADZ). Meat roasted on a skewer; also known as *shashlik* in the Caucasus.

SHOGHKAM. Turnip.

SHOKEP. Stew.

SHOUSHMA. See SESAME SEED.

SIKHDOR. Garlic.

SIMIT. An unsweetened breakfast roll sprinkled with sesame seeds.

SIMPOOG (BADINJAN; Turkish PATLIJAN). Eggplant.

SINI KEUFTEH. See KEUFTEH.

SKINLESS WHOLE-GRAIN WHEAT (Armenian GORGOD). Used in soups and stews, including the traditional *keshkeg* (chicken or lamb and wheat puree) and *anoush gorgodabour* (Armenian pudding).

SOKH. Onion.

SOORJ. Coffee.

SOORJAMAN (Turkish JEZVE; Greek KAFE IBRIKI). A special pot, usually made of brass or enamelware, having a long handle, a narrow neck, and a pouring spout, used for brewing and serving Armenian coffee.

SOU BOEREG. A baked dish of homemade noodle dough with a cheese filling. In Turkish the word *sou* means "water." The dish is so named because the dough is dipped into boiling water before baking.

SOUDJUK (Turkish; Armenian YERSHIG). 1) A highly spiced Armenian sausage. 2) A grape and walnut confection, also known as *sharots* or *chuchkhella*.

SOUNG. Mushroom.

SUMAC (SUMAK, SUMAKH; Armenian AGHDOR; BARBERIS, BAR-BERRY). A reddish-brown berry with a sour taste. It is dried, powdered, and used as a seasoning for meats, or it is crushed and steeped in water to extract its essence. The sumac water is then used in place of lemon juice to flavor certain salads, soups, and stuffed vegetables or leaves.

TAHINI (TAHIN). A nutty-flavored paste made from crushed sesame seeds, used for preparing eggplant and chick-pea dips, Lenten *keuftehs*, and coffee cakes. It may be purchased from Middle Eastern groceries and specialty shops. *Tahini* will keep for years without becoming rancid.

TAHN (Turkish AYRAN). The favorite Armenian summer beverage, prepared with lightly salted yogurt and water and served cold.

TARAMA. Preserved carp roe, light orange in color. It is used to make a very good dip. Sold in Middle Eastern specialty shops.

TARATOR. A somewhat thick sauce made with ground nuts, oil, garlic, vinegar or lemon juice, bread, and seasonings. It is served on fried or boiled seafood and vegetables.

TARGHANA (TARKHANA). A soup mix made with dried yogurt and wheat, used in the preparation of *targhana* soup. A commercial *targhana* is available in Middle Eastern groceries.

TARRAGON (Armenian TARKHOUN). Used widely in Armenian cookery, particularly by Armenians living in the Caucasus, who use it in soups and in fish, meat, and egg dishes. It can easily be grown at home in the garden or in a pot.

TAS KEBAB. Cubed meat (*kebab*), cooked in a pot (*tas*).

TEL KADAYIF (KHADAYIF; Arabic KNAFE). Long strands of very thin pastry, partially cooked and dried, resembling shredded wheat. Sold by the pound in Middle Eastern and Greek specialty shops and bakeries and used to make the delectable *kadayif* desserts. There is no substitute for *tel kadayif*.

TELAHAYS (Turkish TEL SHEHRIEH). Vermicelli.

TERBIYEH. A sauce made with lemon juice, eggs, and broth which is added to many soups, meat stews, meat-stuffed vegetables, or boiled fish dishes before serving.

TEY. Tea.

TITMAJ (Turkish MAKARNA). Macaroni.

TITOUM. Pumpkin, squash, zucchini.

TITVASH (Turkish TOURSHOU). Armenian pickled vegetables.

TOPIG (TOPIK). A Lenten dish made with chick-peas and wheat, with a stuffing of nuts, currants, onions, herbs, and spices flavored with *tahini*.

TSOUG (Turkish BALIK). Fish.

TZAVAR. See BULGHUR.

TZITAYOUGH (TZET). Olive oil.

TZUAZEGH. Omelet.

UNGUYZ. Walnut.

VARYAG. Pullet.

VOLORN. Pea.

VOSB. Lentil.

VOSDRÉ. Oyster.

YAHNI. A method of cooking. The food is braised with onions in olive oil and then, after the addition of water and perhaps tomatoes, cooked slowly until tender.

YEPVADZ. Baked, cooked.

YERSHIG. See SOUDJUK.

Shoppers' Guide

The following is a partial list of stores that carry Armenian food products. Some will accept mail orders. For other sources in or near your community consult your telephone directory for Armenian, Greek, Middle Eastern, or even Italian grocery stores, delicatessens, and bakeries, as well as gourmet specialty shops. If there are any Armenian, Greek, or Middle Eastern churches or organizations in your area, they too can assist you in locating sources for ingredients.

ALABAMA

Birmingham
Bruno's Food Store, 2620 13th Avenue W. 35204
Cash Produce Co., 2216 Morris Avenue. 35203
Sawaya Delicatessen, 1104 S. 10th Street. 35205
Mobile
Lignos Grocery, 160 Government Street. 36602

ARIZONA

Phoenix
Cater-Maid Bake Shop, 1135 E. Glendale Avenue. 85020
Filippo's Italian Groceries and Liquor Wheel, 3435 E. McDowell Road. 85008

CALIFORNIA

Anaheim
Athens West, 111 N. Dale Avenue. 92801
Fresno
Arax Market, 502 L Street. 93721
Hanoian's Market, 1439 S. Cedar Avenue. 93702
Lahmajoon Kitchen, 3358 E. Butler Avenue. 93702
Manukian's Basturma & Soujouk Co., 1720 S. Orange Aveune. 93702
Sunnyland Bulghur Co., 1435 S. Gearhart Avenue. 93702
Valley Bakery, 502 M Street. 93721
Zahigian's Market, 6947 S. Elm Avenue. 93706

Long Beach
Batista Imports, 222 E. 5th Street. 90812
Los Angeles
Bezjian's Grocery, 4725 Santa Monica Boulevard. 90029
C & K Importing Co., 2771 W. Pico Boulevard. 90006
Europa Grocery Co., 321 S. Spring Street. 90013
Greek Importing Co., 2801 W. Pico Boulevard. 90006
Middle Eastern Bakery, 5405 Hollywood Boulevard. 90027
Nassraway's Pastry Shop, 4864 Melrose Avenue. 90029
Oakland
G. B. Ratto & Co. International Grocers, 821 Washington Street. 94607
Palo Alto
José's Delicatessen, 422 Cambridge Avenue. 94306
Pasadena
Kabakian's Bakery, 476 E. Colorado Boulevard. 91101
San Carlos
Bit of Lebanon, 637 Laurel Street. 94070
San Diego
Athens Market, 414 Street. 92101
San Diego Importing Co., 2061 India Street. 92101
San Francisco
Haig's Delicacies, 441 Clement Street. 94118
Hellenic-American Imported Foods & Pastries, 2308 Market Street. 94114
Istanbul Pastries & Imported Foods, Ghirardelli Square, 900 North Point. 94109
Mediterranean and Middle East Import Co., 223 Valencia Street. 94103
Shehrazade Pastry & Candy, 1935 Lawton Street. 94122
San Jose
Hun-i-Nut Co., 789 The Alameda. 95126
San Mateo
Middle East Bakery, 1529 S. B Street. 94402
Santa Barbara
Johnny's Italian & Greek Delicatessen, 636 State Street. 93101
Sunnyvale
Tarver's Delicacies, 1338 S. Mary Street. 94087

COLORADO

Denver
Economy Grocery, 973 Broadway. 80203
Kebab Bakery & Delicatessen, 2703 E. 3rd Avenue. 80206

Danbury
Dimyan's Market, 116 Elm Street. 06810
Hamden
Milano Super Market Inc., 870 Dixwell Avenue. 06514
New Britain
Vittoria Importing Co., 35 Lafayette Street. 06051
Waterbury
Impero Import Co. Inc., 121 S. Main Street. 06702
P & S Importing Co., 36 Canal Street. 06702

DISTRICT OF COLUMBIA

Acropolis Food Market, 1206 Underwood Street N.W. 20012
Aloupis Company, 916 9th Street N.W. 20001
Calvert Delicatessen, 2418 Wisconsin Avenue N.W. 20007
Columbia Delicatessen, 17th Street and Columbia Road N.W. 20009
Hellas Greek Imports, 1245 20th Street N.W. 20036
Skenderis Greek Imports, 1612 20th Street N.W. 20009

FLORIDA

Fort Lauderdale
Flamingo Grocery Inc., 630 S. Federal Highway. 33301
Jacksonville
Joseph Assi Bakery & Delicatessen, 3316 Beach Boulevard. 32207
Farah Imported Foods, 705 McDuff Avenue S. 32205
Miami
Arabic Grocers and Bakery, 123 S.W. 27th Avenue. 33135
Joseph Baratta, 2503 S.W. 8th Street. 33135
Greek American Grocery Co., 2690 Coral Way. 33145
Near East Bakery, 878 S.W. 8th Street. 33130
Pensacola
Stamatelos Grocery, 500 E. Blount Street. 32503
Steve's Superette, 1620 W. Garden Street. 32501
Tampa
Italian Imported Super Market, 2412 N. Armenia Avenue. 33607

GEORGIA

Atlanta
Foxies Delicatessen, 659 Peachtree Street N.E. 30383
George's Delicatessen, 1041 N. Highland Avenue N.E. 30312

Honolulu
Gourmet Bazaar, International Market Place. 96815

Chicago
Akropol Pastry Shop, 2601 W. Lawrence Avenue. 60625
Athens Grocery, 811 W. Jackson Street. 60607
Columbus Food Market, 5534 W. Harrison Street. 60644
Grecian Phoenix Pastries, 5530 W. Harrison Street. 60644
Hellas Grocery Store and Pastry, 2621 and 2627 W. Lawrence Avenue.
    60625
New Deal Grocery, 2604 W. Lawrence Avenue. 60625
Sparta Grocery, 6050 W. Diversey Avenue. 60639
Rockford
Kelly's Food Mart, 1132 Broadway. 61104

Indianapolis
Athens Imported Food Store, 103 N. Alabama Street. 46204
Terre Haute
Bob Corey's Flaming Pit Bar-b-q Steak House Restaurant, 1719 S. 13th
    Street. 47802

Des Moines
Italian Importing Co., 316 3rd Street. 50309

Louisville
A. Thomas Meat Market, 309 E. Jefferson Street. 40202

New Orleans
Central Grocery Co., 923 Decatur Street. 70116
Progress Grocery Co., 915 Decatur Street. 70116
Shreveport
Fertitta's Delicatessens, 1124 Howell and 6301 Line Avenue. 71101 and
    71106

388

Portland
Model Food Importers, 115 Middle Street. 04111
Saco
Boucouralas Brothers, Common and Middle Streets. 04072

Baltimore
H. & H. Importing Co., 518 S. Broadway. 21231
Imported Foods, Inc., 409 W. Lexington Street. 21201
Stella Foods Co., Inc., 3815 Eastern Avenue. 21224
Parkville
Danny's Foods, 7905C Hartford Road. 21234

Belmont
Eastern Lamejun, 145 Belmont Street. 02178
Boston
Laconia Grocery, 908 Washington Street. 02111
Syrian Grocery Importing Co., 270 Shawmut Avenue. 02118
Cambridge
Cardullo's Gourmet Shop, 6 Brattle Street. 02138
Dedham
Homsy Middle East Importing Co., 918 Providence Highway. 02026
Dorchester
Krikor Kalunian, 57 Dix Street. 02122
Quincy
Quincy Syrian Baking Co., 723 Washington Street. 02169
Somerville
Hellas Baking Co., 6 Porter Street. 02143
Watertown
Euphrates Bakery Inc., 10 Mt. Auburn Street. 02172

Detroit
Acropolis Market, 8441 Joy Road. 48204
Athens Bakery & Grocery Co., 527 Monroe Avenue. 48226
Delmar & Company, 501 Monroe Avenue. 48226
Gabriel Importing Co., 2461 Russell Street. 48207

Stemma Confectionery, 514 Monroe Avenue. 48226
Stoukas Imports, 16401 E. Warren Street. 48224
Grand Blanc
Aremia Imported Foods, G-11230 S. Saginaw Street. 48439
Grand Rapids
Russo's Imported Foods, 1935 Eastern Avenue S.E. 49507
Southfield
American Oriental Grocery, 20736 Lahser Road. 48075

MINNESOTA

Minneapolis
The Pavo Co. Inc., 119 N. 4th Street. 55401
St. Paul
Morgan's Grocery, 736 S. Robert Street. 55107

MISSOURI

St. Louis
Heidi's Around the World Food Shop, 1149 S. Brentwood Boulevard. 63117
Italo-American Importing Co., 512 Franklin Avenue. 63101
Lebanese-Syrian Bakery, 3246 S. Grand Boulevard. 63118

NEBRASKA

Lincoln
Leon's Food Mart, Winthrop Road and Ryons Street. 68502
Omaha
A. Marino Grocery, 1716 S. 13th Street. 68108

NEVADA

McGill
The Louis Cononelos Co. 89318

NEW HAMPSHIRE

Manchester
Joseph's Brothers Market, 196 Lake Avenue. 03103
Nashua
Liamos Market, 176 W. Pearl Street. 03060

Asbury Park
Andrew's Delicatessen, 305 Sewell Avenue. 07712
Elizabeth
John's Market, 62 Orchard Street. 07208
Hackensack
Central Food Stores Inc., 63 Main Street. 07601
Jersey City
Gacos Delicatessen, 378 Summit Avenue. 07306
Moonachie
Sahadi Importing Co. Inc., 200 Carol Place. 07074 (This is a major firm
    whose products are distributed nationwide. A catalog is available on
    request.)
Newark
Tom's Ravioli Co., 791 S. Orange Avenue. 07106
Union City
Michael Nafash & Sons, 2717 Bergenline Avenue. 07087

Albany
Paparian's Food Market, 205 2nd Avenue. 12202
Astoria
Ditmars & 35th St. Market, 28-07 Ditmars Boulevard. 11105
Kismet Oriental Pastries Co., 27-02 23rd Avenue. 11105
Bayside
Constantine's Delicatessen, 205-10 48th Avenue. 11364
Brooklyn
George Malko, 185 Atlantic Avenue. 11201
Buffalo
Sammy's Imported and Domestic Foods, 1348-54 Hertel Avenue. 14216
Flushing
Emir Grocery, 135-18 Roosevelt Avenue. 11354
Freeport
Freeport Italian American Delicatessen, 52 W. Merrick Road. 11520
Kenmore
Curtis Imported Foods, 154 Niagara Falls Boulevard. 14217
New York City
Ohannes Aharonyan, 1537 St. Nicholas Avenue. 10033
Balkan Bakery, 1590 St. Nicholas Avenue. 10040
House of Yemen East, 370 3rd Avenue. 10016

K. Kalustyan Orient Export Trading Corp., 123 Lexington Avenue. 10016
Kassos Brothers, 570 9th Avenue. 10036
Macy's, Herald Square. 10001
Middle East & Oriental Grocery Store (Karnig Tashjian), 380 3rd Avenue. 10016
Aleksan Narliyan, 1530 St. Nicholas Avenue. 10033
Turkish American Trade & Development Corp., 16 Fulton Street. 10038
Rochester
International Importers of Fine Foods, 845 Bulls Head Shopping Plaza and 388 Jefferson Road. 14611 and 14623
L & H Superette, 508 Monroe Avenue. 14607
Syracuse
Thanos Imported Grocery, 424 Pearl Street. 13203

NORTH CAROLINA

Charlotte
East Trade Company, 402 E. Trade Street. 28202
Raleigh
Galanides-Raleigh, Inc., Wicker Drive and Campbell Street. 27604

OHIO

Akron
Ellis Bakery, 577 Grant Street. 44311
O'Neil's Department Store Food & Wine Pantry, 226 S. Main Street. 44308
Canton
Canton Importing Co., 1136 Wertz Avenue, N.W. 44708
Cincinnati
Bruno Foods, 4970 Glenway Avenue. 45238
Nettuno Italian Delicacies, 129 E. Court Street. 45202
Cleveland
Athens Pastries & Imported Foods, Inc., 2545 Lorain Avenue. 44113
Sheikh Grocery Co., 652 Bolivar Road. 44115
Syria-Lebanon Baking Co., 716 Bolivar Road. 44115
Columbus
Genoozi's Imported Foods, 4016 E. Broad Street. 43213
Dayton
Athens Greek & Italian Delicatessen, 616 Five Oaks Avenue. 45406
Lebanese Delicatessen, 4163 Salem Avenue. 45416
Toledo
Antonio Sofo & Son Importing Co., 3253 Monroe Street. 43606

Youngstown
Consumer's Market, 141 E. Florida Avenue. 44507

Oklahoma City
Nick's Importing Co., 2416 N. Western Avenue. 73106
Polsano's Delicatessen & Gourmet Foods, 2410 N. May Avenue. 73107
Royal Coffee and Tea Co., 7519 N. May Avenue. 73116
Tulsa
Antone's Imported Foods, 2606-K S. Sheridan Road. 74129

Portland
Downtown Delicatessen, 345 S.W. Yamhill Street. 97204
Pieri's Delicacies, Inc., 3824 S.E. Powell Boulevard. 97202

Harrisburg
Capitol Italian Grocery, 32 S. 4th Street. 17101
Lancaster
Simon X. Mandros, N. Charlotte and W. Lemon Streets. 17603
Philadelphia
Armenian Pizza, 6204 Woodbine Avenue. 19151
Pittsburgh
European Grocery Store, 520 Court Place. 15219
Stamoolis Brothers Co., 2020 Pennsylvania Avenue. 15233
Wilkes-Barre
Adelphia Delicatessen, 19 E. Market Street. 18701
Calamata Groceries, 27 E. Northampton Street. 18701
Middle East Bakery, 316 Hazle Street. 18702

Cranston
Henry's Delicatessen, Inc., 41 Warwick Avenue. 02905
East Providence
Albert Sarkisian, 65 Taunton Avenue. 02914
Providence
K. Barishian, 75 Messer Street. 02909
Near East Market, 41 Cranston Street. 02903

Knoxville
The Cheese Market, 503A Clinch Avenue S.W. 37902
Memphis
Barzizza Brothers, Inc., 351 S. Front Street. 38103
International Gift Corner, 181 Union Avenue. 38103

TEXAS

Dallas
Capello's Imported & American Foods, 5328 Lemmon Avenue. 75209
Houston
Antone's Import Co. (P.O. Box 3352), 807 Taft Street, 8111 Main Street, and 1639 S. Adams Street. 77001
Import Liquor & Food Stores, 910 Preston Avenue. 77002
San Antonio
Paletta's Imported Foods, 202 Recoletta Road. 78216

VIRGINIA

Arlington
Apollo Greek Imports, 4782 Lee Highway. 22207
Norfolk
Excel Market, 3230 Tidewater Drive. 23509
Galanides, Inc., 902 Cooke Avenue. 23504
Richmond
Greek American Importing Co., 518 E. Marshall Street. 23219
Nick's Produce & Importing Co., 504 E. Marshall Street. 23219

WASHINGTON

Seattle
Continental Pastry Shop, 4549 University Way N.E. 98105
DeLaurenti's Italian Market, Stall 5, Lower Pike Place Market. 98101
Spokane
Gino's World Food Mart, N. 126 Washington Street. 99201

WEST VIRGINIA

Charleston
Haddy's Prime Meats, 1422 E. Washington Street. 25301

394

WISCONSIN

Madison

Ben DiSalvo & Sons, 802 Regent Street. 53715

Milwaukee

Greek Pastries by Despine's, 4715 W. Lisbon Avenue and 4320 W. Center Street. 53208 and 53210

Olympia Grocery, 4303 W. Vliet Street and 4322 W. Center Street. 53208 and 53210

Topping & Co., 736 N. 2nd Street. 53203

Index

Lentil(s)
-Bulghur Soup, 28
and Bulghur Stuffing for Grapevine
Leaves, 11
Cracked Wheat Pilaf with, 232
Soup I, 28
Soup II, 28
Stew, Lamb and, 151
and Wheat Patties, 189
Liver(s)
beef, calf's, or lamb's
in Broth, Stuffed Lamb and Wheat
Balls with, 184
and Chick-Peas, Cracked Wheat
Pilaf with, 233
Fried, 16
with Green Peppers and Tomatoes,
Grilled, 140
Lamb and Wheat Ball Soup with,
185
Pilaf (rice), 230
Chicken
and Scallions, Rice Pilaf with, 225
Lokma, 331
Loligov Bami, 271
Loligov Bulghur Pilav, 232
Loligov Gaghamp, 271
Loligov Ganach Lupia, 270
Loligov Havgit, 68
Loligov Printz Pilav, 221
Loligov Simpoog, 272
Loligov Titoum, 272
Lolig yev Sokh Aghtsan, 51
Luleh (Lyulya) Kebab, 160
Lupia Plaki, 259
Lupia Yahni, 260

Macaroni with Lamb, 243
Mackerel, Fried Stuffed, 90
Madzoon, 286
Ginamonov (Tarchinov), 287
Sikhdorov, 288
Madzoonov Gargantag, 334
Madzoonov Keufteh, 182
Mamoul, 328
Mantabour, 34
Manti, 247
Many-Layered Pastry with Filling, 316
Marinated Beef on Skewers, 133
Marinated Broiled Lamb Chops, 126
Mashed Eggplant Salad, 55
Matsnabrdosh, 27
Meat(s), 119–170. see also Beef, Lamb,
Liver, Pork, Soup, Veal
appetizers, with, 14–16, 19, 174
casseroles and stews, 141–145

Meat(s) (cont'd)
dishes, ground, 160–169
egg dishes with, 71–75
and Egg Rolls, 14
Pastries Baked in Broth, 247
Patties, Fried, 161
phyllo pastry filling with, 19
Pies, Armenian, 244
rice pilafs with, 229–230
sandwiches with, 162
Sauce, 293
Cracked Wheat Pilaf with, 234
soups with, 34–39, 181, 185
Tarts, 238
Tongue Salad, 60
vegetables and fruits stuffed with,
196–207
with vegetables, ground, 164–169
wheat keuftehs with, 174–187
wheat pilafs with, 233–234
Meatball(s)
Smyrna, 163
Soup
with Cracked Wheat, 33
Kololik, 33
with Rice, 32
with Rice and Egg and Lemon
Sauce, 33
Melon, Stuffed, 207
Menus, 367–371
barbecue, 371
breakfast, 367
buffet suppers, 370
dinner, 369–270
luncheon, 367–368
meza, 369
picnic, 371
Meza, 1–20
Midia Dolma, 12
Midia Pilav, 226
Mint Tea, 363
Mirkatan, 344
Missahatz, 244
Missov Bami, 152
Missov Bighbeghi yev Loligi Dolma, 201
Missov Boereg, 238
Missov Bras, 150
Missov Derevapatat, 200
Missov Derevi Dolma (Sarma), 200
Missov Dziran, 158
Missov Dziranabour, 39
Missov Gaghamp, 147
Missov Gaghampi Dolma (Sarma), 197
Missov Ganach Lupia, 149
Missov Gangar, 146
Missov Gangari Dolma, 196